Praise for

THE ARGUMENT ABO

IN THE 1980S: GOODS AND ⌐........ .. ..
AGE OF NEOLIBERALISM

"This is a superb book—sharply argued, theoretically astute, richly researched, and beautifully written. I think it will make a real contribution to the study of American literature and culture, contemporary fiction, and potentially to emergent fields that are challenging entrenched ways of understanding materiality. I can easily imagine this book being taught in graduate seminars and think it will gain a readership among students and scholars of US culture."

—Stephanie Foote, editor of
Histories of the Dustheap: Waste, Material Cultures, Social Justice

"Quite brilliantly, and most entertainingly, Tim Jelfs's new book troubles at and unpicks the ways in which *things* and an *argument about things* are conducted across a range of different American fiction written in the 1980s. The book develops a crucially important argument that masterfully demonstrates the importance of the eighties in determining our understandings of contemporary America. It also complicates, significantly and importantly, our appreciation of how neoliberalism inflects older versions of American materialism. Fiction, the book argues, attends to things, everyday objects especially, so as to deliver new ways of reading America and its culture in fascinating aesthetic, political, and philosophical ways. As intelligent as it is beautifully written, Jelfs's book will significantly shape debates about materiality in America."

—Nick Selby, University of East Anglia

"Anyone tired of the usual 'Age of Reagan,' rise-of-the-right narratives that have for too long defined our understanding of the period after the Sixties will be grateful for Tim Jelfs's intervention in *The Argument about Things in the 1980s*. Jelfs takes up the 'long 1980s' by drawing upon an astonishing range of literature, music, and visual art, and he forces us to consider the period not as defined merely by Reagan and neoliberalism, but by the material things present in American culture at the start of our present neoliberal age. It is an incredibly important distinction, and every page bristles with fresh insight."

—Michael Stewart Foley, author of *Front Porch Politics: The Forgotten Heyday of American Activism in the 1970s and 1980s*

THE ARGUMENT ABOUT THINGS IN THE 1980S

Goods and Garbage in an Age of Neoliberalism

By Tim Jelfs

WEST VIRGINIA UNIVERSITY PRESS
MORGANTOWN 2018

ISBN:
Cloth 978-1-946684-23-3
Paper 978-1-946684-24-0
EPUB 978-1-946684-25-7
PDF 978-1-946684-26-4

Library of Congress Cataloging-in-Publication Data is available from the Library of Congress

Cover design by Than Saffel / WVU Press
Cover photograph by Olexandr Taranukhin / Shutterstock

Some material from Chapters 3, 4, and the conclusion appeared in "'Something Deeper than Things': Some Artistic Influences on the Writing of Objects in the Fiction of Don DeLillo," *Comparative American Studies* 9:2 (2011) 146–160. © M.S. Maney & Son Ltd. 2011. Reprinted by permission of Taylor & Francis Ltd.

A previous version of Chapter 4 was published in *The Journal of American Studies* 51:2 (2017) 553–571. © Cambridge University Press and British Association for American Studies 2016. Reprinted with permission.

"Life During Wartime" words and music by David Byrne, Jerry Harrison, Chris Frantz and Tina Weymouth © 1979 WB Music Corp (ASCAP) and Index Music, Inc. (ASCAP). All rights administered by Warner/Chappell Music Holland B.V. Used by permission.

"The Big Country" words and music by David Byrne © 1978 WB Music Corp (ASCAP) and Index Music, Inc. (ASCAP). All rights administered by Warner/Chappell Music Holland B.V. Used by permission.

"(Nothing But) Flowers" words and music by David Byrne, Jerry Harrison, Chris Frantz, Tina Weymouth and Yves N' Jock © 1988 Index Music, Inc. (ASCAP). All rights administered by Warner/Chappell Music Holland B.V. Used by permission.

For Abigail and Lilah

"So, there is a little tale to tell of many things . . ."

O. Henry, *Cabbages and Kings* (1904)

Contents

Acknowledgments / xi
Introduction / 1
1. The Triumph of Neoliberalism / 23
2. After the Great Transformation / 38
3. Rhopography and Realism / 52
4. Matter Unmoored / 77
5. At Peace with Things? / 98
6. All that Fall / 117
Conclusion / 141
Notes / 151
Bibliography / 173
Index / 199

Acknowledgments

Since this book was a long time in the making, the debts of gratitude it has accrued are many and varied. In the American Studies department of King's College London, Dr. Janet Floyd offered invaluable guidance during the earliest stages of the project, while the British Library has furnished me with world-class research facilities and a scholarly homefield for more than a decade now.

An array of colleagues and students in the Department of American Studies and Research Center for the Americas at the University of Groningen exercised more influence on the final outcome of this book than they perhaps realize. Working, researching, and learning alongside you all has helped my thinking on the argument about things evolve, and that evolution would not have been possible at all without institutional support from the Groningen Research Institute for the Study of Culture and Faculty of Arts.

Over several summers, various libraries in and around San Diego have afforded clean, well-lighted places in which to shape the final version of this book, including the Kellogg Library at UC San Marcos, the Geisel Library at UCSD, and the Copley Library at USD. In 2016, I was the recipient of a Global Scholars Award from the Society for Historians of American Foreign Relations, which enabled me to attend SHAFR's Annual Meeting and think more deeply about the kind of interdisciplinary conversations *The Argument About Things in the 1980s* might be able to contribute to in the fields of American Studies and American history.

At West Virginia University Press, Andrew Berzanskis, Derek Krissoff, and everyone else I have worked with on this book have been remarkably proactive, responsive, and supportive, while the anonymous reviewers supplied by WVUP offered exceptionally useful feedback.

Deep personal thanks for everything from pecuniary support to drinks and laughs go to friends and family members on both sides of the Atlantic, but especially to my parents, Bryan and Sue, and to the two new Jelfs that have appeared since I began working on this project: Abigail and Lilah, you are without any doubt the two most luminous presences in this or any life; this book is dedicated to you.

The deepest thanks of all are reserved for Katrina, though, who has seen fit to love me from Prague to London and London to Groningen, rarely even mentioning how much she misses the warm California sun.

Introduction

This is a book about the United States written by a non-American Americanist, and one informed by the interdisciplinary traditions of the field of American Studies. It is an analysis of some of the ways Americans spoke about, wrote about, and pictured material things and their relation to them during the 1980s, a brief (and yet, as we will see, perhaps not so brief) period in the much longer life of a centuries-old cultural argument, at the heart of which lies the suspicion that it is in things and their relations to things that not just Americans but the United States might find themselves and be found, or else lose themselves and be lost. Listen, for example, to the complaints of early Puritan preachers like Urian Oakes: "Sure there were other and better things the People of God came hither for than the best spot of ground, the richest soil."[1] But listen also to the way other settlers met these exhortations with explanations that they had only ever journeyed to the New World in order to catch fish, access land, or otherwise turn a profit.[2] By the 1830s, it seemed to the visiting Alexis de Tocqueville that the people of what were by then the United States wanted to "cling to the good things of the world as if assured they will never die."[3] Subsequently, as often as either its own citizens or outside observers have castigated the US for such an attachment to material things, or insisted that that attachment is inimical to American values, others have equally often celebrated it.[4] Or they have assured themselves that a thoroughgoing engagement with the material things of the world is and always has been central to the nation's self-conception. In the early twenty-first century, figures from the economist Paul Krugman to longshoreman Frank Sobotka in HBO's *The Wire* mourned the loss of a nation that "used to make things"—or that "used to make shit," as Sobotka mournfully puts it.[5] Such a eulogy, with its half-conscious acknowledgement that the finished goods of a great industrial civilization are simultaneously abject, excremental garbage and lost objects of love that stand in for the nation's whole manufacturing and laboring tradition, is no less a part of the argument about things than the more venerable examples cited above. Indeed, such laments offer a much-needed flavor of that argument's complexity.

1

This, then, is the argument about things with which this book is concerned: that recurrent contestation about the proper place of things in the life of the nation. Like smallpox or the silkworm, the argument may well have begun its American life as a European import, since in its most basic iteration, it mirrors the schism in Western thought between idealism and materialism. From Plato onwards, idealist philosophers have de-valorized the realm of matter in relation to that of so-called "metaphysical" or "spiritual" things, a conceptual hierarchy that influenced the Christian theologies of the later Roman Empire and Medieval and Renaissance Europe. St. Augustine, for example, saw "lust for money and possessions as one of the three principal sins of fallen man."[6] Hence the ferocity with which those early Puritan New Englanders began rebuking one another as their settlement enterprise declined towards merely material success. They shared the Augustinian view: seeing one another submit to the lust for things, they feared that New England had proven itself no less committed to mercantile advantage than the numerous other European assaults on the continent in the colonial period. "I discovered a great many islands, inhabited by numberless people; and of all I have taken possession," wrote Columbus to Luis de Sant Angel in 1493.[7] Was such casually rapacious acquisitiveness all the would-be "city on a hill" had to show the world? Sacvan Bercovitch certainly once argued as much, claiming that the Puritans simply "managed more effectively to explain away their greed."[8] The suspicion helped the argument about things establish itself on the North American continent, long before paths of empire began to carry it further West, then South, and in due course, the world over. "It concerneth New England always to remember that originally they are a plantation religious, not a plantation of trade . . . worldly gain was not the end and design of the people of New England, but religion," John Higginson thundered in his 1663 election sermon.[9] By the middle of the eighteenth century, the revivalist preacher James Davenport was organizing a bonfire of the vanities in New London, Connecticut. "Wigs, jewels, fine clothing, and books by worldly divines—anything that caused the soul to turn away from the spirit and toward the idols of this world, were to be cast into the fire," David S. New reports.[10] Davenport later confessed to having been under the influence of some sort of demonic possession.

If Davenport's bonfire was again action on the old European model, reprising that of the fifteenth-century Florentine monk Girolamo Savonarolo, it also shows the intensity with which the exported argument would periodically catch fire over the coming centuries. That the United States was founded, at least in part, upon Lockean property rights, or a version of what C.B. Macpherson called

Argument about things : their role in the life of America ; place in the American character

"possessive individualism," only added to that intensity, especially since that individualism went hand-in-hand with a demand for land.[11] Witness, in 1846, Emerson observing the "famous States" as they managed to provoke, and then win, their expansionist war with Mexico: "Things are in the saddle,/And ride mankind," concluded the sage of Concord.[12] So might have Tatanka Iyotake (Sitting Bull) when, in 1875, he surveyed the wreckage the doctrine of manifest destiny had made of his civilization; instead, he just lamented, of those responsible, that "the love of possessions is a disease in them."[13] On this view, it was the European-American love of things that drove nineteenth-century expansion. One is reminded of the conversation between Socrates and Glaucon in Book II of *The Republic*, in which the interlocutors agree that it is the desire for luxury, for more than just "the necessaries," that causes a state to "enlarge" its borders, as "gold and ivory and all sorts of materials must be procured."[14] The difference was that the possession of American land was understood by many neither as necessarily a luxury nor the consequence of luxury but a guarantor of political rights as much as a source of sustenance or, very frequently, slavery-enabled profit. Indeed, for a slaveholder like Jefferson, the possession and "improvement" of land was both a promulgator of republican virtue and a defense against the vice and corruption he associated with manufacturing and urbanization.[15] As it turned out, after the Civil War, the railroad-led corporatization and enclosure of much of that land was the prerequisite for the development of a mature, heavily industrialized system based around the ever-greater production, consumption, and disposal of things, a condition for entry into the "age of things" of the early twentieth century.[16]

What was true for continental expansion also held true for the extra-continental projection of US power during that most American of centuries: it did nothing to diminish the intensity of the argument about things in American life and plenty to fan it. In "The Significance of the Frontier in American History" (1893), Frederick Jackson Turner celebrated Americans' "masterful grasp of material things."[17] However, as what Turner called "American energy" continued to seek a "wider field for its exercise," both foreign and domestic commentators frequently presented that grasp as too intimate, too limited, a vulgar spur to dominion as much as proof of any more benign form of mastery.[18] There is, for example, a whole school of Latin American literature that excoriates US materialism of that era as a driver of imperialism. "You join together the cult of Hercules and the cult of Mammon," complains Rubén Dario in "To Roosevelt" (1905).[19] Yet even Theodore Roosevelt himself, as he was advocating the turn of the century expansion that so enraged Dario, approved of how he saw the people of his own nation "turn[ing] back to try to recover the possessions of the mind and the spirit" and realizing "that the life of material gain, whether for a nation or an individual, is of value only as a foundation, only as there is added to it the uplift that comes from devotion to loftier ideals."[20] By the middle of the twentieth century, in *The Chrysanthemum and the Sword* (1946), the anthropologist Ruth Benedict had to explain to occupying Americans why it was that the Japanese found it hard to process their defeat at the hands of the United States in the Second World War: "Even when she was winning," Benedict explains of Japan, "her civilian statesmen, her High Command, and her soldiers repeated that this was no contest between armaments; it was a pitting of our faith in things against their faith in spirit. When we were winning they repeated over and over that in such a contest material power must necessarily fail."[21]

After the war, as the mass-producing, mass-consuming United States underwent its long economic expansion, the argument about things in American life only seemed to flaunt its longevity. In 1959, John Steinbeck wrote to his friend Adlai Stevenson and complained, of his fellow Americans and their post-war prosperity, "Having too many THINGS they spend their hours and money on the couch searching for a soul."[22] Shortly before his death, Martin Luther King called on his fellow Americans to "rapidly begin the shift from a thing-oriented society to a person-oriented society," while various critiques of attachments to material things were symptomatic of much of the discourse of the New Left.[23] In "What Is A Hippie?" (1967), for example, Guy Strait spoke of parents who "have thought so long in terms of money and possessions, that they have forgotten how to think in terms of people."[24] "The hippie," Strait declares, "sees a madness in the constant fight to sell more washing machines, cars, toilet paper, girdles, and gadgets than the other fellow."[25] If the argument about things thus appeared to grow in intensity as the global economic and military power of the United States increased, that only illustrates the structural depth of the roots the dispute had lain down in the American experience by the second half of the twentieth century. After all, Strait's list of consumer desirables does not seem so dissimilar to the material vanities Davenport had tossed into his Connecticut fire centuries earlier.

The argument about things has always found expression across not just the cultural mainstream but also sub-cultural and subaltern discursive spheres. Compare, for example, contemporary heteronormative laments for that lost America that used to "make things"—a longing for what one British critic has characterized as "a hologram of a nation where men manufacture the world's goods and women iron their shirts"—with the kind of dilemma sketched out by the gay liberationist Don Kilhefner when considering the plight of LGTBQ citizens in the 1980s.[26] The choice for liberationists, Kilhefner suggested, was between "our assimilation into the mainstream versus our *enspiritment* [sic] as a people."[27] For groups like the Radical Faeries and other gay subcultures, liberation was in danger of taking the form of what one of the Faeries called "an oppressive parody of straight culture," in which an embrace of the material excesses of both mainstream consumer culture and its attendant regime of strict body maintenance risked producing something like an attenuation of the spirit.[28] For Kilhefner, a neo-Platonic-sounding "enspiritment" appeared to be part of the answer, but could that ever involve leaving the flesh and blood of the body behind, especially once embodiment itself had begun to look like a curse? "I don't think anybody really likes their body," Ned tells Felix in Larry Kramer's *The Normal Heart* (1985), a play in which Bruce Niles, the "gorgeous clone that everyone's always after," is eventually dismissed by Felix (in an ironic inversion, perhaps, of F. Scott Fitzgerald setting Daisy weeping over Gatsby's clothes) as having no more to him than "a lot of good looking Pendleton shirts."[29] And what good were those, or even bodies themselves, in the face of something like the AIDS crisis? The artist David Wojnarowicz had some idea, sporting at an ACT UP protest in 1988 a jacket emblazoned, "IF I DIE OF AIDS—FORGET BURIAL—JUST DROP MY BODY ON THE STEPS OF THE F.D.A." Things, then, and a culture of things in which, even long after slavery's formal extirpation, human bodies remain capable of being traded and exchanged, destroyed and remade, have never been free from the gross inequities that have long scarred the American continent. Poor bodies, female bodies, queer bodies, black bodies, all therefore often stand in quite different relation *to* things and *as* things when compared to their less marginalized counterparts.

*

Although far from exhaustive in their scope, the chapters that follow trace several aspects of this argument about things across various parts of the political, cultural, and intellectual life of the United States during the 1980s, by which I somewhat paradoxically mean a period that ranges from some time in the mid-1970s to the prosecution of the Persian Gulf War. And if that temporality sounds rough around at least one of its the edges, that is because the era in question has necessarily elusive origins. For by "1980s," I really want to signify not just a decade but something like the opening phase of the "age of neoliberalism." And it is difficult to say where and when that age, or even its "opening phase," definitively began, in part because neoliberalism can itself be difficult to define. If we simply take the term as referring to that congeries of now more or less regnant beliefs about the role of the state vis-à-vis financial markets and the role of markets vis-à-vis society that has been characterized by its critics as "free market fundamentalism," did the rise to dominance of those beliefs begin in Chile in 1973, when a CIA-backed coup ousted Salvador Allende and paved the way for the experiments of "the Chicago Boys"?[30] Or in the latter years of the 1970s, perhaps, when Californians staged a consequential tax revolt, and President Jimmy Carter first began deregulating important sectors of the US economy? We might go back even further. After all, many of the ideas associated with what we now know as neoliberalism were hardly new when the Mont Pèlerin Society first met in the Swiss Alps in April 1947, and as I will show in a subsequent chapter, at least one branch of the complex causal root system that belongs to the hegemonic ideology of our time can be traced to the period in the 1930s when US consortia began striking oil in the Middle East. By the Carter era, that historical development would prove indirectly responsible for what looks in retrospect like the mainstream reanimation of the argument about things in American life, some of the origins of which themselves run back, as we have already seen, through Puritan New England to Ancient Greece and the birth of Western philosophy. The discursive and conceptual risks of infinite regression in pursuit of definitive points of origin are thus considerable, and perhaps we ought simply to allow that whatever neoliberalism is (and what it *is* is something we will return to), its roots are flung far in space and time and leave it at that.

But something *did* nonetheless happen over the course of the 1970s that looks in retrospect like the ragged dawn of something like a neoliberal age and the beginning of a decade that may in some ways still be yet to end. For while the origins of the present age may prove elusive, its conclusion is hardly any more determinate. Indeed, the 1980s form such a crucial part of the story of how we arrived at the crisis-hit present that the present feels at times like nothing so much as a version of the earlier decade writ large: a dream, or nightmare, of debt-drenched deindustrialization, financialization, imperialism, and material inequality, from which many US and global citizens are trying unsuccessfully to awake.[31] It is true that the policy shift towards what we now know as neoliberalism was initiated not under the Reagan administrations of the 1980s but under the single term of Carter's presidency, and that the ideological thrust of that shift has extended throughout the 1990s to the present day. However, it was in the 1980s that the political and cultural course of the following decades was determined, which is why some commentators on American culture have already used the decade as a kind of historiographical synecdoche, the part that stands for the whole of all that the elite embrace of the doctrines of neoliberalism has wrought in the United States. "I thought I was writing a period piece about the 1980s in America," Michael Lewis claimed, referring back to the success of his book *Liar's Poker* (1989) in an article he published in the wake of the 2008 financial crisis: "Not for a moment did I suspect that the financial 1980s would last two full decades longer."[32]

Lewis wrote under the assumption that the 1980s, or the "financial version" of them, at least, must finally be ending. After the calamitous regulatory and ideological failures that contributed to the 2008 crisis, one can understand why he thought that would be the case. Even Alan Greenspan, Chairman of the Federal Reserve from 1987 to 2006, acknowledged in the aftermath of the worst financial calamity since the Great Depression that he had "[f]ound a flaw in the model that I perceived is the critical functioning structure that defines how the world works," a *mea culpa* that recalled Louis Althusser's definition of ideology as "the imaginary relationship of individuals to their real conditions of existence."[33] Whether the 1980s have actually ended, however, remains open to dispute. The basic operating model of political economy that lies at the heart of neoliberalism, and the influential roles that model assigns to such things as the state, markets, societies and citizens, remains largely unreformed at the time of writing, even after the onset of a global financial crisis and the painfully slow "recovery" from the Great Recession that followed. So, although for reasons of both scope and narrative circularity, I end my own analysis in what follows neither in 2008 nor 2016 but in 1991, I do so in the full knowledge that for all that has obviously changed between the beginning of the 1990s and today, we may in some ways still be stuck in what Leigh Claire La Berge has called a "long 1980s."[34] It is almost as if, as Francis Fukuyama first argued in 1989, history really had ended there.[35]

One of the things historians used to think they knew about this new historical sticking point was—to rehearse the narrative in fairly crude form—that after the "idealism" of the 1960s had soured in the late 1960s and early 1970s, and after the 1970s themselves had offered little more than drift and uncertainty in national life, some important tonal change took place in the 1980s as "Americans overall felt less mopey and less gloomy, less idealistic and more materialistic."[36] Or to put it even more crudely, one of the things historians thought they knew about the 1980s was that it was a decade in which something called materialism "came back in style."[37] To be sure, understandings of the era are certainly evolving and important work on rescuing accounts of the decade from the long shadow cast by President Reagan is still emerging.[38] Nevertheless, many popular and scholarly conceptions of the period still seem to agree that "the materialism of the 1980s" was itself a socio-cultural or even psycho-social fact, and that it therefore follows that if Tom Wolfe could label the 1970s the "Me" decade, then the 1980s were in some meaningful sense what Gil Troy has called the "Mine All Mine Decade."[39] So much, in fact, appeared obvious both in the 1980s and very shortly after they had ended. See the 1991 *Time* magazine piece that proclaimed that the decade following the 1980s was about to witness a profound change in cultural attitudes: "After a 10-year bender of gaudy dreams and godless consumerism, Americans are starting to trade down. They want to reduce their attachments to status symbols, fast-track careers and great expectations of Having It All," *Time* announced. "In place of materialism, many Americans are embracing simpler pleasures and homier values."[40]

Setting aside the dubious nature of *Time*'s prediction about pleasures and values, it is difficult to know exactly what "materialism" signified in this context. *Time*'s invocation of godlessness was empty rhetoric. Even today, the United States appears remarkably god-fearing: in the 1980s, which saw the entrenchment of the religious right as a powerful socio-political force in American life, religiosity held firm, with the percentages of respondents to Gallup polls describing themselves as having no religion never rising above single digits.[41] As for consumerism, this phenomenon was in itself far from unique to the 1980s. Large swathes of the United States had been functioning as part of a consumer society since at least the 1920s and perhaps as far back as the Industrial Revolution, as a vast literature on the history and meaning of consumerism in the United States and elsewhere has amply demonstrated.[42] In the world's largest capitalist economy, one can always measure economic activity, of course, and note that since for much of the middle part of the decade, the American economy was booming, the aggregate number of acts of capitalist exchange was likely on the rise.[43] Is that, then, what we really mean by "1980s materialism," some empirically verifiable and historically significant triumph of Milton Friedman's vision of the marketplace and market exchange as the basic organizing space and principle of American life respectively, notwithstanding the impact of the work of critics like Christopher Lasch, who had in the late 1970s already bemoaned the nation's "culture of competitive individualism" and "acquisitive materialism"?[44] Is that why some historians of the era count the growth of shopping malls as indicative of materialism's coming "back into style"?[45] If so, how precisely does that growth sit in relation to wider material conditions, namely the shifting geospatial configurations of an already extensively global capitalism that has long formed the object of study of historical materialists?

Such questions are worth posing if only because they highlight the insufficiencies inherent in some of the ways it is tempting to think about the phenomenon of "materialism" in the 1980s. For if decades are necessarily vulnerable to caricature, and if, as Charles Ponce de Leon has argued, the 1980s have proven especially susceptible in this regard, the relations between Americans and the things they made, used, and consumed in the period with which this book deals have also been particularly poorly served.[46] For that reason, my analysis of the argument about things in the 1980s is predicated on a deliberate effort to move beyond reductive understandings of "materialism," precisely because such an emphasis neglects the extent to which the most significant triumph witnessed in the 1980s, even or especially in the elongated form with which I deal with them here, was surely at least partly ideological. The ascent of the ideas associated with neoliberalism, after all, has been just that: a triumph of once discredited beliefs about markets, politics, and human behavior that won acceptance, as Mark Blyth has argued, at a time of pronounced uncertainty among elites and policymakers by offering such constituencies the kind of ideational certitude that has, in turn, resulted in a set of changes as pronounced and consequential as any since the Great Depression.[47] That is not to say that neoliberalism's triumph was necessarily experienced as such at the time it was happening, nor that it has been total or irresistible. Nor, indeed, is it to deny that ideology is rooted in material conditions and produces material effects. It is instead to emphasize the dynamism with which what we call "matter" and what we call "ideas" can interact, while drawing attention to the fact that the very division between the two terms is exceedingly problematic. How else to explain the peculiar phenomenon that, as Robert M. Collins has noted, the 1980s saw the flourishing of both *the idea* of "materialism" and what Ronald Inglehart has called "postmaterialist" politics, in which *still obviously material* concerns like racism, feminism, LGTBQ rights, and the environment decisively trumped Harold Laswell's older vision of politics coming down to the no less material question of "who gets what"?[48] On this view, and given what we know now about how effectively real wages were restrained from the mid-1970s onwards, the statistic cited by Troy that showed that eighty percent of college freshmen "desired wealth" in 1987 (compared to a mere forty percent in 1967) might indicate not so much the moral decadence of "1980s materialism" as students' keen-eyed sense of where things were likely headed.[49]

In any event, the binary opposition between matter and idea, a foundation of Western thought on which the positing of materialism as a socio-cultural or psycho-social fact ultimately rests, only gets us so far, I would contend. First, we need to think instead about the emergence of some of the ideas associated with neoliberalism as a result of a reconfiguration of global capitalism that took place in the 1970s that was itself rooted, as we shall see, in some of the peculiar ironies of American imperialism. And to the extent that, as Perry Anderson has recently argued, American imperialism may itself be a phenomenal blend of the ideal and material, we also need to see that reconfiguration as a networked process of both matter and ideas.[50] For if one of the enduring puzzles connected to the triumph of neoliberalism remains how it has ever been able to get away with calling itself "new" when it was mainly a "warmed up" version of much that had gone before, in earlier phases of capitalism, part of the answer lies in the particular set of material conditions that happened to obtain when the ideas associated with neoliberalism began to gain currency in elite circles in the 1970s.[51] And these conditions, as we shall see, had much to do with the internal contradictions of the United States' exercise of geopolitical power during the Cold War era, when a series of strategic decisions made in that exercise of power helped to ensure that from the mid-1970s onwards, networks of agency remarkable in their complexity and global in their reach would play an important role in the ideological triumph of neoliberalism in the United States.

For anyone interested in the late twentieth-century United States, one of the problems with conceptual models that fail to take account in their approach to the 1980s of the complex, networked interplay between whatever "the material" is and whatever we suppose it is not is that they have tended to script simplistic interpretations of what much visual, literary, and other forms of culture were doing in their engagements with things in the era. And make no mistake, whatever "materialism" might really mean, American culture was certainly engaged with material things throughout this period. What kind of material things? Those that the philosopher Martin Heidegger once rather vaguely called "particular things, these and those things," or, somewhat less vaguely, those found in "that sphere of things in which we know ourselves immediately at home [. . .] things as the artist depicts them for us, such as Van Gogh's simple chair with the tobacco pipe which was just put down or forgotten there." These are the things, to put it another way, that the philosopher and art critic Arthur C. Danto has called part of the *Lebenswelt*, or life-world.[52] Of course, in the context of the late twentieth-century United States, the objective repertoire of American culture extended far beyond the chairs and pipes of Heidegger's philosophy. Think of the vacuum cleaners and basketballs in Jeff Koons's work of the 1970s and 1980s, or the bravura opening of Don DeLillo's *White Noise* (1985), with its description of "a long shining line" of station wagons arriving on the campus of the fictional College-on-the-Hill, their roofs laden "with boxes of blankets, boots and shoes, stationery and books, sheets, pillows, quilts; with rolled-up rugs and sleeping bags; with bicycles, skis, ruck-sacks, English and Western saddles, inflated rafts."[53] Everyday objects, con-sumer goods, the paraphernalia of daily life; or perhaps just the things that comprised what George Carlin's famous comedy routines of the era simply called "stuff": define them as you may, these and the vast volumes of waste they were generating in a mass-consuming, mass-discarding culture, are all impli-cated in the "things" of my title.

That such things should have featured in American cultural production in the era is unsurprising; they were, after all, undeniably and characteristically part of the late twentieth-century American cultural scene. More surprising, however, is the lack of nuance or variety in a great deal of the cultural criticism produced in response to those things and their cultural representation, at least in the 1980s themselves. Somewhat reductive versions of Lasch's argument informed critical assessments of much of the seemingly representative visual and narrative culture of the period that were often characterized by a deep unease about the relationship between culture, material goods, and capitalist consumerism. To cite just one example of the general critical mood, Alison Pearlman has shown how "[t]he emergence of Julian Schnabel, David Salle, Jean-Michel Basquiat, Keith Haring, Peter Halley, and Jeff Koons as 'art stars' in the 1980s, aroused art critics' most explicit fear of the time: that art no longer opposed consumer culture."[54] In part this had to do with these new artists' status as celebrities and the vast sums their work was trading for in a booming art market, which is to say the commoditization of the work itself.[55] However, it was also related to the direct use that an artist like Koons was making of con-sumer goods in his work, which, as Pearlman put it, was either celebrated for "making a statement about the impossibility of making art that could transcend its inevitable commodification" or else criticized for indulging in what Hal Foster called "the phantasmagoric, sensuous qualities of consumer products."[56]

There is a genuine dilemma here. On the one hand, in an era in which Hollywood blockbusters, television soaps, and a handful of pop megastars accounted for large parts of mass-produced media markets that were already remarkable in terms of both their domestic and their global penetration, it was impossible to ignore the fact that much culture itself was, as the Frankfurt School had argued had long been the case, heavily industrialized and commercialized, just another thing to be bought and traded. Hence the fear among critics of what Michael Clune has called the "utopian" school of Marxist and Marxist-influenced criticism that much culture inevitably ended up just producing "more capitalism." And hence Hal Foster's own contention that what the art of the Duchampian "readymade" had itself already suggested, decades before the dawning of the age of neoliberalism, was that "art in a capitalist society cannot escape the status of a commodity."[57] On the other hand, there is also something deeply problematic about a critical approach to the cultural representation of consumer goods that forecloses interpretations lying outside the unremitting binarism accurately set out by Pearlman. This is not to preach as an alternative to such an interpretative impasse the kind of emptily hip cultural studies criticism caricatured by Terry Eagleton as abandoning critique completely, but it is to argue that criticism of, say, literary fiction in the period needs to be more discriminating and nuanced than that of the critic who claimed that not only young "bratpack" writers like Jay McInerney and Bret Easton Ellis, but also older writers like Raymond Carver and Ann Beattie, were all writing "fictions of acquisition," in which "[w]hat seems to be important is not what happens to you, but how many items you can list to quantify and therefore establish your legitimate claims as a sufferer."[58] Such sweeping claims, like Bruce Bawer's similarly disdainful complaint of the so-called "bratpack" fiction of the decade—that its narrators were "more likely to give a detailed run-down on the contents of a given character's cupboard or clothes closet [. . .] than to provide a coherent and convincing set of clues to the contents of that character's soul"—have found their way into general histories of the 1980s, but read now like disturbingly homogenizing efforts to ventriloquize critics' own concerns about the role of things in American culture and life, which often evince what anthropologist Daniel Miller has described as the tendency to view "the relation of persons to objects" as "in some way vicarious, fetishistic or wrong."[59]

*

Two evolving and important bodies of literature have helped scholars begin to see things somewhat differently now, setting the stage for an approach to the argument about things that might usefully complicate the vision of 1980s culture as simply confirming or critiquing the "terminal" materialism that critics have argued has long blighted capitalism.[60] The first is that associated with the material turn in the humanities. Literary and cultural critics like Bill Brown, who in the late 1990s began arguing for a kind of "methodological fetishism," a willingness to begin (if not necessarily end) scholarly inquiry with material culture and the question of things, have been central to this turn, alongside a fairly recent stream of theoretical work originating in the field of science and technology studies with Bruno Latour and others.[61] But such work ought also to have served as a conduit through which scholars have begun to (re)discover a diverse, interdisciplinary, and already very well-established literature on things and our relations to them, including an American scholarly and intellectual tradition that had, in fact, always taken things seriously and had long urged others to do the same. Books like Siegfried Gideon's *Mechanization Takes Command* (1948) and John Kouwenhoven's *Made in America* (1948), for example, stressed the importance of acknowledging the influence that man-made artifacts and technologies had had on the development of modern American civilization. Kouwenhoven would later argue that his own discipline of American Studies had been too concerned with words at the expense of things, while by the mid-1990s, one scholar working in a related field was complaining that much material culture-based work remained "scholarship no one knows and no one heeds."[62] And yet, by then, as Brown noted in the essay that introduced what he called "thing theory" to the scholarly world, we were already living in a time in which "you can read books on the pencil, the zipper, the toilet, the banana, the chair, the potato, the bowler hat."[63]

It may have been more accurate for Brown to have claimed that by then, we were already living in a time in which anthropologists, historians, archaeologists, social psychologists, and others had for years been trying to get scholars to think about things in ways that went beyond the well-rehearsed critiques of consumption and consumerism.[64] Today, by contrast, that crucial battle seems to have been won, and won, as we shall see, at a potential cost, at least in the eyes of the material turn's critics. For the history of the world can now apparently be told in just one hundred objects, and academic publishers are selling slim volumes of "object lessons" on everything from remote controls to shipping containers, all part of a process that has seen things regain epistemological respectability while transforming understandings of them from mere objects to agentic entities that intervene in and structure our lives in perhaps surprising but not necessarily "vicarious" or "fetishistic" ways. Intriguingly, such ways of looking at and thinking about things, which critics like Andrew Cole have attacked precisely because of their fetishism, traverse any imagined boundary between the popular and the scholarly.[65] Audiences may pore over compulsively accumulated masses of other people's "stuff" on reality TV shows like *Hoarders* while simultaneously reading important sociological studies on how such behaviors are in fact about maintaining connections with people and not just with things.[66]

If it has taken the critical humanities a long time to reach such a point, that may be because, while earlier responses to many cultural representations of things often evinced a lingering disapproval not only of things but of both our attachments to them and the market processes that so often mediate those attachments, the "materialism" such critiques decried was not always all that heavily invested in the material at all. Instead, some of the most influential accounts of how we lived in the early years of neoliberalism have tended to focus on the fact that the entire global economy was, as early as the 1970s, in the midst of an epochal transformation heralded by the effective "dematerialization" of transnational capital flows and even of things themselves.[67] Capital, of course, has long demonstrated an apparent tendency towards dematerialization, whether in the infamously "phantasmagorical" form of Marx's commodity or in the form of money itself, which has evolved from coins made from precious metals to pieces of paper representing quantities of those metals to free-floating fiat currencies unmoored from any obligation to material convertibility at all. By the mid-1970s, increasingly mobile financial capital was appearing in the form of the electronic "waves and charges," or the already digitized "green numbers on the board" noted in the pages of DeLillo's *Players* (1977), a novel published more than half a decade before the same writer would catalogue the material cornucopia of middle American life in *White Noise*.[68]

While such a rendering, itself made possible by developments in technological communications, was commensurate with the process of "time–space compression" that David Harvey argued lay at the heart of postmodernity, it seems to me that the rhetorical hyperbole of some of the most influential theorists of the postmodern once risked calling into question whether in the age of such super-mobile, digitizing capital anything "material" was really still there at all.[69] Indeed, looking back now not on Harvey's work but on some of the other critical literature on postmodernity proliferating in the 1980s, one finds a radical rhetorical destabilization of the materiality of not only money and finance capital but of things in general. Consider, for example, how Jean Baudrillard wrote in *America* (1988) as if his book's eponym was itself nothing less than a "giant hologram," in which "things seem to be made of a more unreal substance; they seem to turn and move in a void as if by a special lighting effect, a fine membrane you pass through without noticing it."[70] The roots of such rhetoric can be traced back to Marx's analysis of the commodity fetish, which Peter Stallybrass has argued "inscribes *im*materiality as the defining feature of capitalism."[71] And given that the thought of theorists like Baudrillard emerged in part out of an ideological worldview understandably interested since at least the late 1960s in the destabilization of the capitalist systems it critiqued, it may not be surprising that much of that rhetoric has also had the effect of contributing to a kind of conceptual dematerialization of still obviously material things, even as it engaged with the systems of production and consumption of material goods that remained at the heart of capitalism in the late twentieth century.

The consequence of all this was a certain critical inattentiveness to the material qualities of material things, even when what was purportedly being critiqued was "materialism." As Brown notes, it was not until the 1980s that Baudrillard himself "declare[d] that just as modernity was the historical scene of the subject's emergence, so postmodernity is the scene of the object's preponderance."[72] By that point, however, the objects in question often seemed only coincidentally material. See, for example, the influence of semiotic understandings of consumer society, in which sign-values are unrelated to any material qualities a thing might possess. Or consider the striking cultural and intellectual assimilation of notions like Baudrillard's "simulacrum," a term which Fredric Jameson also uses in his influential conceptualization of postmodernism to describe "the object world itself." The term has itself had a destabilizing, dematerializing effect, the idea of the copy of a copy of which there is, in fact, no original having informed countless (mis)readings of the culture produced in the "long 1980s" as dominated almost to the exclusion of all else by reflections on the two-dimensional, media-generated image unmoored from material reality.[73] In fairness to Baudrillard, what such critical recyclings of the concept tended to miss was that what is lost in "the precession of simulacra" (and without the absence of which it would still be possible to distinguish representation from reality) is not the physical, material world ("the war is no less atrocious for being only a simulacra—the flesh suffers just the same") but the metaphysical: "It is all of metaphysics that is lost [. . . The real is now] no longer really the real, because no imaginary envelops it anymore."[74]

From the 1990s onwards, then, the time has appeared ripe to acknowledge, as both Walter Benn Michaels and the novelist Tom McCarthy have recently reaffirmed, that matter still matters in the age of neoliberalism, even as finance capital appears increasingly to render itself nothing more than waves and charges passing imperceptibly through the air, and even if such matter only assumes the abject forms of the pencil stubs and "[p]aper accumulated underfoot" that DeLillo noted still continued to characterize Lyle's work on the floor of the exchange in *Players*.[75] In this sense, perhaps what the "material turn" most importantly offers a reconsideration of American culture's engagement with things in the 1980s is an awareness, as Alan Bilton has claimed of the fiction of the decade, that it may in part be characterized by a sense of the tension between the materiality of things and the apparently increasing immateriality of capital.[76] To neglect the former in our critical fascination with the latter would be to neglect the stubborn materiality of so much of the warming world that still surrounds us, or what Brown, quoting Georg Lukács, has identified as the "thingness of things."[77] It would also be to neglect the no less important point, often missed by critics, that the things with which American culture was engaging in the 1980s were by no means all examples of the commodity form, regardless of how hard or otherwise culture itself might have been struggling to escape from its own commodification.[78] Thus, if we need to remember that matter still abides—that it exhibits, as Jane Bennett has it, the Spinozan quality of *conatus*, even in the days of electronic capital and the apparent digitization of all human and social relations—we also need to remember that not all things found in American culture in the 1980s were fetishes.[79] And as a later chapter will make clear, even some of those things that *were* might have been speaking to an aestheticism and/or eroticism of everyday objects that had little to do with their status as saleable commodities.

Aside from work associated with the material turn, the second body of literature that makes a reexamination of American culture's engagement with things in the 1980s even possible is that on neoliberalism and the neoliberal era itself. In the fields of intellectual history, labor history, political science, political economy, critical theory, and cultural and literary studies, a burgeoning, multidisciplinary literature is emerging that has tried to account for some of the schismatic changes wrought in the fabric of US social, political, intellectual, economic, and cultural life by the dawning of what I earlier referred to as the age of neoliberalism in the mid to late 1970s.[80] As the term "neoliberalism" has itself caught on, circulating across a wide range of discursive spheres, it has understandably provoked questions as to its precise definition. For most of its critics, it still signifies something "more than an intellectual swearword," but what, exactly, and why have some begun to question the use of the term?[81] In the lectures gathered together in *The Birth of Biopolitics*, Michel Foucault traced the roots of neoliberalism as far back as the emergence of liberalism itself "around the middle of the eighteenth century," and the birth of what Foucault called a "principle of limitation" intrinsic to "the art of government."[82] As Philip Mirowski has argued, Foucault's analysis, enshrined in lectures delivered in 1978–79, was remarkable both for the earliness of its perspicacity and the extent of its vision, for the French post-structuralist "was the first to appreciate the vaunting ambition of the neoliberals to recast not just markets and government, but the totality of human existence."[83]

Something more than a mere approach to political economy, then, neoliberalism, at least by Mirowski's account, is a "relatively discrete subset of right-wing thought situated within a much larger universe" of rightist political philosophies that experienced a resurgence in the 1970s and 1980s.[84] It is related to, but distinct from, both libertarianism and classical liberalism in that in its pursuit of the extension and entrenchment of that "principle of limitation" with regard to the operation of supposedly "free" markets and in defense of property rights, it nonetheless rejects the "minimalist night-watchman state of the classical liberal tradition" in favor of a "set of proposals and programs to infuse, take over, and transform the strong state."[85] In this sense, neoliberalism is both programmatic and self-contradictory, glaringly different in its theory and practice. For its well-regimented, disciplined adherents cry freedom and a small, non-interventionist state, while, since the 1970s at least, actively and carefully organizing themselves around and within the physical and ideological spaces of the state and the rich ecosystem of think tanks and other institutions that surround it. And if, as I have already intimated, one of the reasons neoliberalism may be hard at times to delimit or define is because both its origins and the causes for its ascendancy are themselves diffuse, there are still distinct streams, or "sub-guilds," of neoliberal thinking that, as Mirowski has shown, were all well-represented in the initial formation of the Mont Pèlerin Society, the still-extant home of what Mirowski calls the "Neoliberal Thought Collective," founded by Friedrich Hayek and other like-minded thinkers in 1947.[86]

Scholars like Mirowski and Dieter Plehwe have schematized the major tributaries of neoliberal thought ("Austrian-inflected Hayekian legal theory, the Chicago School of neoclassical economists, and the German ordoliberals"), adumbrated their shared tenets, historicized those tenets' diffusion, and shown just how resilient neoliberalism has proven since the 1970s.[87] For my own purposes, what is most important is not to attempt to reify "neoliberalism" into a willed coherence that glosses over its diffuse origins, its internal tensions, and

17

attentive to its heterogeneity

its inconsistent practices as it has continued to articulate its ultimately rather narrow views on freedom, individualism, and property rights. Rather, what counts is how neoliberalism and its ascendency have come to be understood as perpetuating their own cultural logics that attempt to convince us that we all live and ought to live in markets rather than societies, and must therefore adapt ourselves and our every way of life to recognition of that fact. This is why some cultural critics have deployed the term "capitalist realism" to describe not only neoliberalism's ideological insistence that there is no alternative to its own once decidedly alternative vistas but also the "realist" cultural mode that now appears as something like neoliberalism's aesthetic signature.[88] By using such a term, Mark Fisher and others eschew the once dominant concept of "postmodernism" as no "longer contain[ing] the referential capacity required for contemporary analysis."[89] Meanwhile, other important work on cultural politics in the neoliberal age by scholars such as Walter Benn Michaels and Adolph Reed, Jr. raises the possibility that one of the reasons historians of the 1980s have sometimes found themselves describing American life in the period as simultaneously materialist, postmodern, *and* postmaterialist is that as not just an approach to political economy, but an ideology, neoliberalism has shown itself able to embrace purportedly postmaterialist, post-1960s values like cultural diversity, individual freedom, and even the definitive end of "grand narratives" as the ideological veneer under cover of which massive upward transfers of wealth and power have been taking place, both domestically and globally.[90]

If this is the case, one is left with the sense that those disavowing the term either for strategic purposes or because they find it too amorphous to be useful risk playing into their ideological opponents' hands. For it well may be in its very diffusion, and in its complex and far from complete evolution from a set of beliefs held by a cadre of out-of-favor intellectuals in the 1940s to the key determinant of the supposedly common sense ideological frame within which so much politics now takes place, that whatever "neoliberalism" is draws at least some of its ideological resilience. On the other hand, perhaps deploying the term or not ultimately makes less difference than we might think. After all, some of the scholars whose work has been most valuable in documenting in some granularity the ascendancy of what often goes by the name of neoliberalism have not always used the term themselves, preferring instead to narrate the organization of a well-funded network of political and business interests since the 1970s in terms of the politics of a new right and accommodationist center and center-left. Such work is not necessarily weakened by the omissions. Was

Howard Jarvis, the leader of the "Prop 13" campaign in California that slashed property taxes in 1978, a neoliberal? Was Barry Goldwater, when he shepherded his own version of small-government thinking to catastrophic electoral defeat in 1964? Were Ayn Rand, Alan Greenspan, or Ronald Reagan? Does it always necessarily matter?

The point is that to speak of living in a neoliberal age is not meant to legitimate a neo-McCarthyite hurling of epithets, a naming-and-shaming of one's ideological antagonists, nor to pretend that what is on offer in this book is anything like an exhaustive anatomy of either neoliberalism or the present era. It may instead come down to the deployment of what the philosopher Bertrand Russell once called a "linguistic convenience," or what we might alternatively think of as an expeditious historiographic shorthand. After all, for the purposes of what follows, there may very well be occasions when the term could arguably be substituted for, say, "(late) capitalism," "(post)postmodernity," or "(post)postmodernism," to the extent that these can all themselves be used to denote some of the same material, ideological, and cultural forms that global capitalism happens to have helped produce in the present age. The key point is that we live in an era in which ideas associated with neoliberalism have achieved a purchase they previously did not have, and that certain global structural conditions have contributed to that development. I leave it to the reader, in any case, to determine whether my terminologies offer sufficient analytical or strategic weight, merely proposing that, to the extent that it has emerged in concert with the material turn without yet being put in direct conversation with it, the sprawling literature on neoliberalism surely demands new ways of thinking about American culture's engagement with things in the 1980s, ways that are skeptical of claims about "materialism" as a socio-cultural or psycho-social fact, but equally skeptical of how the once-hegemonic discourse on the postmodern de-emphasized the materiality of things. To that end, the chapters that follow are predicated on the interpretative assumption that in combination with the emerging literatures on the material turn and neoliberalism, attention to the cultural and discursive history of the United States, a willingness to consider the phenomenon that we often mistake for "1980s materialism" across what Wai-Chi Dimock has encouraged literary scholars to think of as "deep time," opens up important new perspectives on the relationship between American culture and material things in the opening phase of the age of neoliberalism.[91]

For that reason, the remainder of this book explores how, even as the geopolitically rooted and admittedly still-partial triumph of neoliberalism entrenched deeper into the heart of a supposedly democratic nation forms of domination and dispossession that are themselves familiar from the history of imperialism both on and away from the North American continent, a peculiar epiphenomenon of the reconfiguration of capitalism that took place at the beginning of the "long 1980s" was an intensification—or at the very least, a rendering more prominent—of the argument about things in American life. This, indeed, may be the root of the conception of the period as peculiarly "materialistic," for if materialism itself will always be difficult to measure, and if attempts to measure it can always be subject to critique, it is undeniable that a certain discursive fixation on the question of material things and Americans' relation to them did indeed occur in the period. Recall, for example, how keenly Jimmy Carter insisted in 1979 that he and his fellow citizens had learned that "owning things and consuming things do not satisfy our longing for meaning."[92] As we will see, it was an observation powerful enough in the realm of national political discourse to ensure that George H. W. Bush was still publicly musing on its implications nearly a full decade after Carter first made it.

And by the time Carter did first make it, the argument about things was itself as much an "old staple of American culture" as anything so hard to define as "materialism."[93] Beyond political discourse, American narrative and visual culture had its own important, if often under-acknowledged or else misunderstood, contribution to make to that argument. For far from the unremittingly abject, inert dross—far from the mere "dreck" as Gore Vidal once characterized it—of some prominent cultural and political critics' caricature; far even from the easily malleable disdain that penetrating Marxian analyses have fostered for the phantasmagoric qualities of the commodity in a capitalist system, the goods and the garbage rendered in the culture of the part of the seemingly endless decade with which this book deals are remarkably polyvalent, communicating a series of aesthetic and epistemological positions on the part of their creators that move beyond straightforward critiques or celebrations of the supposed "materialism" of the age.[94] While the prevailing accounts of a society given over to materialism might be reflected in some mainstream cultural expression, something quite different was afoot as far as many other cultural representations of "particular things" were concerned in the first decade-and-a-half or so of neoliberalism's ascendency. Indeed, many of the renderings of things to be found in the art and culture of the period posed a series of consequential questions not only about capitalism in the neoliberal era but also about art, death, thought, war, and ultimately, that thing—or argument—that is the United States itself.

As we will see, then, many of the things rendered in American culture of the 1980s spoke, albeit against considerable critical resistance, of forms of dispossession that were more than merely material; they also whispered intimations of cultural and civilizational collapse. If they appeared, in the ways that some producers of culture rendered them, to help to construct a sense of the self, they did not do so at the expense of visions of that self as already part of wider social networks that crossed time and space. In this sense, even today, some of the things with which this book is concerned perform—or might be made to perform, if only we let or made them—a vitally important corrective function, underscoring the under-appreciated and potentially irresolvable complexity not only of things but also of the argument about things in American life. Often they expose the crudity of the way that argument has been conducted in far too many discursive spheres and thus show how part of the art of culture in the age of neoliberalism might be its capacity to render a depth of conceptual detail to the most pressing of public debates, revealing as it does so the limits of straightforwardly anti-materialist or neo-Platonic discourse, at least as far as any politics of opposition or resistance to the dictates of neoliberalism go.

Working across and between relevant disciplines, incorporating elements of literary, historical, political, and cultural analysis, and at the same time deliberately putting into conversation with one another scholarly discourses that have far too often taken place independent of one another, the discussion that follows has both a thematic and a roughly chronological structure. It begins by fixing upon one thing in particular: a single bottle of oil sat on a desk in Eastern Saudi Arabia in the middle of the 1950s, written into a book that was not published until the beginning of the 1970s. That starting point will enable us to dwell in Chapter One on the role of things, including the imperial pursuit of and global trade in things, in establishing some of the broader conditions that facilitated neoliberalism's ideological triumph in the United States. From there, we will be able to observe in Chapter Two the pronounced effect that the shifting configurations of global capitalism had on the conduct of the argument about things in political discourse as the "long 1980s" got underway, as well as some of the ways that mainstream culture dealt with, or failed to deal with, the transformation of global capitalism as that culture, in its turn, contributed to the argument about things. Chapter Three shifts the focus away from the profound structural changes coeval with the triumph of neoliberalism to consider how the aesthetic rendering of everyday consumer goods functioned, and was interpreted, across a range of cultural texts, from the art of Jeff Koons, the music of Talking Heads, and the fiction of Don DeLillo to the new and often-derided forms of literary realism that were emerging in the work of writers like Raymond Carver and Bobbie Ann Mason, as well as "brat pack" authors like Jay McInerney.

Chapter Four turns its attention to trash, exploring the ways that garbage provoked the expression of a certain archaeological consciousness across multiple forms of cultural expression, as politicians, writers, and artists were forced to confront the personal and civilizational implications of emerging knowledge about just how long-lived discarded matter previously assumed to be ephemeral would turn out to be. Chapter Five, meanwhile, considers the uneasy peace that American culture appeared to have made with things, at least in some quarters, by the end of the Cold War, examining the advent of a new epistemological respectability attached to everyday things alongside a close textual analysis of the writings of Nicholson Baker, whose highly idiosyncratic work challenged the popular myths of the mindlessness of materialism while also registering indirectly the profound shift in the structure of global capitalism that had occurred since the 1970s. Chapter Six examines the cultural weight exerted by the memory of the Vietnam War up to and including the early 1990s, suggesting that if, by that point, elites in the United States appeared to be imagining in things and through them a new immaterial vision of the future, they were doing so even as producers of culture sought to remind the nation of the oppressive weight of the capitalist and imperialist structures on which the subsequent history of the nation has shown any such future would still depend. My conclusion considers the contribution such cultural renderings of things have made to the argument about things and highlights some of the implications of that contribution for those that would seek to critique or otherwise resist "the world that neoliberalism has actually produced."[95]

CHAPTER 1

The Triumph of Neoliberalism

In 1971, the Middle East Export Press, based in Beirut, Lebanon, published *Discovery! The Search for Arabian Oil*. Its author was Wallace Stegner, the celebrated environmentalist and writer of the American West. In the mid-1950s, Stegner had accepted a commission from Aramco, the American Arabian Oil Company, to write the history of that consortium's successful search for oil on the Arabian Peninsula. That search had begun in 1933, when the California Arabian Standard Oil Company (now Chevron) started prospecting in the Kingdom of Saudi Arabia. Aramco, which was formed when Texaco, Exxon, and Mobil joined the California firm's endeavors, in part to avoid the US government acquiring a major share of the company, initially saw little to be gained from publishing the fruit of Stegner's efforts, sitting on his manuscript for ten years before eventually publishing it in fourteen installments in *Aramco World*, its in-house journal.[1] There is nothing to suggest that Stegner, whose literary environmentalism earned him honorary life membership in the Sierra Club and who would be instrumental in the passage of the 1964 Wilderness Act, was at all embarrassed by the work he had carried out for the consortium as a pen-for-hire, and by the early 1970s, he was evidently happy for it to be published in book form, supplying the Beirut publishers with a new introduction.

The tone of that 1971 introduction is fascinating. The writer who had so zealously defended the conservation of American wilderness writes up this all-too-consequential tale of resource exploitation in surprisingly positive terms, even a decade-and-a-half after his association with the oil giant had ended. "American oil development in the Middle East has been, all things considered, responsible and fair," Stegner explains, insisting that "Aramco can congratulate itself on a record that is a long way from being grossly exploitative or 'imperialist.'"[2] For all the environmentalist associations that cling to Stegner, those assignations of fairness and moderation had little, in fact, to do with the ecological interests of the Earth (which mankind had only just somewhat presumptuously granted its own "day" at the time Stegner was writing).

Rather, they had to do with the way the power of corporate America had brought to Saudi Arabia what Mark Twain in his sardonically anti-imperialist mode had once called "the blessings of civilization."[3] Those blessings extended in this case not just to the cutting-edge engineering techniques perfected by corporations like Bechtel but also to the development programs and "social engineering" projects that Stegner presents as part-and-parcel of the oil industry's hunt for profit on the Arabian Peninsula.[4] These included "training and health programs," allegedly generous employee benefits and savings programs, and an entire division of the company focused on Local Industrial Development, which led the Eastern Province of Saudi Arabia "into the American consumptive pattern and the productive patterns that supply it." For that is what, Stegner avers, "the Saudis themselves wanted—what, ultimately, they will not be denied."[5] The sum total of such efforts was almost as extensive in its local effects, Stegner suggests, as "Europe's Marshall Plan."[6]

Consider in this context the "bottle of black crude oil" that sat on the desk of an official involved in the management of the Tapline, the Bechtel-built Trans-Arabian Pipeline. It was there, according to Stegner, to remind the official "what business he was in."[7] Even amidst all that corporate-led social and developmental uplift, Stegner's account of which reads now like an unintentionally ironic iteration of what Kipling in the late nineteenth century infamously called the "white man's burden," was it really likely that the manager might lose sight of the profits that were accruing from the commodity buried deep beneath his feet? Either way, it is clear what that bottle of oil itself was trying to do: narrate a story about the essential goodness of the United States and of the things it was both making for the world and taking from it by the early 1970s. At the same time, however, Stegner's mise-en-scène does offer, in spite of the corporate-financed conditions under which it was produced, an important reminder of the complexities of American imperialism in the 1970s. For, as we will see, one way to understand that bottle of black crude is as a material and symbolic embodiment of a geopolitically rooted reordering that was to have a profound effect on American life, ushering the nation into a phase of disorientating inflation that would give fresh impetus to a well-established feature of American cultural history while more or less ensuring the triumph of the now-hegemonic ideology of neoliberalism.

*

From the late nineteenth century, thinkers as diverse as J. A. Hobson, Lenin, Joseph Schumpeter, and Hannah Arendt understood "imperialism" as a process by which private capitalist interests of one sort or another successfully enrolled the powers of the state in defending those interests.[8] Thus, the history of the East India Company's commercial exploitation of the Asian subcontinent had become the history of the British raj, that of various plantations along the Eastern seaboard of North America, British America, and, in due course, the independent but expansive United States. A version of such imperialist processes had already informed American literary culture, as can be seen from a work like *Cabbages and Kings*, by O. Henry. Based on the author's own experiences in Honduras, Henry's narrative, a deeply ironic saga of late nineteenth-century American imperialism, unfolds in the fictional Central American republic of Anchuria and opens with the image of a "small adventurer, with empty pockets to fill, light of heart, busy-brained . . . bearing an alarm clock with which . . . to awaken the beautiful tropics from their centuries' sleep."[9] The collection of interlinked stories that follows is set against the backdrop of the kind of profit-led imperialist incursions into the nominally independent republics of Central America that would see the hard power of the United States deployed again and again in defense of "US interests" in the early 1900s: "Gentlemen adventurers throng the waiting-rooms of its rulers with proposals for railways and concessions. The little *opéra-bouffe* nations play at government and intrigue until some day [sic] a big, silent gunboat glides into the offing."[10] Thus Henry reminds us that these often at-first very minor key imperial adventures were frequently tales of things and the profits that could be made from them. Think bananas, and banana republics. Think too of the history of the United Fruit Company, but think also of the two-way traffic in things that inevitably emerges from such endeavors, with the agents of Western capitalism carrying with them on their quests for commodifiable resources all the alluring accoutrements of modern manufacturing, the equivalent of Henry's "small adventurer's" alarm clock.

Dwelling on Henry's text sheds some light on Stegner's if only because, at first glance, Stegner's work mirrors aspects of the earlier writer's, albeit stripped of their irony. Listen, for example, to Stegner wax lyrical about what Aramco's oil prospectors brought to "eastern Saudi Arabia": nothing less than a "revolution of *things* . . . For whatever they may think of the nations which produce and possess them, whatever distaste they have for their beliefs, their dress, and their politics, no people in history has been able to resist for half an hour the *things* that people like this small contingent of geologists bring with them."[11] Woodrow Wilson had made a similar claim about the power of (American) things some decades previously, the historian-turned-politician having once instructed an audience of businessmen to "go out and sell goods that will make the world more comfortable and happy, and convert them to the principles of America."[12] Once framed in this context, it is hard not to see the bottle of black crude that Stegner invoked in 1971 as merely the latest enabling commodity in the long tale of Western imperialism, with Bechtel and the oil companies in the role of Virginia planters or the gentlemen adventurers of O. Henry's earlier tale.

Indeed, the place occupied by things in such narrative meditations on imperialism *à l'Américaine* points toward one explanation, not only for the presence of Aramco and Bechtel in the Middle East in the mid-1930s but also for some of the central features of the world situation of today. After all, much of the suffocatingly close geostrategic engagement with the region that has seen repeated military and political interventions on the part of the United States has been predicated on the perceived strategic importance of being able to exercise some degree of control over the supply of oil from the Gulf region. This was made explicit in January 1980, when President Carter pronounced that an "attempt by any outside force to gain control of the Persian Gulf region will be regarded as an assault on the vital interests of the United States of America, and such an assault will be repelled by any means necessary, including military force."[13] Decades earlier, the CIA had orchestrated a coup in Syria after the sitting government refused to ratify the terms of an agreement with the Trans-Arabian Pipeline company.[14] In 1953, the same agency conspired with British intelligence services to reverse the nationalization of Iranian oil by overthrowing the democratically elected Mossadegh.[15] The Carter Doctrine thus formalized and extended a strategic process that has meant that today, one form "the big, silent gunboat" off the coast of O. Henry's Central American Republic takes in the Middle East is that of the US Navy's Fifth Fleet, permanently stationed since the mid-1990s in Bahrain, the oil-rich island state fewer than twenty miles off the coast of Al Khobar, which, as Stegner relates, is a city the discovery of oil in Eastern Saudi Arabia raised out of little more than "a couple of palm-thatch fishermen's *barastis*."[16]

If in his account of Aramco's quest for Arabian oil Stegner takes great pains to insist that this was no "imperialist" endeavor, he takes even greater pains to distinguish American activities in the region from older European models of state-supported economic exploitation, stressing that the United States government "was so far from being involved" in the search for oil that "it didn't even have a representative in Saudi Arabia."[17] Putting to one side the fact that Stegner was unlikely to have known, writing in the mid-1950s, the true extent of the CIA's presence within Aramco itself, nor to have been able fully to grasp the still-developing web of relations that would see Western "democracy" increasingly underpinned by the oil-rich autocracies of the contemporary Middle East, it is fair to say that the US government is now more than sufficiently represented in the region, projecting its military and political power in a way that simultaneously indicates the sheer extent of the agentic potency of oil: conjuring up cities and ships, resentments and wars as efficiently as any earlier incarnations of imperial objects of desire.[18] In this sense, what spices and opium were to other geographic locales at earlier historical moments, so oil has proved to the Middle East since the end of the Second World War, a period in which the United States has assumed its own version of the imperialistic role once played by the older European powers in the region, proving itself as it does so no less powerlessly at the behest of things and the profits that might accrue from them than those earlier powers were in their own time. It was not just, as Stegner seemed to think, the case that "trade followed the flag," but as theorists of the causes of empire had explained, that trade sought out things and the state followed dutifully behind.[19] As Timothy Mitchell has argued, the thing at the heart of the whole process is and remains oil itself, "whose energy is the force that oil firms seek to master and whose location, abundance, density and other properties shape the methods and apparatus of its control."[20]

In elucidating those methods and that apparatus, Mitchell has shown how "the major oil companies, which were the first and largest of the new transnational corporations of the twentieth century, established their global presence at the historical moment when the old [European] system of empire, built up originally through colonising corporations, was finally disintegrating."[21] For Mitchell, this was itself part of a longer historical process involving the "engineering [of] political relations out of flows of energy" that has seen the shift from coal power to oil power in turn transfer political power further away from organized labor in the West, which had previously been able to use its physical capacity to shut down or otherwise interrupt the flow of coal to demand, and achieve, "improvements to collective life."[22] The material properties of the fuels in question were central to this process. The fluidity of oil, which enabled it to be drilled, traded, and transported via far less labor-intensive, and far-more grid-like, networks of derricks and pipelines has effectively disabled this political process, enabling instead a set of political relations that has seen the global power of transnational corporations, still attended by the military power of the US, operate in concert with more local forces of repression in the form of autocratic (and in the case of Saudi Arabia, familial) national governments.[23] By means of such processes, Mitchell relates, the infrastructure of the modern state of Saudi Arabia has been developed, while the political power of its workforce has been constrained. Thus, oil energy and Aramco may well have built the nation's "towns, road system, railway, telecommunications network, ports and airports, and acted as banker to the ruling family and investor in Saudi enterprise," but oil energy and Aramco also conspired with the Saudi monarchical kinship-state to repress Arab workers' demands.[24] Indeed, the year after Stegner first composed his account of Aramco's endeavors in the Arabian Peninsula, a general strike saw Saudi workers demand a constitution, labor unions, political parties, and "an end to Aramco's interference in the country's affairs."[25] They also demanded the closure of the US military base that had been established at Dharhan. The outcome was, perhaps, predictable: "Aramco's security department identified the strike leaders to the Saudi security forces, who imprisoned or deported the organisers."[26]

There are, though, risks in seeing the modern geopolitics of oil as a mere case of history repeating well-established patterns of Western imperial domination. For in retrospect, we might equally think of the contents of the bottle on the executive's desk as bespeaking Western vulnerabilities as much as Western power. In 1971, the same year Stegner's work for Aramco was finally published in book form, the landmark Tehran and Tripoli agreements more or less ensured such vulnerability by formalizing a far more powerful role for the governments of Middle Eastern oil-producing states in setting oil prices.[27] The agreements mandated significant increases in the commodity's price per barrel and determined that for the first time, producer states would take in tax more than a fifty percent share of the profits generated from oil sales. King Ibn Saud of Saudi Arabia had himself been a pioneer in this regard, negotiating a 50/50 split of revenues with Aramco as early as 1950, which was perhaps why Stegner's corporate-sponsored account of Aramco's story in the Arabian Peninsula repeatedly gave embarrassingly Orientalist voice to fears about the perils posed by "emotional nationalists."[28] The dread specter of what Stegner disapprovingly called "willful nationalization" had also led to the Anglo-American intervention in Iran in 1953; and nationalization, too, would in time be Aramco's fate, the company being taken under full control of the Saudi state in 1980.[29] That, however, was not before the economic vulnerability of the West to imported oil had been demonstrated in the two oil shocks of the 1970s, the first in 1973–74, the second in 1979, when the leaders of Saudi Arabia and other oil-producing states, now organized into the OPEC cartel, increased oil prices.

Such considerations complicate the view of that bottle of black crude in important ways. What was going on in the 1970s was in one sense the result of classic "resource imperialism."[30] And yet, as we have seen, this was not just the imposition of some rigidly determined, all-pervasive, top-down Yankee control in areas of the globe (the Middle East, South East Asia) in which the crumbling dominion of the older European states necessitated a passing of the imperial baton to the United States. Instead, we were witnessing the emergence of a new system of global market integration and interdependence that marked the end of the Bretton Woods era, the transition towards the present age, and the latest phase in an American form of imperialism that would see the United States itself become increasingly vulnerable to only apparently exogenous shocks reverberating down what G. K. Kiernan identified in the late 1970s as a "new main line of American expansion, economic and political" that had been established in the oil-rich nations of the Middle East from the 1930s onwards.[31] For what was really crumbling was the Bretton Woods system, which had survived from the end of the Second World War until the "Nixon shock" of August 1971, when Nixon introduced wage and price controls, hiked import duties, and took the dollar off the gold standard.[32] In spite of such semi-protectionist maneuvers, designed in part to protect an overvalued dollar, by the end of the decade, deep integration of the world's oil markets was a fait accompli precisely because demand for the commodity continued to spiral and the activities of corporations like Aramco and the Anglo-Persian Oil Company (now BP) over previous decades had helped to prime the pump of the "oil power" that OPEC nations would later wield. Energy self-sufficiency, which Nixon called for after the 1973 oil shock, was simply not viable by that point, nor desirable from a transnational oil company's point of view, and so American imperialism found itself vulnerable to the nascent economic power of rapidly developing nations over which it exercised no formal dominion.

Should we understand this complex set of affairs as something like a postmodern imperialism? Like latter-day Stegners, some historians of the oil politics of the 1970s still shy away from anything that smacks too much of American empire.[33] Leftist critics like Michael Hardt and Antonio Negri, meanwhile, have revised earlier understandings of the phenomenon by conceiving of "Empire" as a power structure that has in some sense left the hegemonic nation state far behind it.[34] Others, like Sam Gindin and Leo Panitch, suggest there is an American empire with the power of a nation state still very much at its heart but that it took until well after the end of the Cold War for the United States to begin exercising anything like true dominion over the global capitalist system.[35] Mitchell's analysis speaks of a "combination of a variety of social logics and forces" when describing configurations of power in the "age of oil," within which the conduct of the United States in the Middle East stands out on account of "the breadth of its involvement in the use of violence across the region, its increasing reliance on wars of attrition as a normal instrument of politics, and its efforts to prevent the resolution of conflicts."[36] Yet Daniel J. Sargent's somewhat less radical account of the early stages of the present era adds to such debates important insights into the extent to which any attempts by US policymakers to behave imperially during this period of the Cold War were in fact subject to a range of "ironic" effects, which may itself be just a milder term for what Chalmers Johnson in his work on American imperialism calls "blowback."[37] For example, Sargent quotes Henry Kissinger's reflections on the emergence of powerful oil states in the region and the pressure they brought to bear on the West through the weaponization of their oil resources. Kissinger's tone was both offensively imperious and genuinely perplexed: "It is ridiculous that the civilized world is held up by eight million savages. . . .We are now living in a never-never land in which tiny, poor, and weak nations can hold up for ransom some of the industrialized world."[38] The early years of Bretton Woods had seen US trade surpluses efficiently recycled via Marshall Plan aid into Western European purchases of US manufactured goods and Middle Eastern oil. By the 1970s, European and Japanese manufactured goods were beginning to compete with American ones. Even the so-called "third world" was sufficiently powerful to inflict serious damage on the West at the same moment that the American war in Vietnam was demonstrating how similar asymmetries would play out on the bloodiest of Cold War battlefields. Now this, surely, was not how empire, nor even Kennanite containment, was supposed to work out. Or perhaps it is how empires have always worked out? In any event, Kissinger's confusion in the face of the world taking shape in the 1970s is symptomatic of just how complex the relation between capital and state would become throughout the neoliberal era.

It is thus impossible to view Stegner's bottle of oil either in the light of gentle American benignity that the author's writing of it attempts to cast or in the grimmer, wholly deterministic shades that an anti-imperialist impulse might tend to call forth. Instead, it is a representative marker of a set of transformations that we now know were about to take effect in the world and, at the same time, an embodiment of some of the dark ironies of American imperialism. After all, in Sargent's telling, it was the US desire to bolster Iran and Saudi Arabia as twin pillars of regional security in the Middle East that led policy-makers to view developments like the Tehran agreement with little concern. The petrodollars that accrued to Iran and Saudi Arabia allowed them to buy US-produced arms with which they could ensure "stability" in the region, guard against Cold War incursions by the Soviet Union, and recycle dollars back to the US.[39] Both Judith Stein and Chalmers Johnson have shown how similar trade-offs between economic and geostrategic interests contributed to the hollowing out of the US steel industry in the 1970s, as the strategic impor-tance of East Asia to US military plans led trade negotiators to allow Japanese and Korean steel to enter the US domestic market without insisting on recipro-cal arrangements.[40] In an even more acute irony, the petrodollars pooling in the Middle East in the 1970s would soon be reinvested, via New York invest-ment banks, in Latin American sovereign debt, supposedly safe bets that, when they failed, would eventually leave the field clear for the imposition of the neo-liberal "Washington consensus" across much of Central and South America.[41]

In this way, the nuances of US military imperialism combined with capital's inherent restlessness were already somewhat unexpectedly conspiring toward the material reordering of the global political economy, offshoring ever-larger proportions of production and taking the first tentative steps toward the present, post-Cold War configuration, in which more and more goods are made neither in one country nor another but, thanks to market integration, containerization, and global supply chains near-rhizomatic in their geographical complexity, in a place called "the world." In fact, by the 1970s, what were already beginning to emerge out of the ruins of Bretton Woods were some of the principal contours of a new "world," in which highly organized, hyper-mobile capital would hold the whip-hand over the increasingly disorganized, state-disciplined, and demoralized forces of labor. As a result of this changing configuration, the US role was already significantly different from what it had been in the preceding post-Second World War decades. Increasingly, that role was no longer to manufacture the things that the world needed or wanted; instead, if the emerging system were to function, it had to consume them like never before. That fundamental fact is what explains balance of trade figures that, according to the federal government's census figures, have seen the United States import more than it exports every year since 1976; in 2015, the trade deficit was as high as $500 billion, or $762 billion counting goods alone.[42] In work similar in some ways to Mitchell's, Jefferson Cowie has brilliantly documented just how well-established capital's restless quest for docile (and therefore profitable) labor environments has been on the North American continent, his study of RCA showing how production shifted from New Jersey in the 1930s to Indiana in the 1940s, Tennessee in the 1960s, and Mexico in the 1970s.[43] It is instructive to think about the kind of complementary movements that were also afoot on the global level by the 1970s, driven both by oil and the United States' geostrategic aims. Just as the exploitation of the CIA-enabled coup in Chile in 1973 by the "Chicago boys" saw Cold War strategy facilitate the earliest experiments with neoliberalism, Cold War policy vis-à-vis both the Far and Middle East played its part in ensuring that ever-higher proportions of oil and steel production went the same way as so much manufacturing plant.

This was less, then, a case of the postmodern dematerialization of capital and more a matter of its spatial reconfiguration. Things were not vanishing into thin air; they were merely learning how to inscribe ever more complicated spatial trajectories in a complex, rapidly globalizing system that would mean Americans would soon be less and less likely to encounter the things of their world at the start of those things' lives. Ever-dwindling proportions of the population, in fact, would have the dubious honor of working in steel mills or oil refineries or on factory floors, places in which technological change was already a threat to their continued presence. Bouts of economic nationalism were to break out as American workers and consumers found themselves not so much alienated from the fruits of their own labor as confronted by those of others'. With the final abolition of outflow capital controls in 1974, hot money was free to flow where it could, while towns and communities built on industry and once sustained by the short-lived magic of capital were left to ruin. The nature of Americans' relation to things was thus by the mid-1970s already being transformed by forces and networks of agency both remarkable in their complexity and brutal in their effects.

*

But if the "average" American's role in this emerging system was going to be to consume the things of the world, that mythical figure needed to be able to afford what the world had to offer. And the central problem that this emergent global order faced in the 1970s, the phenomenon that informed not only the design of the Nixon shock but the efficacy of the two oil shocks that would follow it, looks in retrospect like the most potent of all the energies we might imagine stoppered up in that bottle of black crude that Stegner depicts perched on the oil executive's desk. For although the Arab-Israeli conflict was the key precipitating factor in prompting the first oil shock and the Iranian revolution the second, the inflationary effects of both shocks were to be arguably even further-reaching than the ongoing failure to resolve the regional conflicts of the Middle East, providing the material conditions for a second "great transformation" in the relation between markets and societies that we can recognize now as key to the triumph of neoliberalism. And while the inflation that plagued the 1970s was multifactorial, and the political stripe of economists and economic historians still among the best ways to determine what many of them see as the main driver of that inflation, several recent analyses take the view that it was rapidly escalating energy prices rather than pressure from union-backed wage demands or expenditures on the war in Vietnam that were the primary cause of double-digit price increases that were witnessed throughout the decade.[44] This was, in the view of modern monetary theorist Warren Mosler, a "cost-push" inflation, in which prices rose because "everything is ultimately 'made out of food and energy' and hikes in those costs work through to everything else over time."[45] That is not to say labor power and war expenditures did not play a part, but that the most vital component of the transformationally high levels of inflation of the 1970s was the global oil price, which increased approximately five-hundred percent between 1970 and 1980 before tumbling again in the mid-1980s. This suggests a double valence to the potency of crude oil, for that substance proved simultaneously powerful enough first to run a global economy and then, in concert with the policy prescriptions of the neoliberals, to change the world so many of us now live in.

And once they began to be realized from 1973 onwards, the inflationary and ideological consequences of that potential were certainly remarkable. Karl Polanyi wrote in his 1944 magnum opus, *The Great Transformation*, of the "double movement" by means of which the market became at least partly disembedded from society in the nineteenth century only to provoke a dialectical drive towards either fascism or the kind of social protections from the market's injurious effects associated with the New Deal and other Western welfare states. What Mark Blyth has argued Polanyi did not foresee was that this process could be repeated in reverse, which was precisely what happened when neoliberalism emerged in the 1970s and 1980s as the ideological antidote to the failure of "embedded liberalism" to continue producing profit, a failure ensured by the elite perception of the oil-powered inflation of the 1970s as severe enough to merit a form of economic sadism as the supposed short-cut to a return to stability and prosperity.[46] For the monetary response to high inflation launched by the Federal Reserve of restricting the money supply in such a way as to ratchet up interest rates provoked the deep and injurious recession of the early 1980s but was itself just part of a wider package of measures that an avalanche of data has shown has resulted in nothing less than the upward redistribution of vast sums of wealth to the economic elite.[47]

By at least one account, this happened because, in a stagflationary environment in which prices were rising and profits and perceptions of the potential for future profits were being squeezed, partisans of the "free market" were able to capture first large parts of the rich ecosystem of ideological apparatuses that surrounds the state and then the state itself. By such means, they attempted once again to "disembed" the object of their affection from society, bringing us ever-closer to what Wendy Brown has described as the "extension of economic rationality to all aspects of thought and activity," a new iteration of what Polanyi decades ago dubbed the "stark utopia" implied by "the self-adjusting market."[48] On the domestic level, political scientists have taken the 1971 Powell memorandum, in which the Virginia corporate lawyer and thereafter Supreme Court justice Lewis Powell complained in a memo to the United States Chamber of Commerce of the plight of business interests, as a rallying cry that was heeded by business and corporate interests as they revolutionized their own capacity for political organization in the 1970s and 1980s.[49] "One does not exaggerate to say that, in terms of political influence with respect to the course of legislation and government action, the American business executive is truly the 'forgotten man,'" claimed Powell.[50] In the years that followed, such interests organized themselves to remarkable effect, repeatedly exerting sufficient pressure to ensure that the legislative and regulatory "drift" of policy across various levels of government would remain overwhelmingly in their favor throughout the "long 1980s," a move consonant with the supply-side economics and deregulatory fervor that has characterized the entrenchment of so much neoliberal doctrine in the United States.[51]

Be all that as it may, any assessment of this second great transformation needs to give due credit to the sheer potency of the fossil fuel that also helped create the peculiar conditions that encouraged policymakers finally to turn to a set of what were previously minority-held ideas that managed to link the broad concept of personal freedom with a "belief in private property and the competitive market" and an embrace of the ongoing globalization of capital, a consequential ideological shift the material impetus for which we might want to imagine, if only in part, as already lurking and waiting to be realized in the hydrocarbons contained in Stegner's executive's bottle, perched on that desk in the mid-1950s.[52] After all, among the constituencies that did not suffer from the upward spiral of oil prices in the 1970s were the scions of longstanding US oil interests like Richard Mellon Scaife and Charles and David Koch, major benefactors of the network of think tanks like the Heritage Foundation and the Cato Institute that have done so much to promote some of the tenets of neoliberalism.[53] In this sense, it is perhaps not just oil itself but the whole crisis-and-response network of class conflict, imperialism, Cold War strategizing, valuable hydrocarbons, Middle East politics, inflation, and ideological mobilization that has helped create the long neoliberal moment that we are still experiencing. If oil was by no means the only motive force in operation, it was a significant agent in the transformation nonetheless.

Contributing factors.

*

In truth, had one even been able to secure a copy of Stegner's book in 1971, no prolonged meditation on that bottle of oil would have predicted the sheer extent of the influence of the inflationary power of the precious hydrocarbons it contained. For at the very same time that it was precipitating the most significant ideological shift of the last half-century, oil-powered inflation—or at least, the profound reordering of global systems of which that inflation was both symptom and cause—was also affecting the discursive life of the nation, stoking a pronounced reanimation of the argument about things in American life. After all, it was the economic misery apparently visited upon the American people by the painful emergence of the new disposition of capitalism's global resources that eventually led to President Jimmy Carter telling the American people in a televised presidential address in July 1979, in the midst of the second oil shock, that "we've discovered that owning things and consuming things do not satisfy our longing for meaning. We've learned that piling up material goods cannot fill the emptiness of lives which have no confidence and purpose."[54] The electoral sequel to Carter's "malaise" or "crisis of confidence" speech is well known. The following November, he was voted out of office, comprehensively defeated by Ronald Reagan as both gas shortages and the Iranian hostage crisis dragged on, whereupon the nation found itself entering a decade in which, in the words of one recent history of the period, the United States would find itself "awash in things" and given over to a culture of "things for everyone."[55] On this view, Carter's speech is of interest precisely because it went unheeded. It was as if, eschewing Carter's puritanical asceticism, the nation instead fell *en masse* for the sunny prosperity gospel preached by his successor and, what is more, found itself thoroughly relieved to have done so, at least in some accounts. "For years we have been taught not to like things. Finally somebody said it was OK to like things. This was a great relief," remarked no less of an authority on the national temper than David Byrne of Talking Heads in the mid-1980s.[56]

By then, of course, the "long 1980s" were well underway, and just such rhetorical invocations of "things" and Americans' relations with them were to prove a discursive feature of the age. In 1986, for example, Wall Street arbitrageur Ivan Boesky infamously used a commencement address at the University of California, Berkeley to articulate a position on things and their acquisition that could not have been further from Carter's: "Greed is all right, by the way. I want you to know that. I think greed is healthy. You can be greedy and still feel good about yourself."[57] In the same year, Boesky confessed to his part in a multi-million dollar insider trading scandal and was sentenced to three years in prison, his speech allegedly providing the inspiration for the maxim used in Oliver Stone's *Wall Street* (1987) that "Greed is good."[58] Michael Lewis's *Liar's Poker* (1989), a first-hand account of the life of a young bond trader working for Salomon Brothers, appeared to capture the spirit of the times, at least on Wall Street: "They valued profits," Lewis wrote. "And money. Especially money, and all the things that money could buy."[59] In his 1989 inaugural address, as if concerned that he had become too intimately associated with such a view of things during his years as Reagan's vice president, President George H. W. Bush asked his fellow Americans: "But have we changed as a nation even in our time? Are we enthralled with material things, less appreciative of the nobility of work and sacrifice?" His answer was clear, direct, reassuring: "My friends, we are not the sum of our possessions. They are not the measure of our lives. In our hearts we know what matters."[60]

Bush's words were an implicit response both to the analysis laid out by Carter nearly a decade previously and the sustained cultural discourse on things that had followed it. But they were also, I want to suggest, something else. For such pronouncements, emanating from and referring back to some of the most prominent political and cultural figures of the age, have been central to understandings of the 1980s as an age given over to "materialism." Similarly, the rejection of Carter and the embrace of Reagan, or the elevation of characters like Boesky, Donald Trump, Lee Iacocca, Sam Walton, or even the Madonna of "Material Girl," to important historiographical exemplars of the spirit of the age, have all tended to form part of the familiar narrative about the supposed "materialism" of the 1980s. They risk doing so at the relative expense of the consequences and implications of the deep recessions that bookended the 1980s, or the bailout of financial institutions and upward redistributions of wealth that were also taking place in the decade. There was, in any case, evidently more than simply "materialism" going on here. It is more accurate to say that the very prominence and form of an explicit discourse on things that itself seems closely tied to questions of national identity, particularly because such discourse flourished both in the face of inflation and the shift towards neoliberalism, suggests that what was happening was not so much an embrace of materialism on the part of the nation's population at large as an epiphenomenal reanimation, rooted in an epochal reconfiguration of global capitalism, of that very old argument about things in American life to which politicians, producers of culture, and other commentators had long been contributing.

Thus, if we tend to see the 1979 speech in which Carter inveighed against piling up material goods as somehow remarkable, we might in some ways be better off thinking of it as representative, both of the long-running argument about things and the "long 1980s" in general. From this perspective, far from falling on deaf ears, Carter's so-called "malaise" speech in fact established as peculiarly prominent what has remained a central preoccupation of the political and cultural discourse of the age of neoliberalism: things and Americans' relation to them. One question that remains to be answered in much finer detail, however, is the extent to which such political and cultural contributions to the argument about things were themselves registering (or else failing to register) the true extent and nature of some of the changes that the simultaneously material and ideological triumph of neoliberalism was already in the process of ushering into the life of the nation by the late 1970s. What, for example, was the relationship between the anti-materialist rhetoric of his "malaise" speech and Carter's own well-documented role in the transition towards neoliberalism? And how did American culture appear to respond to the structural transformations afoot, both in the late 1970s and the decade that followed?

CHAPTER 2

After the Great Transformation

There is a fine poem by the Objectivist poet George Oppen, published in the late 1960s, called "Of Being Numerous" (1968). It begins, "There are things/We live among 'and to see them/Is to know ourselves."[1] The poem, which is a late modernist meditation on what it was to live in the simultaneously democratic, capitalist, and imperialist United States in the 1960s, as well as a late twentieth-century response to both Whitman's "Song of Myself" and T. S. Eliot's "The Waste Land," treats of the self and that self's consciousness of itself, of others, and of the nation to which it supposedly owes some sort of allegiance. The lines that open the poem thus induce two related thoughts of some significance for both this chapter and the chapters that follow: the first about the primacy of subject–object relations in constructing a sense of self; the second about the role played by such relations in determining a sense of a nation. To the extent that they meditate on the latter, the lines are themselves contributions to the same long-running argument about things in American life into which Jimmy Carter would so memorably intervene in 1979. For Oppen, the existential self was knowable in its relation to things; for Carter, scaling up to the cultural level the clinical view that the "narcissism" Christopher Lasch had written about stemmed from "blur[ring] the boundaries between the self and the world of objects," this was precisely the problem in a nation plagued in the late 1970s not so much by capitalism per se as by a globalizing capitalism entering a period of crisis.[2] And however divergent in ethos these claims about things and our relations to them might be, it is the central argument of this book that they are both most profitably understood as contributions to the same cultural debate.

But were Oppen and Carter in fact participating in the same debate? An obvious objection is that politics and culture represent distinct discursive arenas that might inflect in different directions at different times, and that what we are thus dealing with here is not one argument but two, or even several arguments. Such an objection prompts reference to the question of disciplinary perspective, for it is perfectly possible to see in place of one long argument about things in American life a series of quite discrete debates occurring in different discursive spheres at different times. Another way to answer the objection, however, is to say that the obvious contextual distinctions that exist between, on the one hand, a thought framed in the discursive context of avant-garde, experimentalist poetry and, on the other, one framed in a televised presidential address are very much to the point of the cultural historical claim I am trying to make and much of the cultural analysis that will follow. For it is surely the remarkable prominence of the discursive engagement with material things and Americans' relations with them as much as that engagement's no less remarkable pervasiveness that makes it appear that a significant reanimation of the argument about things in American life was definitively underway as the imperially derived, oil-powered inflation of the 1970s gave way to the entrench-ment of the doctrines of neoliberalism.

The poetry of George Oppen, after all, had belonged to an obscure artistic avant-garde, that of the Objectivist poets who not only followed William Carlos Williams's dictum that there should be "no ideas/but in things," but actively sought to make "things" out of the poems they themselves made. Just one decade later, operating, as Natasha Zaretsky has intimated, under the influence of his own inadequate reading of the work of Lasch, a sitting president broached the question of things and Americans' relation to them in the way that Carter did. [3] To have Carter's successor-but-one, George H. W. Bush, return to the same theme once he found himself on the cusp of the presidency might speak on this view to the discursive breadth and historical depth of the kind of argument about things that I have claimed has long characterized the cultural and discursive history of the United States. And even if it fails convincingly to do that, it still nonetheless shows that a definitive attempt to dwell on the meaning and significance of Americans' relation to things was certainly front and center of the national discursive stage at important points in the "long 1980s." Thus, whether we choose to see contextually distinct speech acts like Oppen's and Carter's as parts of the same conversation or else contributions to more circumscribed ones, both perspectives are themselves distinct from those that see the 1980s as an era simply given over to "materialism." For they both equally recognize that the *discourse* on that supposed materialism, which appears frequently to include a strategic co-option of the anti-materialist rhetoric of the New Left of the 1960s, was of itself as culturally significant as the kind of social attitude surveys that historians have cited as proof of the decade's mania for material things.[4] Moreover, in either scenario, there is a weight of circumstantial evidence to suggest that whatever else this discursive engagement was, it

certainly looks in retrospect like a cultural epiphenomenon of the shifting configurations of the global capitalist order.

Just consider once again some of the material conditions out of which
Carter's "malaise" speech emerged. The late 1970s saw not just soaring inflation
but low growth and high unemployment, hence the coinage of that noxious
portmanteau, "stagflation." In 1979 itself, in a textbook example of imperial
"blowback" caused by the fall of the US-backed Shah of Iran decades after he
had been installed in power with Western support, the United States found
itself in the grip of the second oil shock. Queues of motorists battled for access
to gas priced at ever-higher levels in an inflationary environment that tended
to prompt consumers to either purchase today what might have increased in
price, if not tomorrow, then uncomfortably soon, or else use the newly available but already rapidly expanding markets in personal credit and private
finance to do so.[5] After a Camp David retreat at which he had surrounded himself with political and intellectual advisors, Carter addressed the nation as if
the material circumstances with which Americans were struggling were simply
symptomatic of a supposedly far "deeper" problem. "In a nation that was proud
of hard work, strong families, close-knit communities, and our faith in God,"
Carter told his television audience, "too many of us now worship self-indul-
gence and consumption. Human identity is no longer defined by what one
does, but by what one owns."[6]

Notwithstanding the main thrust of his own rhetoric, Carter's speech, just
like a seventeenth-century Puritan jeremiad prompted by bad harvests, is obviously about those material things that are invoked even as their significance is
denied.[7] "It's clear that the true problems of our Nation are much deeper—
deeper than gasoline lines or energy shortages, deeper even than inflation or
recession," Carter claims; and yet his speech is a response to those same material circumstances. Indeed, in some ways, the speech's incorporation of aspects
of the form of the jeremiad reads like a deliberate attempt to spiritualize a
material crisis.[8] Take the manner in which Carter's words mirror what Sacvan
Bercovitch has shown to be the essentially affirmative nature of the jeremiad as
a rhetorical form, and how, when it comes to that part of his jeremiad in which
he points the way out of the crisis, Carter dwells less on spiritual concerns and
returns instead, somewhat bathetically, to the realm of material things, pro-
moting in the light of the US's increasing dependence on foreign oil not just
energy conservation measures, but, like Nixon before him, a boosting of
domestic extractive industries and an increase in worker productivity.[9] It is an
interesting historical quirk: the troubles besetting capitalism at the end of the

1970s prompting presidential recourse to an early modern rhetorical form and what looks like a reignition of the argument about things in the nation's political discourse.

Whatever its origins, the deployment of that argument obviously had its political uses, or so Carter had hoped. Indeed, the initial public reception of the speech was positive, but soon soured in the face of critical commentary. Such commentary was perhaps no less than it deserved. After all, bearing in mind the role his administration played in assisting neoliberalism's ascendency, there is something rather trite in the disdain Carter manufactured for the merely "material." By the late 1970s, and partly as a result of the political organization of business interests touched upon above, the widening of class inequalities and the redistribution of wealth up the income ladder were already underway in the United States. That was a fact hidden in plain sight: "The standard of living of the average American has to decline," stated the Chair of the Federal Reserve, Paul Volcker, shortly after his appointment.[10] Like Thatcherism in Europe, the adoption in the 1980s of the precepts of monetarism and "Reaganomics" was obviously pivotal to hastening those outcomes, but such an acknowledgment should not obscure the contributions made by both successor and preceding administrations of the purported center and/or center-left throughout the West over the course of the "long 1980s."

Thus, it is important to remember that when, in August 1979, Volcker began the aggressive attempts to tame inflation that raised interest rates to eye-watering levels subsequently unheard of in the age of neoliberalism, he did so as a Carter appointee. Similarly, if Reagan's policy prescriptions were recognizably neoliberal (deregulation, privatization, and reductions in both corporate and personal tax rates), the earliest moves in this direction were made under Carter, whose administration oversaw both tax cuts and the deregulation of key sectors of the economy in a bid to foster the desiderata of less state control and more "competition." And these were moves that had significant consequences as far as "material things" were concerned. The 1978 Revenue Act, for example, reduced corporation and capital gains taxes, while the Natural Gas Policy Act of 1978 deregulated the domestic gas markets through a phased lifting of price ceilings, incentivizing domestic producers to bring more energy to markets that had already proven themselves at the mercy of the geopolitical instability the conduct of US foreign relations helped to bring about.[11] The Motor Carrier Act of 1980, which certainly expedited the speed and ease with which goods could be trucked throughout the United States, did so to the material detriment of truckers themselves, with the costs in significantly reduced wages

41

repeatedly identified by the Federal Trade Commission as amply compensated by the benefit that deregulation brought to "society" as a whole.[12]

Such moves, remember, were coming from the party of the New Deal and are difficult not to interpret as evidence that Carter's "anti-materialism" was at least partly strategic, his fervent but mistaken belief that the federal budget deficit was responsible for the inflation that plagued his administration notwithstanding.[13] But truckers' paychecks were of perhaps less concern to him and the new centrists of the Democratic Party in the 1970s than their party's association with organized labor might suggest. Senator Dale Bumpers of Arkansas, for example, famously cast the vote that killed labor law reform in 1978, destroying the hope of overturning restrictions on organizing that had been in place since the passages of Taft Hartley Act in 1947.[14] Moreover, if the nation's problems really went "deeper" than material things, what was there to make of Carter's articulation, just months after the "malaise" speech, of his foreign policy doctrine vis-à-vis the Persian Gulf and the oil supplies emanating from it? That ethically, things were worthless except for that vital commodity worth fighting and dying for that Aramco and others pumped out of the deserts of Saudi Arabia at whatever rates were most profitable? Perhaps G. K. Kiernan's quip that the oil wells of the Middle East were the region's true "holy places" as far as the United States was concerned was nearer the mark than even Carter would have cared to admit.[15] At the very least, one can certainly understand the appeal of a figure like Reagan, railing during the 1980 presidential campaign against "an energy policy based on the sharing of scarcity," insisting we "do not have inflation because—as Mr. Carter says—we have lived too well." It was not "their confidence" they were losing but "their shirts," Reagan told his fellow Americans.[16]

Yet the years and decades that followed showed that many of them had far more to lose, and that if Carter's words on the material crisis were cynical, Reagan's were hardly any less so. For among rhetorically effective descriptions of the problems faced by Americans as those of "flesh and blood," there was also in Reagan's speechmaking as he was about to be elected to office plenty of cant about the supposed "spirit" of the nation and the simultaneously inflationary and stagnating effects that over-regulation and the economic size of the state and its fiscal deficits were having on that spirit.[17] Indeed, it was more the regulatory burden that Carter had already begun dismantling than the complex of global forces described in the preceding chapter that stood in the way of energy independence, according to the incoming president. For that reason, his fellow Americans ought just to burn more coal and embrace nuclear power still further, irrespective of the partial meltdown at Three Mile Island in March 1979. Only the size of military spending needed increasing as far as the state was concerned, Reagan explained, and after the deep, Fed-induced recession of the early 1980s, the topography of the already emergent modern-day economy of the United States began to grow more sharply visible than ever, including the increasing deindustrialization of the Northeast and Upper Midwest and rise of the Sunbelt, as manufacturing outside of the defense industry continued to shrink as a proportion of US economic activity; the concomitant erosion of labor power, most powerfully and symbolically illustrated in Ronald Reagan's summary dismissal of striking air traffic controllers belonging to the PATCO union in 1981; and simultaneously, the prodigious growth in the financial services sector.

This was a period that was to be characterized by rising inequality, soaring sovereign and private debt, and, as an ever-growing literature has begun to argue, the ideological and material erosion of the postwar institutions in which many Americans had invested their faith. Whether through a paradoxically merger-friendly approach to anti-trust enforcement, further deregulation of the banking sector, or simply a willed failure to regulate trades in the kind of innovative financial products that would eventually lead to the 2008 crisis, corporations and financiers were empowered as never before, the efforts business interests put into political organization in the 1970s now paying off handsomely. The results for the nation at large, and for the argument about things, were less clear-cut. As early as 1983, Bruce Steinberg warned that the "mass market" was "splitting apart," while critiques of the "paper entrepreneurialism" of investment bankers and traders like Boesky and junk bond king Michael Milken as an essentially unproductive social parasitism became common currency later in the decade.[18] "Rarely have so few earned so much for doing so little," Robert Reich observed, while a *Washington Post* columnist spoke in one of the best traditions of the argument about things when flaying the disgraced Milken with a string of accusatory negations: "The man produces nothing. He manufactures nothing. He has dug no wells, cut no record, made no movie."[19]

*

But what, then, of those who *were* still manufacturing things, including culture, as the shift towards neoliberalism gathered pace? Movies, television, popular music, and even the odd blockbuster novel surely had as much of a contribution to make to the argument about things as political speeches or media commentary? The film industry is an interesting place to start answering that question because it too was shifting in this period from a "golden age" of American auteurs to the higher-grossing era of summer blockbusters and endless sequels. In the late 1970s, the pro-union movie *Norma Rae* (1979), for which Sally Field won an Oscar, certainly exhibited a sense of what might be lost in the turn that capitalism was taking, but Paul Schrader's *Blue Collar* (1978) offered a more penetrating meditation on what it was actually like to "make things" in the United States during a time when to do so was already beginning to look like a case of being in the wrong place at the wrong time as far as the history of capitalism was concerned. The movie's narrative unfolds in the setting of the Checker cab plant in Kalamazoo, Michigan, not so as to enable a meta-fictional nod to the screenplay that made Schrader's name, that of Martin Scorsese's *Taxi Driver* (1976), but because, on Schrader's own account, the working conditions in other auto plants were too labor intensive to permit filming at all, at least as far as the "big four" producers were concerned, all of whom he approached for co-operation when he came to make the movie. "They're making 50 cars an hour, and there are two work shifts and one maintenance shift, and they said, 'You tell us you can do it, but we know you can't,'" Schrader explained in an interview with *Cineaste*.[20] This was a loss, he agreed with the interviewer, because it meant it was more difficult to "convey the abrasive nature of working conditions" in a typical auto plant in the late 1970s, in which the "mass specialization" that had characterized much industrial production since the days of Frederick Winslow Taylor still often meant workers were doing the same rote task over and over again.[21] The Checker plant, by contrast, produced only twenty-five cabs a day, an approach to production that provided, in combination with the goodwill of the management, both the space and the time that Schrader needed to craft his movie, large proportions of which were shot on and around the Checker production line itself. In the film, whether through the abuses of a tyrannical foreman, a corrupt union, a recalcitrant drinks machine, or even a spray-painting facility that, in collusion with the union itself, proves fatal, the working lives of those who still ushered the nation's goods into being are shot through with an anomie leavened only by an inter-racial class solidarity that all too swiftly proves itself no match for the powerful forces and institutions arrayed against it.

The plot of the movie turns on the decision of Richard Pryor's Zeke, Yaphet Kotto's Smokey, and Harvey Keitel's Jerry to rip off the safe in their union's headquarters, whereupon they discover not the tens of thousands in cash for which they were hoping, but a measly $600 and a notebook filled with suspicious bookkeeping entries: the real money, it transpires, was already being made from money itself, in the form of an illegal lending operation the union has been running. The workers' attempts at blackmail swiftly come to naught and the movie ends with Smokey already dead and Zeke and Jerry more or less ready to kill one another, class solidarity in tatters. Their motivations in even attempting the heist are, I suppose, mainly material. Zeke's primary gripe with the union appears in some scenes to be about racial discrimination, but the economic conditions of the late 1970s rank high among his concerns. "It ain't the wages. It's the prices," Zeke explains to his union boss, even before he is confronted with an IRS demand that he repay thousands of dollars owed for claiming assistance for children that do not exist. Jerry works evenings at a gas station but is unable to afford the braces his daughter needs for her teeth. When, in a remarkable scene, he comes home to find her gums bloodied after she has tried to fashion some of her own, he resolves to get the money he needs. Taking on more credit is one option; theft, another.

Credit, which in the legal form of home loans, personal loans, and credit card debt, has been one way American workers have sought to offset the decline in their wages over the course of the age of neoliberalism. It also sits at the emotional center of the film: a three-person articulation of male despondency that takes place after an adulterous evening of cocaine-fueled debauchery. "Credit's the only thing you can get free from the company," drawls Jerry, even as a huge billboard advertising the aggressively grilled Pontiac Phoenix looms behind him, visible in the early morning light through the open blinds of Smokey's apartment. "You got a house, fridge, dishwasher, washer-dryer, TV, stereo, motorcycle, car. Buy this shit. Buy that shit. All you've got's a bunch of shit. You don't even own it. You can't give it back because it's already broke down." This is the world of things denuded of any other value than as a means to keep extracting the price of their own labor from workers like Jerry, for as Smokey has already revealed, the real reason that he keeps going back to the plant, even after moments of coked-up clarity in which he tells himself he is not going to, is because "the credit man needs your paycheck." Mary Douglas and Baron Isherwood may well have been about to explain that the consumption of goods communicates participation in the social process; for that brief moment, Jerry sees things, and the argument about things, quite differently.[22] But that comes before his daughter lacerates her own gums with wire in her effort to straighten out her teeth, as if to prove Reagan at least half-right when he spoke of inflation as a problem of flesh and blood.

If *Blue Collar* took material inequities seriously, rather than waving them away with ethereal talk about the spirit of the nation, this was not a virtue it shared with much mass culture of the "long 1980s." Some important exceptions stand out, of course, such as the work of the photojournalist Mary Ellen Mark. Shooting in the social realist tradition of Dorothea Lange, and reminding those who cared to notice that the deprivations of the late 1970s and early 1980s witnessed dispossession and immiseration on a scale unseen in the United States between the Great Depression and the Great Recession of recent years, Mark photographed homeless youths in Seattle in 1983, co-producing with Martin Bell the harrowing documentary *Streetwise* (1984), and then, in a 1987 collaboration with the journalist Anne Fadiman, shooting haunting portraits of the Damms, a homeless family in California.[23] Later, Roseanne Barr's long-running sitcom took the genre back to a working class milieu it seemed to have more or less abandoned since the cancellation of Norman Lear's *All in The Family* in 1979. Nor, of course, should Bruce Springsteen's work of the mid-1980s, nor Tracy Chapman's folk-rock protest songs later in the decade, be ignored. If Springsteen's songs are still held to capture the sense of disenfranchisement and dislocation that has descended on white working class males since the 1970s, Chapman's multi-million-selling, Grammy-winning, eponymous debut adds some necessary complicating detail to that picture. For songs like "Fast Car" and, even more obviously, "Mountains O' Things" tell stories of intersectional material dispossessions that clarify that to be poor, female, and black made it even harder to participate in the culture of abundance and "things for everyone" of historiographic myth.

For the most part, however, mainstream culture tended to narrate the rising socio-economic inequality that was hardly new to the United States but was certainly already being exacerbated by the structural transformations of the domestic economy in such a way as to make material class divisions either sources of irony and/or easily resolvable forms of narrative conflict, as if poverty were just another identity category to be accepted or overcome by love. Madonna's "Material Girl" (1984), for example, is often quoted as exemplifying much of the supposed ethos of the era, but commentators frequently miss the have-your-cake-and-eat-it cynicism of the accompanying music video, which is all the more regrettable given the emphasis rightly placed on the emergence of MTV and the music video as significant developments in the culture industry in the 1980s. A fine example of what Simon Reynolds has called "retromania," the "Material Girl" video has it both ways as far as the argument about things is concerned, undercutting its slick homage to

Gentleman Prefer Blondes (1953) and the unabashed material greed of the lyrics with a framing narrative of a behind-the-scenes romance between Madonna and a male studio executive. The latter learns that the real way to win the "real" Madonna's real heart is not, in fact, to lavish her with expensive gifts, but to make out that you drive an old pick-up truck while offering her nothing more than a hand-picked bunch of daisies as a token of your affection. The caricature of the gold-digging, female arch-materialist, the latest iteration of the Lorelei Lee character played by Marilyn Monroe in the 1950s musical, was and should only ever be a comic fantasy, just a little harmless, role-playing fun, this narrative frame makes clear.

Note, however, that this was a mere two years before Ivan Boesky gave his infamous commencement address legitimizing greed—white male greed, at least—and three before, in *Wall Street*, Oliver Stone's intentions notwithstanding, Michael Douglas's villainous arbitrageur, Gordon Gekko, seduced sufficient numbers of young male hearts to ensure the investment banks of Wall Street would stay well-stocked with Ivy League graduates for years.[24] What chance did Martin Sheen's dying-breed union dad stand against such a seductively anti-heroic surrogate father as Gekko, at least as far as large parts of the movie's fan base were (and remain) concerned? Michael Lewis reports a similarly perverse response to *Liar's Poker*, a memoir he had hoped would discourage talented young graduates from aspiring to work on Wall Street. He was alarmed to find many who corresponded with him about his book could dream of few finer things, writing to ask him for career advice.[25] No wonder, perhaps, that Bret Easton Ellis ended up raising the stakes even higher in *American Psycho* (1991), in which the eponymous Patrick Bateman is imagined and perhaps imagines himself as a serial killer working not on mergers and acquisitions but "murders and executions."[26] For that offense against good taste, and for the large advance he was able to secure on the novel, the author himself became controversial, just as the newly emergent genre of gangsta rap, which in another world might have prompted serious political action to address some of the social conditions it described, instead induced moral panic about its glorification of violence and that ever-present scourge, "materialism." This was in spite of the fact that, as Johnathan Munby has argued, the "all-consuming amoral conspicuous materialism" of gangsta rap is entirely consonant with what others have long seen as values and identities "central to the American dream."[27] Indeed, there is sufficient contiguity in these representations of two markedly different sectors of the nation's population (the new robber barons of Wall Street on the one hand and the self-described "gangsters" of the inner cities on the other) that their coeval emergence begins to look like an early cultural articulation of a claim more recently made by Nils Gilman that the contemporary era has witnessed "twin" insurgencies against the state, that of the criminal and (what is to all intents and purposes the same thing) that of the plutocrat.[28]

With its caricature of both New York street life and the pretensions of the city's moneyed and political elites, Tom Wolfe's *The Bonfire of the Vanities* (1987) feigned to take in much of this and more while disdaining almost all of it equally. Both a would-be-Dickensian "social novel," initially serialized in *Rolling Stone*, and a before-the-fact realization of the literary manifesto Wolfe would later publish in favor of the idea of the kind of realist fiction that "stalked" what Wolfe called "the Billion-Footed Beast," *Bonfire of the Vanities* invoked the earlier, anti-materialist conflagrations of Savanorala and Davenport in its own title while reducing 1980s New York to a mess of social and ethno-racial stereotypes. Henry Lamb, a young African American, is injured when Sherman McCoy, Wolfe's WASP antihero, a junk bond trader like Milken, takes a wrong turn into the Bronx with his mistress. Wolfe's novel charts the ensuing court case. Spike Lee would cover the street-level tensions of New York with considerably more socially aware, though in some ways no less garish, aplomb in *Do The Right Thing* (1989), a movie that, like Schrader's *Blue Collar*, tells of the damage racial and class tensions can exact while also illustrating how both such conflicts and lethal state violence serve to provoke the kind of urban conflagrations and, to outsiders, near-inexplicable crimes against property that had blighted major US cities before and would do so again. For what starts as a dispute in a Bedford-Stuyvesant pizza place about why there are no pictures of African Americans on the wall degenerates in the urban broil of the hottest day of the summer into a localized riot after cops murder a local resident, Radio Raheem, by putting him in a chokehold.

In the mid-1970s, in protest at budget cuts deemed necessary by the threat of bankruptcy proceedings, police had taken to distributing leaflets at New York's airports warning travelers of the difficulties they may face in keeping their "property intact" if they dared to venture into the city itself.[29] It was a vision of one of the nation's most iconic cities as itself something like a maelstrom or raging bonfire in which no thing would be safe from destruction. While Wolfe and Lee both in their different ways offer representations of an urban inferno that, in its combustible tensions, continued to imperil things themselves deep into the "long 1980s," it is perhaps no surprise that the neoliberal response to the kind of problems such culture documents has been the gentrification of urban space. For while riots, as Martin Luther King claimed, are the language of the unheard, they are also a cry of the dispossessed. And if, for many, the problem with the dispossessed is the all too real threat they might pose to other people's "stuff," then the answer, according to the logic of neoliberalism, appears to be to deny them access to even the kind of urban spaces in which they might ever be able to realize that threat. After all, to the neoliberal imagination, there can be few greater crimes than a crime against property. How then to understand the scene in *Do The Right Thing* in which Lee's pizza delivery man, Mookie, throws a trash can through the window of Sal's pizza place? As J. J. Masters has argued, the rendering of what he calls "the infernal city" is qualitatively different in *The Bonfire of the Vanities*, in which "Wolfe rewrites class struggle as the agonistic conflict between wealthy Anglo-Americans and an increasingly racialized Other."[30] The wealthy, it has transpired, had already set in train ways to douse the flames, not through the redistribution of their own wealth downwards but by transforming larger and larger swathes of the city into places where poor people simply could not afford to live, for a single Sherman McCoy, market prices have long indicated, is worth countless pizza delivery men.

The sheer cynicism of much of the mass culture participating in the argument about things in the long 1980s is impressive to contemplate. It is not that it exhibits a lack of cognizance about the domestic effects of the global transformation underway. Nor that it has nothing to say about those effects when it sees them. It is rather the ersatz nature of some of the gestures such culture makes in the direction of critique. Consider one more example from the end of the period with which this book deals. *Pretty Woman* (1990), a Hollywood retelling of the Pygmalion myth, saw Julia Roberts's call girl Vivienne effect a metamorphosis in Richard Gere's Edward, transforming him from an amoral corporate raider dismantling companies for profit to the whitest of white knight investors keen not only to protect the ageing Ralph Bellamy's shipbuilding company from hostile takeover but also, as Bellamy's character puts it at the end of the film, to build "great big ships" together. As with "Material Girl," gender roles and sexual politics were to the fore here, but while Madonna appeared simultaneously to celebrate and ironize commodity fetishism, the nature of Edward's transformation in *Pretty Woman* gives voice to that same "nostalgic materialism" that today yearns for a lost America that used to "make things," as if returning there might of itself smooth away class inequality, which is, after all, the pseudo-obstacle that never-too-convincingly stands between Vivienne and Edward, putting one in a limousine and the other out on the streets in the first place.

Taken in the round, the foregoing examples can be read as an illustration of just how swiftly American culture came to terms with the dictates of "capitalist realism," the understanding that permeates both the political ideology of neoliberalism and its characteristic cultural modes that there is simply no alternative to the world that its own logical precepts insist we must now inhabit, regardless of the material inequalities such logic consistently perpetuates.[31] If Schrader's movie, with its pessimistic view of a labor force divided against itself by the machinations of both factory and union bosses, now looks like one of the more effective examples of critique that mass culture had to offer in the era, that may be because it reminds us that the status quo prevailing before neoliberalism definitively achieved its ascendency was itself no utopia, nor had it ever been. Moreover, it also offers in retrospect a bracing antidote to the nostalgic materialism of the early twenty-first century. Schrader's characters already sensed amid the stagflation of the late 1970s that they were caught in a post-Fordist trap whereby the shortfall between their wages and living costs meant they could only function as the producer-consumers of American capitalism's very best dream of itself by taking on debt. They had no faith in an organized labor movement that was about to embark on the precipitous decline that has seen union membership rates plummet since a centrist Democratic Party allowed, not for the last time, labor law reform to die a legislative death in Congress. All worthy exceptions notwithstanding, much mass-produced, mass-consumed American culture of the "long 1980s" simply went through the motions as far as commenting on the local effects of the geopolitically rooted, inflation-led transformations of the era were concerned, either ironizing a caricature of the same "materialism" that Jimmy Carter had decried before losing the presidency, or else finding itself unable, as much of it still finds itself unable, to imagine any alternative to the structural changes in American life other than "making things," by which is very frequently meant returning working class men and women to standing on a production line: back at the start of the trap, with a racialized urban underclass that never even made it into that trap in the first place either out on the streets or in other inner-city spaces from which neoliberalism would increasingly begin to cleanse them.

In this context, the bouts of economic nationalism that saw the condemnation, boycott, and even destruction of certain foreign-made goods in the long 1980s take on an altered complexion. In 1980, when running unsuccessfully for the Republican nomination for president, John Connally, one of the architects of the Nixon shock, came on like a racist Howard Beale, the mad-as-hell TV anchor played by Peter Finch in *Network* (1976): "If we can't come into your markets with equal openness and fairness as you come into ours, you had better be prepared to sit on the docks of Yokahama in your little Datsuns and your little Toyotas while you stare at your own little TV sets and eat your mandarin oranges, because we've had all we're going to take!"[32] "Buy American!" campaigns flourished, and newspapers across the nation featured reports of attacks against foreign-made imports. In a February 1982 story about a troubled Ford aluminum-casing plant in Sheffield, Alabama, *The Philadelphia Inquirer* recounted how "a visitor parked his rented Toyota in the plant parking lot and returned to find it covered with trash," while the "local Datsun dealer found knife scratches in the shiny new finish of five cars on his lot."[33] For better or worse, it seemed, some Americans had already decided not so much that to see things is "to know ourselves," but that "to make things was to be ourselves."

Admittedly, some of this may well have been nothing more than violent xenophobia. In 1982, Vincent Chen, a Chinese American, was murdered by two unemployed auto-workers in Detroit, while reports in May 1986 of the apparent bombing of bulldozers clearing the site on which Hitachi was poised to build a new manufacturing plant in Norman, Oklahoma ominously stated that the motive was unclear.[34] This came at a time when such foreign direct investment may have represented the best hope many Americans had for returning to a working world in which they "made things," rather than the one that had already been envisaged by Walter Mondale in 1982, when he conjured a dystopian future in which "jobs will consist of sweeping up around Japanese computers and spending a lifetime serving McDonald's hamburgers."[35] The point is not to vindicate a post-industrial cultural politics of resentment, xenophobia, and racial division by dressing it up in the garb of a nostalgic materialism that is itself deeply problematic. It is instead simply to note the diminishing expectations that the triumph of such nostalgia, after the triumph of neoliberalism, implies. For some of the workers in the late 1970s Checker cab factory in *Blue Collar* averred they were working not in a "plant" but on a "plantation"; today, for too many, it looks more like the Garden of Eden.

CHAPTER 3

Rhopography and Realism

Under what obligations, if any, do artists find themselves when it comes to the argument about things in the age of neoliberalism? Is it at all fair to demand of them that, in their renderings both of things and our engagements with those things, their works should evince what the literary critic Kenneth Burke once termed "answers to questions posed by the situation in which they arose"?[1] Ought they, as Burke proposed of "any work of critical or imaginative cast," "size up [those] situations, name their structure and outstanding ingredients, and name them in a way that contains an attitude towards them"?[2] Reflecting on something like this question, Walter Benn Michaels, who has invested considerable energy in recent years bemoaning American literature's failure to critique the "situation" ushered in by decades of neoliberalism, has offered an interesting interpretation of a series of photographs by Viktoria Binschtok depicting the accumulated marks on the wall of a Berlin unemployment office. For Michaels, whose complaints about the work of novelists like Philip Roth, Toni Morrison, Jonathan Franzen, and others has been that they have demonstrated little interest in writing "about the world neoliberalism has actually produced," a photograph like Binschtok's "Wand 1" does just that by avoiding an explicit focus on the victims of neoliberalism—in this case, the absent unemployment claimants—and instead concentrating on the counter-intuitively beautiful marks those claimants had left behind as they leant against the wall awaiting the determination of their eligibility for unemployment relief.[3] In adopting such an aesthetic strategy, Michaels argued, Binschtok achieves a double distancing effect:

> the photograph establishes a distance from its subjects, and seeks to mirror that distance with the one it establishes from its viewers, making it impossible for us to identify by giving us no one to identify with, making the question of who its viewers are and how they feel as irrelevant as the question of who its subjects were and how they felt. What it

wants instead is to establish a space of its own, to make itself autonomous.[4]

Although Michaels describes this desire on the part of this piece of art as "the opposite of how we usually think about the relation between politics and art," his point is not that Binschtok's photograph is apolitical. On the contrary, its representation of a "structural" part of the increasingly unequal world neoliberalism has made in such a way as to create not just a representation but, simultaneously, an "autonomous" aesthetic space itself constitutes a political comment on that world. An image like "'Wand 1,'" Michaels argues, is "a picture of the labor market" that also "imagine[s] its own autonomy from that market" by aspiring towards the condition of beauty: "Today, we might speculate, it's only insofar as art seeks to be beautiful—seeks, that is, to achieve the formal perfection imaginable in works of art but not in anything else—that it can also function as a picture not of how, if we behaved better, we might manage capitalism's problems, but rather of capitalism as itself the problem."[5] The formal perfection of art, the implication seems to be, is what exposes the structural imperfections of the neoliberal regime to critique.

One need not agree wholeheartedly with Michaels's critical aesthetics to see their implications for the contributions that American culture was making to the argument about things at the beginning of the "long 1980s," when neoliberalism was so firmly establishing itself as the hegemonic approach to political economy in the United States. The preceding chapter voiced frustration with the failure of mainstream culture to offer much in the way of critical analysis of the changes taking place in the resolutely material global processes that were so profoundly affecting American life. This chapter, by contrast, meditates for the most part on somewhat more experimental forms of culture. Perhaps there was an artistic and cultural avant-garde making more critical interventions into the argument about things in the "long 1980s," not necessarily by pondering the structural changes in global affairs per se but by reflecting, and reflecting upon, the goods circulating through American lives in the era? Perhaps artists, musicians and writers were subjecting such things and their fellow citizens' relations to things to forms of critique more nuanced and penetrating than those offered by both their political leaders and much of mainstream American culture? Or even rendering them in such ways as to achieve through that rendering an aesthetic autonomy that exposes the imperfections of capitalism manifest in the early years of neoliberalism, as per Michaels?

I frame these possibilities in the form of questions only because the answers to them remain so uncertain. As we will see, artists, musicians, and writers were certainly engaging with the consumer goods and everyday objects that populated American life, an aesthetic engagement with objects that may have looked at times like a (dis)engagement from the human subjects that used and consumed them. It is by no means clear, however, that they were doing so for the sole purpose of critique. Nor can any failure to do so on their part be attributed merely to the fact that culture was itself an industry. Instead, it often had more to do either with a studied and at times genuinely baffled ambivalence on the part of producers of culture that was rooted in their far-reaching aesthetic fascination with the things of a culture of mass consumption as almost anthropologically representative of that culture; or else a perception on the part of such artists and writers that such things had, for them, an aesthetic value that, even when it enabled them to approach or attempt a humanistic critique of the lives of Americans under the changing conditions of a new age, was met with considerable critical resistance. And as we will see, some of that resistance, which was predicated on a suspicion of the *rhopographic*, the aesthetic rendering of small and trivial things, is at least as important in understanding the fate of American culture's engagements with things in the "long 1980s" as culture itself.

*

From the late 1970s onwards, Jeff Koons began exhibiting art featuring consumer goods in the form either of found objects or representations of such goods that playfully altered their scale and material composition. His series *The New*, for example, was dominated by mounted or encased vacuum cleaners lit by fluorescent tube lighting and identified by their product names: New Hoover Quik Broom, New Hoover Celebrity IV, and so on. By the middle of the decade, Koons was displaying cases of Spalding and Wilson basketballs suspended in a specially devised liquid that made them look like they were hovering in mid-air. The title of these pieces also featured brand names: Spalding Dr. J Silver Series, Wilson Supershot, for example. Koons incorporated into such installations advertising materials, including promotional posters. The Du-Champian gesture of displaying such goods as art in a way that made them look like quirky reinterpretations of store window displays was not missed by critics. But what did such things mean? We can certainly read *The New* as a wry commentary on the phenomenon of planned obsolescence, which had long been a feature of capitalist consumer culture. We might even note, for example, that as far as it was possible to tell (and more than one commentator of the period complained that it was already becoming increasingly difficult to tell), some of the products produced under the Wilson and Spalding brand names that featured in Koons's work were themselves already subject to the globalization of supply chains, much to the dissatisfaction of economic nationalists.[6] Was this work, then, commenting on that? The chances seem slim, but Koons has retrospectively claimed that the posters advertising sports shoes featuring African American basketball stars that formed part of such installations were intended to draw parallels between art and professional sports as routes towards a social mobility that was already dwindling when his works were conceived. As Koons put it, "white middle-class kids have been using art the same way that other ethnic groups have been using basketball—for social mobility. You could take one of those basketball stars, Dr. Dunkelstein, or the Secretary of Defense, and one could have been me, or Baselitz, or whoever."[7] That's right: just as basketball represented a way out of poverty for black youths in the 1980s, so conceptual art offered the same for struggling former commodity brokers like Jeff Koons. Was this a joke? Was the appeal of such art something to do with that joke? Or were these objects simply diverting—beautiful, even—to look at, in a way that may or may not have offered commentary on the systems that produced them, because they had, as Arthur C. Danto has put it in reference to the work of other artists, succeeded in "transfiguring the commonplace"?[8]

Critics themselves were and have remained conflicted about such work. A reasonably favorable interpretation of the late 1980s claimed that Koons "invested" his objects "with the kind of desire the artist believes consumers feel for the objects they covet and acquire," while also noting the unsettling effect of pronouncements from Koons that "I believe in advertising and media completely." However, the same critic also observed that "what side you ultimately feel the artist is on has everything to do with how convincing you find the work."[9] More hostile interpretations have argued that Koons is nothing more than a fraud, a kind of "cargo cultist" of the commodity fetish, while Alison Pearlman has pointed out that one can hardly take Koons's public pronouncements at face value: "There is a pattern to Koons's statements. They are designed in the media-ready forms of quotable soundbites and they combine self-aggrandizing comparisons, exaggerated claims to mass communication and appeal, and unqualified affirmations of capitalism."[10] They are deliberately provocative, in other words, and deliberately unsettling as far as the critical reception of the work goes, offering those attempting to interpret that work no easy way out of the uncertainties they are designed to foster.

Such artistic strategies, of course, were not new. Perhaps that was the point. After all, Koons's self-presentation, as Pearlman has observed, was "a more aggressive and extreme version" of the persona that Andy Warhol had cultivated from the early 1960s to his death in 1987.[11] But on an even more fundamental level, such work engaged questions about the aesthetic value or otherwise of consumer goods that had been so dramatically raised by Pop years previously. Indeed, it is easy now to forget just how fiercely some critics opposed the Pop Art associated with Warhol when it first arrived on the American scene. In the early 1960s, for example, Gilbert Sorrentino trashed Pop by arguing that the Abstract Expressionism that had preceded it was "a *valid form of painting*, where the values of good and bad may be applied. These values have no meaning when applied to work which, in itself, has no value, unless one wishes to concede that this ketchup bottle is 'better' than this cupcake."[12] Note the focus on objective repertoire here, which was always part of the point of Pop: a deliberate turning back to the world of things, and especially those all too "commonplace" things that were already filling American lives in the 1960s and hardly went away, even as the complex global systems that produced and brought them to market were being reconstituted from the 1970s onwards. One of the leading Pop artists, Robert Indiana, had framed the new art as a "turn back to some less exalted things like Coca-Cola, ice-cream sodas, big hamburgers, supermarkets and 'EAT' signs" after the journeys into psychic depths pursued by the practitioners of Abstract Expressionism.[13] In this sense, much of the objective repertoire of Koons's work of the "long 1980s," the parade of vacuum cleaners and basketballs, teapots and telephones giving way to stainless steel statuettes of Bob Hope and kitschy, material reimaginings of inflatable pink rabbits, constitutes a continuation of Pop's aesthetic project.

Pop Art's supporters had long previously acknowledged the resistance such a project was likely to face. Gene Swenson had complained in defense of Pop art that "criticism has generally refused to say that an object can be equated with a meaningful or aesthetic feeling, particularly if the object has a brand name."[14] Swenson was referring to art history's traditional disregard for representations of mere material objects. Even the objects depicted in still life painting, for example, had traditionally been considered a particularly lowly form of aesthetic subject matter; indeed, the entire still life mode was once considered a form of rhopography, from the Greek *rhopos*, meaning small or trivial things.[15] If the Cubists' turn in earlier decades of the twentieth century towards certain objects was, as Alan R. Solomon argued in the 1960s, accepted on the grounds of formal experimentation, what was striking about Pop was its willingness to expand the repertoire of figurative subject matter even further, to include what Solomon called "a range of distasteful, stupid, vulgar, assertive and ugly manifestations of the worst side of our society."[16] Add to that the sense that much of the objective repertoire of Pop Art dealt with things that the heteronormative and patriarchal structures of US society coded as feminine (soap boxes, say) or infantile (comic strips), and Koons's art seemed, in its mere choice of subject matter, deliberately designed to expand that provocative repertoire further still.

But the analogue with Koon's work does not end on the level of subject matter. After all, critics' hostility to Pop was only increased by its use of representational techniques that sought to mimic the impersonal, mechanical (re)production processes of mass culture, such that what it was the Pop artists wanted to say about such material was forever unclear and ambiguous, its purposes as blank and inscrutable as Andy Warhol's carefully crafted public persona. Had Pop Art been an ironic critique of consumer culture, a celebration of that culture, or about something else entirely? Again, critics differed in their response to that question, and in time, Koons's habit of having things manufactured for him rather than making them himself engendered a similar lack of consensus in the critical reception of his art. Was this just a question, as Warhol had put it, of "liking things," or was the best to be hoped for an art of such things that acknowledged their allure while also ironizing or satirizing it? If so, what if that satire was undertaken in such subtle ways as to render the art, which was itself commodifiable, forever hostage to the vagaries of its own reception? After all, *Wall Street* and the movies that have followed in its wake have bred as much fandom for the glamor and liberatory promise of a life in high finance as moral outrage over the social consequences of arbitrage and vulture capitalism. How, then, could critics be sure whether those visiting the "neo-geo" exhibitions of the work of Koons and others were hip to the ways it may or may not have been commenting on the conditions of its own existence rather than simply indulging in the allure of the *rhopos*? They could not be, just as they could not be sure of "which side" the artist was on, and such uncertainties were and have remained central to the aggressively provocative ambivalence of Koons's never less than unsettling art.

At the same time, one reason the answer to such questions as Koons's art posed may not even matter was that for many producers of avant-garde culture, the sense of ambivalence they felt towards the object world of the United States in the "long 1980s" was entirely genuine and sprang from aesthetic responses that need to be distinguished from acts of critique. It was David Byrne of Talking Heads, for example, who said of the 1980s that they were a moment in which "somebody said it was OK to like things," a deliberate Warholian echo from a former student at the Rhode Island School of Design. And there was also an important *rhopographic* element to the avant-garde art-punk that Byrne was creating with bandmates Tina Weymouth, Chris Frantz, and Jerry Harrison throughout the period. This was a band whose second album went by the name *More Music About Buildings and Food* (1978) and whose presiding genius, in an interview he took the trouble to conduct with himself, once observed, "I try to write about small things. Paper, animals, a house."[17] That was only half-true, of course. A song like "Life During Wartime," from *Fear of Music* (1979), was at least in part "about" the very big thing articulated in its title but achieves some of its finest effects through the combination of the unrepentant funk of the song's music, its purported theme, and the lyrics' attentiveness to a banal and almost Pop-like objective repertoire: "I got some groceries,/ some peanut butter,/To last a couple of days." Is this in any way serious? One might have asked something similar of "The Big Country" (1978), in which Byrne looked down from the windows of an airplane to see more or less the entire interior of the nation fragmented into so many discrete things ("Places to park by the factories and buildings./Restaurants and bar for later in the evening"). But there is no joy to be had down there, a "truth" delivered with the strategic timing of a thing-focused punchline: "And I have learned how these things work together./I see the parkway that passes through them all./And I have learned how to look at these things and I say,/I wouldn't live there if you paid me." Was this a satire on hyper-urban Manhattanite sensibilities or a mere expression of the same? The novelist Johnathan Lethem holds that such a lyric "beg[s] to be taken literally," while the historian Bruce Schulman has insisted, of "Life During Wartime," that the lack of seriousness was part of the point, for the way its "performers and their audience joked about (and danced through) a nightmare landscape" was symptomatic of the late 1970s themselves.[18]

The point is that such critical disagreements over the music's prevailing tone require no resolution precisely because, as with Koons and Warhol, the ambivalence towards the "less exalted things" of late twentieth-century life in the United States was an important aspect of the art of Talking Heads throughout the "long 1980s." Alienation and anomie, a quizzical bafflement, even, may ripple through a track like "Once in A Lifetime" (1983), but by the time of the release of the movie, book, and album *True Stories* (1986), Byrne would also write, of "a huge trade mart devoted to the microelectronics industry" that had just been built in Dallas, Texas, "You feel like you're laughing at it and admiring it at the same time."[19] As if to clarify that such admiration for the representative things of late twentieth-century American culture was at least partly in earnest, by the time of "Nothing But Flowers," from the band's final studio album *Naked* (1988), Byrne was turning the environmentalist ethics of Joni Mitchell's "Big Yellow Taxi" on their head, envisioning a post-capitalist return to Eden that found the singer bemoaning the imagined loss of cars and factories, shopping malls and real estate, dreaming of "cherry pies/Candy bars, and chocolate chip cookies," an all-American objective repertoire as redolent of the confectionary in Wayne Thiebaud's paintings of the early 1960s as any of Warhol's art. "If this is paradise," observed Byrne of this new Arcadia, "I wish I had a lawnmower." The real "nightmare landscape," such a vision proposed, might in fact be the one that capital leaves behind.

To search in such art as that produced by Byrne and Talking Heads for a far-reaching critique of the structural conditions that had made of the United States a land of Dairy Queens and 7-Elevens, of discount stores and microwaves, was beside the point. For Byrne was apt to satirize moral scolds' objections to a commercially dominated, increasingly privatized built environment far more savagely than he was the material culture and *rhopos* of the late twentieth-century United States itself, if indeed he was even satirizing the latter at all. Such ambivalence, which was at times near-anthropological in its poise, was also characteristic of aspects of the work of the novelist Don DeLillo in the long 1980s. *White Noise* (1985), for example, in which what DeLillo called the "almost Pop Art atmosphere" of a local supermarket plays an important symbolic role, teems with *rhopographic* detail, such as the image of an infant child "seated on the [kitchen] counter surrounded by open cartons, crumpled tinfoil, shiny bags of potato chips, bowls of pasty substances covered with plastic wrap, flip-top rings and twist ties, individually wrapped slices of orange cheese."[20] The seventeenth-century "ornate" still lifes (*pronkstilleven*) of Dutch artists like Frans Snyders and Adriaen van Utrecht, frequently sought to depict the material abundance of the Dutch burgher class by using luxurious arrangements of food to produce "still lifes of the table" (*ontbijtjes*).[21] In DeLillo's arrangement, the overflowing arrays of fruit, vegetables, and freshly slaughtered poultry of the *pronkstilleven* have been replaced by a cornucopia of the kind of brightly colored, highly processed, over-packaged foods presented as the standard diet of middle class American families in the 1980s. There is certainly something Pop-like to such written arrangements, but it is not simply the detail's object matter. For if Pop Art for Warhol was "liking things," for his contemporary, Roy Lichtenstein, it was equally "'an involvement . . . with things we *hate*."[22] Similarly, when DeLillo's ironically named narrator, Jack Gladney, claims that the things he and his wife buy at the supermarket ("the familiar package designs and vivid lettering, the giant sizes, the family bargain packs with Day-Glo sale stickers") bring a sense of "security and contentment . . . to some snug home in [their] souls," it seems difficult to be certain, as it often was with the public pronouncements of Warhol, Koons, or Byrne, just how ironic or otherwise he was really being in his attitude to the consumer goods that fill his family's life and DeLillo's novel.[23]

To be clear, it is not that one *cannot* extract critique from such cultural renderings of the things filling many American lives in the "long 1980s" if one so desires. Many of DeLillo's most perceptive critics, in fact, have done just that. It is that any critique that is so extracted tends to do considerable damage to the delicately balanced ambivalence of the work itself. When we read DeLillo describe his sense, referring to an average supermarket in the mid-1980s United States, "that something transcending is about to happen . . . in the midst of all this brightness," ought we to assume he was only joking?[24] The fact that he very likely was not joking, but that one, perhaps, could never quite be sure either way, speaks to how such cultural renderings of things function. For although they might not have been received as such by some anxious critics keen to ventriloquize cultural representations of things as embodying their own distaste for the gaudy forms of consumer capitalism in the United States, such renderings appear to hold the cultural power of capitalism in something like due reverence, hesitant to approach it as merely, to use Walter Benn Michaels's term, a "problem" and more as the source of a legitimate aesthetic wonder that might itself very well be problematic but that also tells us something important about how American life was being lived in the early years of neoliberalism's hegemony. In this sense, they embody what Marx had long ago claimed was true of the commodity, namely that it "appears at first sight an extremely obvious, trivial thing, and easily understood, [yet . . .] it is a very strange thing, abounding in metaphysical subtleties."[25] The supermarket, in which Americans came to purchase the goods they needed and desired, supposedly executing their sovereign choices in a place of exchange, might thus easily seem a site of genuine mystery and transfiguration. At the same time, what such an aesthetic might be most profitably criticized for is an aestheticization of everyday, vernacular things that was so committed to seeing to the supposed mysterious heart of the national culture that it eventually got stuck to the point of fixation on those things, not in an effort to imagine another world through them, as with the example of Michaels's interpretation of Binschtok's photographs, but because it had convinced itself, as an anthropologist might, that such things really represented that culture.[26]

To put it another way, what had made Andy Warhol the artist he was, Arthur Danto has written, was an endeavor to "paint what we are."[27] But why assume that "what we are" could still (or ever) be found where Warhol in the early 1960s and others in the long 1980s thought they had found it, in the *rhopos* of everyday commercial life? Why assume that to see such things was really in any meaningful sense "to know ourselves," understood on the cultural, rather than individual, level? Warhol, Danto insists, genuinely did like things, especially Campbell's soup and Coca-Cola, which tasted good and struck the artist as in some way democratic because, as he famously said, "You can be watching TV and see Coca Cola, and you can know that the President drinks Coke, Liz Taylor drinks Coke, and just think, you can drink Coke too. A Coke is a Coke and no amount of money can get you a better Coke than the bum on the corner is drinking. All the Cokes are the same and all the Cokes are good. Liz Taylor knows it, the President knows it, the bum knows it, and you know it."[28]

But that presumably did not obtain in situations where people had no TV to watch or could not even afford a Coke to drink. And what if, increasingly, what the United States made were not what the novelist John Updike's Rabbit Angstrom called "good goods," like Warhol's democratic Coke, but "bums on corners," the victims, as we have seen, not merely of "ironic" imperialism and reconfigurations of global capital but also of a centrally planned recession followed by the ideological entrenchment of a disembedded liberalism that famously claimed to see government as a problem and had, thus, to cite one particularly egregious example, slashed federal housing subsidies by eighty percent, as the Reagan administration did from 1981 to 1989, while simultaneously lowering the effective tax rates of the wealthiest Americans?[29] All of which is to wonder what, if anything, such a *rhopography* of American abundance, an aesthetic fascination with the kinds of things that seemed to emblematize American culture, ultimately had to say to the poverty and dispossession that existed in the midst of that abundance.

*

Real poverty had long struggled to attain cultural visibility in the United States, as Michael Harrington had pointed out in *The Other America* (1962), a book published, it is useful to remember, right around the time Pop Art was bursting exuberantly onto the American art scene. It is thus unsurprising that what much of the art that placed *rhopos* at the heart of its vision of American life in the "long 1980s" failed to register was that access to the "expansive mass consumption web" so vital to what Lizabeth Cohen has called the "consumer's republic" was to be more difficult for many Americans to achieve without the artificial stimulant of debt, even as global capitalism reordered itself in such a way as to render US consumer demand a vital cog in the post-Bretton Woods system.[30] Cheap imports, falling wages, declining labor power, and rising personal debt could all compensate to a certain extent, and consumption and consumerism would hardly go away, but in an era in which the often invisible problems of structural poverty and inequality were to become no less representative of American life under neoliberalism than supermarkets and shopping malls, an art with a different focus was desperately needed as far as documenting the relation of Americans to the things they lived among was concerned, one that did not attempt to reduce American life down to a handful of representative consumer goods and that was also interested less in those goods as signs in a semiological system signifying either difference or uniformity and more as parts of the real habitus or *Lebenswelt* of American lives in the era. For among those things, real people were actually living—or in many cases, struggling to do so.

The photographer William Eggleston, who collaborated with David Byrne on the book accompanying *True Stories*, indicated one way in which this might be done, simply by acknowledging that the United States remained a vast and various terrain, the apparent uniformity of its commercial culture notwithstanding. Eggleston's *The Democratic Forest* consisted of more than 13,000 images that invested heavily in object culture, often at the expense of the human subject, but without ever wholly abandoning the latter. To be sure, this vast project incorporated elements of portraiture, but the bulk of the images focused on the built environment and the world of things. In this respect, the work mobilized the paradox inherent in much still life art, which, as Mark Seltzer has framed it, "excludes the human subject" because "it is precisely the human subject . . . to which the still life at every point makes reference and pays homage."[31] Eudora Welty, who by her own account had once photographed aspects of the United States she would otherwise never have seen under the auspices of the New Deal-era Works Progress Administration, made a similar point in the introductory essay she wrote for Eggleston's project:

The extraordinary thing is that in all these photographs, wonderfully inclusive and purposefully chosen as they are, you will look in vain for the presence of a human being. This isn't to say that the photographs deny man's existence. That is exactly what they don't do. Everywhere you find the vividness of his presence: Here's a close-up of an outdoor cooker and a bloody hatchet laid down upon it, called "Near the River." Here's the already stripped and de-wheeled front end of a red sports car, at rest under a tree by the Interstate; its radiator grille bites the dust. It seems a personal artifact, like an upper plate of a set of false teeth that's been lost on someone's way between one place and the next.[32]

Such imagery, which is more invested in picturing a nation than a "system," speaks of lives that cannot be defined down to the ways and habits of consumerism, lives that in some cases were, throughout the 1980s, liable to be falling free of the "web" of postwar mass consumption not out of some Thoreauvian dedication to a simpler life but out of dispossession and poverty. For, as Welty put it, one "indelible exception" to Eggleston's focus on things was "the young child photographed standing alone on a desolate street corner in some city: he stares back at the camera with the gravity of the homeless. He, too, is tenaciously present in other scenes while remaining invisible."[33] This image, which might sound like something from the Great Depression, was in fact very much of its time, for although federal government estimates were far lower throughout much of the 1980s, there may have been more than 2 million homeless people throughout the United States, among them countless children.[34] Eggleston's work in this way offers us a vital, social realist insight into parts of the United States in the "long 1980s" that have tended to go unseen beneath superficial interpretations of the era as a time of empty materialism and endlessly ironic postmodernism.

Similar occlusions have dogged understandings of American literary culture's engagements with things in the "long 1980s." Until relatively recently, literary scholars found it difficult to conceptualize much literary production of the 1980s as anything other than "postmodern," as a result of a crude periodizing schema that saw what Robert Rebein has called a model of "realism giving way to modernism giving way to postmodernism" as *the* way in which the whole of American literary history from the nineteenth century up to and including the present day was to be interpreted.[35] Yet the radically experimental literary postmodernism of the 1960s and 1970s, of the kind associated with meta-fictionists like William Gaddis, John Barth, Robert Coover, or Thomas

Pynchon, had long seemed to some important writers on (and of) the American scene the equivalent of what Abstract Expressionism had been to Pop: a highly problematic turn away from the world and the things of the world that facilitated an over-absorption not so much in the mysterious spaces of psychic interiors excavated by the Abstract Expressionists but in the mirrored, endlessly self-referential realm of language. For that very reason, scholars such as Rebein have usefully begun to conceptualize the 1980s as marking an important moment of departure on the part of many authors away from some of the preoccupations of literary postmodernism, heralding instead a widespread resurgence in more representational and realist modes of fiction.[36] Just as Pop had turned back to the world of things in the early 1960s, so too were "new realist" writers of the 1970s and 1980s, like Raymond Carver, Ann Beattie, and Richard Ford, turning back to parts of that world as they decisively rejected the self-reflective aesthetic impulses traditionally associated with literary postmodernism.[37] More recently still, in her work on the financial fiction of the "long 1980s," Leigh Claire La Berge has argued that "the transformation of the United States into a financialized, leveraged, and ultimately, neoliberal society" occurred "in tandem and in tension" with both the "canonization of postmodernism as an aesthetic mode" and the kind of "revanchist realism" championed by a would-be latter-day Dickens like Tom Wolfe.[38] In the wider reaches of literary culture, of course, realism had no more really gone away than "the real" itself, notwithstanding Wolfe's own grandiose claims or an earlier critical habit of squeezing various forms of realism into a capacious definition of postmodernism that, as James Annesely has argued, risked becoming "a catch-all, a category that is used in so many different circumstances that it loses its explanatory power."[39] With all that in mind, perhaps all we are talking about here is a belated critical acknowledgment of realism's continued contribution to the narrative culture of the nation in an age in which the discourse on postmodernism had proved so prominent.

That said, many critics did consider the literary realism that emerged as the 1970s gave way to the 1980s markedly different from that which had gone before. This, various judges decided, was not simply "realism" but "neo-Realism," or "minimalism." As other, often younger writers began publishing work that was either directly influenced by Carver, in particular, or else shared important aspects of his literary aesthetic, this taxonomy of 1980s realisms was expanded further to include such novel classifications as "K-Mart realism," "bratpack fiction," "hick chic," and what Barth only half-ironically referred to in 1986 as "post-Vietnam, post-literary, postmodernist blue-collar neo-early-Hemingwayism."[40] Barth was satirizing the mania for labeling that had seemed to attach itself to many of these new developments in American literary realism. Nevertheless, the broad literary phenomenon that he referred to as "minimalism" incorporated a range of writers whose work shared important formal characteristics, including, perhaps most importantly, what Mark Hoberek has recently described as "a neo-Hemingwayesque aesthetic of terseness and excision."[41]

Aside from this terse, laconic style, another culturally significant aspect of the work of Carver and other "neo-Realists" of the 1980s was the way their fiction prompted some of the most revealing examples of critical resistance to the invocation of the *rhopographic* witnessed in the era. For many literary critics, like the art critics who had been uninterested in the aesthetics of the Coca-Cola bottles, Brillo boxes, or Campbell's soup cans of the Pop era, the incorporation of brand names into much of the "neo-Realist" writing of the "long 1980s" was a particular sticking point. In his introduction to *The Best American Short Stories* (1988), for example, Mark Helprin felt compelled to note that brand names appeared in "about a third" of the short stories he read in preparing the volume. This was part of a sustained complaint about the literary aesthetics of the new realist writing. "Why are so many minimalist stories about despicable people in filthy unkempt garden apartments filled with ugly bric-à-brac, where everyone smokes, drinks, stays up all night and is addicted to coffee? . . . Why are their lives intertwined inextricably with brand names?" Helprin asked.[42] The apparent snobbery in such complaints may have been more aesthetic than political, with the defensible thrust of Helprin's argument being that the new realist writing did its characters a disservice by presenting their lives as unremittingly drab. This was still nonetheless a critique of aesthetic inclusion, with the realists' willingness to include in their art the real things Americans lived among—things the critic appeared to hate, to echo Lichtenstein—a distinct target of Helprin's ire.

Raymond Carver saw similar attacks on his own work as inherently political, especially those emanating from Hilton Kramer's conservative journal, *The New Criterion*, in which one reviewer accused Carver not of a drab realism but of "saddling" his characters "with his idea of a desperate lower-middle-class fate."[43] "Certain right-wing critics don't like my writing, in particular, people associated with Hilton Kramer's *The New Criterion*," Carver told an interviewer in 1987, complaining in another interview about a neo-conservative critic saying that he was afraid my stories were going to give a false impression of America—to the Americans, as well as to people in other countries [. . .] Because under the Reagan administration, you see, people should be happy, people shouldn't be suffering, or out of work, or sick of their jobs. This critic was saying that we shouldn't write about people who are dispossessed and unhappy, and whose lives have gone bust.[44]

Another minimalist, Frederick Barthelme, was probably more accurate when he wrote that the new writing that had initially been heralded by the emergence of Carver was being subjected by the end of the decade to attacks from "every political and literary angle."[45] Regardless of the angle in question, a recurrent complaint was the uncritical, unironic way this writing treated the things of its era, whether "ugly bric-à-brac" or objects of consumer desire, an offense compounded, it seemed, by the flat, paratactical, often present-tense style that was a hallmark of this writing. "Catatonic realism," one critic called it; "assembly-line fiction," claimed another, without any apparent irony in an era of deindustrialization.[46]

Such critics were not wrong that the inclusion of the common objects of everyday life, even if they happened to take the form of brand name goods, was indeed central to the effects the new realism was attempting to achieve. Carver, for example, made the claim that it was "possible, in a poem or a short story, to write about commonplace things and objects using commonplace but precise language, and to endow those things . . . with immense, even startling power."[47] This is hardly a claim that many critics would have considered at all controversial if applied to Hemingway or Chekhov, two writers to whom Carver's work has frequently been compared. So why would it be any different if the "commonplace things" happened to be the brand-named goods that were indisputable parts of contemporary life in the "long 1980s"? Even if brand names were less conspicuous in Carver's fiction than in that of those who were influenced by him, the conviction that such common goods might be incorporated without a necessarily ironic intent into realist writing of the era constituted an important part of Carver's impact on literary culture. Writing shortly after Carver's death in 1989, Jay McInerney revealed that what Carver had conveyed to him and others was a sense "that literature could be fashioned out of strict observation of real life, wherever and however it was lived, even if it was lived with a bottle of Heinz ketchup on the table and the television set droning." As McInerney put it, "This was news at a time when academic metafiction was the regnant mode."[48] Critics had already made strikingly similar observations, again drawing on the object world. Reviewing Carver's influential collection, *What We Talk About When We Talk About Love* (1981) at the start of the 1980s, for example, Thomas LeClair invoked the image of "a bottle of beer and a can of Spam on a metal kitchen table" as characteristic of Carver's fictional milieu, while Arthur M. Saltzman claimed in a scholarly study of Carver that the world depicted in Carver's stories was "a terrain of fast food, used cars, and garish billboards," signifiers of what Saltzman called, as if this was in itself either remarkable or necessary to explain, a "world immediately recognizable as proletarian America."[49]

This was, then, something like Eggleston's "democratic forest" in literary form. But it is important to understand that the *rhopos* that featured in the new realist writing of Carver and others was doing more than achieving what Roland Barthes once called "reality effects," more or less meaningless details, the sole purpose of which was simply to further a sense of the work's verisimilitude.[50] For the best of this writing carried—and still, in fact, carries—remarkable social and aesthetic charge, as well as historicizing some of the epochal structural changes discussed in earlier chapters more effectively than much culture of the era. Take a story such as "Are These Actual Miles?", which appeared in Carver's first published collection, *Will You Please Be Quiet, Please?* (1976), and recounts events surrounding the forced sale of a car by an alcoholic husband and his wife.[51] It is a tale of dispossession, of a bankrupt couple shedding goods, liquidating one of their assets before the courts take it from them, as their lawyer has assured them will happen if it is not sold:

> Leo and Toni still had furniture. Leo and Toni had furniture and Toni and the kids had clothes. Those things were exempt. What else? Bicycles for the kids, but these he had sent to his mother's for safekeeping. The portable air-conditioner and the appliances, new washer and dryer, trucks came for those things weeks ago. What else did they have? This and that, nothing mainly, stuff that wore out or fell to pieces long ago.[52]

This is certainly literary realism: the setting, in an unnamed American town or city, is domestic, identifiably middle class, and the events related represent the active unraveling of the house, home, and mythical stability of the nuclear family of postwar America. Within that essentially realist aesthetic, material objects evidently function on one level as technical markers of a particular domestic, middle- or lower middle-class milieu. In this context, it is worth noting that it was not until *What We Talk About When We Talk About Love* (1981), a collection published the same year that Reagan entered the White House, that, according to Rebein, Carver "finally began to receive national recognition as a major writer."[53] The coincidence of these two events has not gone unnoticed, with Carver's widow, Tess Gallagher, describing after his death how his rise to prominence "had happened to coincide with the fact of the poor having essentially been told to take care of themselves [. . .] Already the hope, even for middle-class people, of owning a home or of sending their children to college, had begun to slip from their grasp, while this reality for working-class people had hit earlier. If they were out of work and uninsured and fell ill, well it was just their tough luck."[54] Note that the implication is not so much that Carver's work and the aesthetic impulses behind it were necessarily conscious responses on his part to some of the social realities that came with the entrenchment of neo-liberalism in the United States. After all, Carver had been working on and publishing stories with varying degrees of success since the late 1950s and early 1960s, and throughout the 1970s.[55] Rather, what Gallagher was implying here was that regardless of some critics' motivated resistance, the emergence and elevation of Carver to the position of a writer of good critical standing itself represented a pronounced cultural reflex against aspects of the contemporary economic and political scene as it was playing out in the United States from the mid-1970s onwards, an acknowledgement that things were not as they should be and that literature might very well have an obligation to document that fact.

However, this was not just a response to subject matter and narrative milieu. For the material dispossession of Leo and Toni is matched by the stylistic dispossession of Carver's prose: Carver's sentences, and his narrative, are stripped of any sense of abundance or excess, just as the couple's home appears to be in the process of being slowly relieved of the material goods, including (in excruciating circumstances) the car, that had marked Leo and Toni's previous sense of financial security. From this point of view, the financial liquidation of the objects in the story, the ever-dwindling inventory of Leo and Toni's goods, and the way such events are related are parts of an aesthetic of politically engaged social realism. The "goods" in the story were not just things used and consumed by his characters, but the things that, increasingly, they stood to lose, or bankrupt themselves in the hope of holding onto, as the United States entered a period of increased economic inequality that continues to this day. The laid-off fiberglass factory worker (Leo) and door-to-door encyclopedia seller (Toni) of "Are These Actual Miles?," along with many of the other characters in a collection that features and is narrated by waitresses, postmen, and salespeople of one sort or another are representative of the troubled economic times the American working and middle classes were entering at the dawn of the age of neoliberalism. So too might the style in which such events are narrated, in its sober-minded, conspicuously unostentatious economy, be interpreted as a gesture of aesthetic solidarity towards such characters. The experience of such financial insecurity was certainly familiar enough to Carver. The son of a sawmill worker, he was married by the age of eighteen. Both his first wife and he worked a variety of jobs over the course of a marriage that Carver characterized as defined by work, poverty, and his own alcoholism: "In those days I always worked some crap job or another, and my wife did the same. She waitressed or else was a door-to-door saleswoman. I worked sawmill jobs, janitor jobs, delivery man jobs, service station jobs, stockroom boy jobs—name it, I did it."[56]

Still, to present Carver's work as shaped only by this kind of class-conscious social realist fictional aesthetic fails to do justice to much that is most interesting about his fiction as far as the argument about things is concerned. G. P. Lainsbury frames the key point well when he argues that Carver is more invested in "the poetic truth of the content of the individual lives that make up these statistical, abstract populations than the mere demographic rendering of the social conditions within which such lives were being lived."[57] Carver's vision of those lives transcends grim economic determinism, as the recurrence of the trope of the liquidation of household goods in a story like "Why Don't You Dance?" illustrates. In this story, a man arranges his household furniture out in his front yard, complete with electrical connections provided by an extension cord so that "[t]hings worked, no different from how it was when they were inside."[58] These goods may or may not be, as David Kaufmann has argued, "a fetish of his former relationship," but it seems clear that his willingness to sell the items off at prices of their naming to a young couple passing by who assume he is having a yard sale is indicative of problems that extend beyond the economic, and are more likely to be rooted in his heart or his head than in his wallet or bank account.[59] It is typical of Carver's style that the question of precisely what those problems might be goes unanswered throughout the story. As David Applefield has observed, in Carver's work, such details manage to "reverberate like symbols, cultural icons, large metaphors" at precisely the same time as they remain "just well-observed objects and gestures from life."[60]

The well-documented product of the collaboration between Carver and his editor Gordon Lish, this aesthetic effect is achieved as a direct result of the relationship between common objects and language in his texts, and is also part of a distinctly masculinist literary aesthetic. This can be seen in a story like "A Serious Talk," an earlier working title for which was simply "Pie," and in which a dropped pumpkin pie becomes a material surrogate for a man's inarticulacy. The pie is just one of six appropriated by an estranged husband called Burt from his wife's home: "one for every ten times she had ever betrayed him."[61] He returns the next day, the pie still on the pavement where he dropped it, with "things he wanted to say, grieving things, consoling things, things like that."[62] "The thing was," Carver writes, "they had to have a serious talk soon. There were things that needed talking about, important things that had to be discussed."[63] Burt does not leave before appropriating another object, an ashtray that, despite the domestic use to which it has been put, was "not really an ashtray" but a stoneware dish.[64] Indeed, the only concrete example offered of the kind of "thing" Burt wants to say to his wife is to "tell her the goddamn ashtray was a goddamn dish."[65] Common objects, in this story, take the place of language, and to the extent that Bert communicates at all, he does so through and by means of material things: taking the pies and ashtray, severing the phone line with a kitchen knife. But if Burt communicates through things, so too, on an artistic level, does Carver, using these objects and Burt's interaction with them to articulate an emotional disturbance that he, Carver (or, at times, as we now know, Lish), chooses not to articulate in words, at least not at any length. Indeed, with its suggestion that each pie, for Burt, equates to ten of his wife's "betrayals," the story seems to include an element of hyperbole quite uncharacteristic of the rhetorical strategies usually deployed in Carver's fiction; and yet this moment of overstatement, implicitly ascribed to Burt rather than to Carver or his narrator, also speaks to a sense of internal emotional derangement, giving just a glimpse but no more of an inner life in which all sense of proportion and clarity has been lost.

In stories such as this, even the smallest, seemingly trivial objects could be read, as Vivian Gornick has read them, as something like the external material signifiers of a particularly male psychic disorder, a kind of desperate, tongue-tied, ham-fisted, emotional inarticulacy that is not a thousand miles away from the attacks on symbolic property that characterized other responses to different forms of dispossession in the "long 1980s," from Toyota cars to storefront windows.[66] At its darkest outer reaches, such a disorder might account for the sickening attack on two young women with a rock at the end of "Tell the Women We're Going." More frequently, it takes the less extreme form witnessed in "Vitamins" from *Cathedral* (1983), in which the narrator, after a brief but unconsummated romantic entanglement with his wife's colleague, finds himself unable to stop knocking things over in his bathroom: "I knocked some stuff out of the medicine chest. Things rolled into the sink [. . .] I knocked down some more things. I didn't care. Things kept falling."[67] In both cases, the object world provides things for these men to hold onto or fail to hold onto as they struggle to exert any sense of control over increasingly fractured and disordered lives. The objects they reach out to simply offer confirmation of—rather than compensation for—their troubled inarticulacy, especially when those objects are those that populate the domestic spaces of the home. This was not, then, simply a question of aesthetic flattening. Rather, it is about a depiction of objects in a deliberately restrained mimetic style that is supposed always to refer to something other than the objects depicted, something unspoken and unspeakable but redolent of an inability to find a home in the world in which things are not constantly subject to disruption and instability. In this sense, as critics such as Gornick and Stanley Elkin observed, Carver's work might actually be more accurately criticized not for a lack of affect, as some of its most hostile detractors proposed, but for an excess of it. For Gornick, for example, Carver was writing "the kind of story that is famous for a hard surface beneath which spreads a contained flood of sentiment."[68] Or as Elkin put it, "People get it wrong about minimalism. Those characters are anything but affectless. Every little thing sets off their feelings."[69]

*

It is difficult to overstate just how influential the example of Carver's writing proved to be in the 1980s, and if the way he incorporated common objects into his work attracted both critical acclaim and disparagement, the same mixed reception greeted some of those younger writers that emerged in his wake. Jay McInerney's *Bright Lights, Big City* (1984), for example, with its present tense, second-person narration, imported variations on the "neo-Realist" aesthetic from the often unnamed, lower middle class cultural and geographic settings of Carver's stories into a milieu with which McInerney himself was more familiar: the 1980s Manhattan that lay at the heart of the new "yuppie" culture. Like Bret Easton Ellis's *Less Than Zero* (1985), McInerney's novel was published after the recession of the early 1980s had subsided, in the midst of Reagan's resounding reelection to a second term, and when ideas of the 1980s as a new Gilded Age were already firmly in place.[70] Speaking of and to these times, McInerney, like Ellis, was understandably more apt to feature the kind of designer goods and status symbols used and consumed within the world of which he wrote than the lowly Heinz ketchup bottle he later invoked in his appreciation of Carver. This, David Kaufmann, has argued, was "the first Yuppie bestseller," shifting "more than 300,000 copies in the two years after it was published."[71] As a result, references to Cartier watches and Ray Ban sunglasses are a conspicuous presence in *Bright Lights, Big City*, serving on one level as markers of socio-economic milieu in much the same way as the "commonplace" objects encountered in Carver's fiction.

But traces of the other aesthetic uses to which Carver put objects in his stories are also evident in McInerney's narrative. The novel concludes, for example, with its unnamed, second-person narrator walking down New York's Canal Street at dawn on a Sunday morning, not having eaten since Friday night, blood streaming from nostrils much abused by cocaine. He smells the scent of fresh bread, which recalls a memory of his mother baking the same, and ends the novel by exchanging his Ray Bans for a bag of warm rolls from the back of a bakery delivery truck. "You will have to learn everything all over again," the novel ends.[72] Is this an allusion to Rainer Maria Rilke's "Archaic Torso of Apollo," which ends, "You must change your life"?[73] Or is it rather an echo of Carver's own echo of Rilke in "Fat," which ends with its narrator, a waitress, insisting, mistakenly or otherwise, "My life is going to change. I feel it"?[74] The bread roll itself recalls Carver's "A Small Good Thing," in which a couple grieving for the loss of their young son eat freshly made bread with a professional baker, the cake they ordered from him having never been picked up after their son is hit by a car on his birthday. Moreover, it is also clear that the bread rolls in McInerney's novel are intended to function in a similar way to objects in Carver's stories. In the absence of any explicit elucidation of the narrator's thoughts and feelings, they are supposed to serve to point McInerney's readers towards the extent of his narrator's grief at his mother's death, which had up until then lain more or less concealed.

There is certainly something heavy-handed and manipulative about the way McInerney achieves that effect in a narrative of this length, such that it feels less like the case of psychological repression that Kaufmann has intimated the author is attempting to present, and more like a case of the deliberate, drawn-out withholding of information from the novel's reader.[75] Of course, the same criticism might be leveled by some critics at Carver; however, in Carver's work, the sense of narrative economy on which such effects are based appears more organic to the aesthetic of the work as a whole, and more suited to the short story form, within which there is simply less space for readers to chafe against an author's evasiveness. Moreover, the objects with which McInerney achieves his effect are made almost too rich in their associations with home and motherhood to do anything but dispel the imprecise symbolism that Carver saw himself generating through his depiction of things. In this sense, the disdain of contemporary commentators who accused writers like McInerney of essentially colluding in, rather than resisting, what appeared to be the all-pervading commercialism, "materialism," and inherently superficial ethos of the era, seems peculiarly misplaced. "What stands out is an assimilation, to the point of wholesale adoption, of advertising culture. Labels, name brands, surface signs, have become the sole social referents," wrote one critic, of what she called "the youthcult fiction of the 1980s," while a 1987 *Newsweek* article claimed that the work of both Ellis and McInerney offered "the intellectual nourishment of a well-made beer commercial."[76] But the concluding scene of the novel involves the conspicuous inscription of a hierarchical relationship between, on the one hand, Ray-Ban sunglasses and, on the other, a food item explicitly associated with ideas of home and motherhood, for which those sunglasses are given up and traded in. The implication is clear: that the kind of brand-named, designer goods apparently valorized by a culture of consumption and consumerism are, in fact, of little value compared to those symbolically resonant objects for which the narrator exchanges them.

Compare the depictions of objects in Bobbie Ann Mason's *In Country* (1985), set in and around Paducah, Kentucky, in the summer of 1984. The novel deals with the efforts of its narrator, a recent high school graduate, Samantha (Sam) Hughes, to comprehend what both her Uncle Emmett and her father, who died in Vietnam, experienced in the war. Sam inhabits an environment in which the material and linguistic details of late twentieth-century consumer capitalism are brought very much to the fore. In some ways redolent of Eggleston's photography, the novel opens on a cluster of roadside restaurants and gas stations described by the kind of invocation of brand names that so displeased some critics: "Exxon, Chevron, and Sunoco loom up, big faces on stilts. There's a Country Kitchen, a McDonald's, and a Stuckey's."[77] Sam and her Uncle Emmett drink Cokes and Pepsis, while characters make passing references to the respective merits of Betty Crocker and Duncan Hines food products. *In Country* is less elliptical than Carver's narratives, at least in the sense that Sam frequently articulates her thoughts and feelings about her attempts to understand at second-hand the experience of the war. Vietnam itself takes the place of the unknowable and unspeakable in the novel, and though hardly florid, Mason's style is somewhat more metaphorically expansive in *In Country* than Carver's had been at its most terse and pared down at the beginning of the decade.

Despite such differences, Mason was very much considered a writer of the Carver school in the first half of the 1980s, even though she, like Carver, disliked the implications of the term "minimalism" that was most frequently used to describe the new realist writing of the 1980s.[78] Given the novel's western Kentucky setting, when conservative critic Jonathan Yardley coined the pejorative term "hick chic" in the same year that *In Country* was published, reporting a novelist friend asking him, why "in a nation full of yuppies, conservatives and materialists" rural poverty was supposedly "all the rage," Mason's work may well have been what he had in mind.[79] Subsequently, the question of how best to interpret the sheer weight of mass cultural references in *In Country* has generated considerable debate among scholars and critics of Mason's novel. Some have argued that it simply shows how any sense of regional specificity had been subsumed by the 1980s beneath a homogenizing wave of mass culture.[80] Mason herself, however, was quite explicit about how little interest she had in using such references to critique the prevailing culture. "I think what writers typically do is throw these [mass cultural] references in to make a comment on the culture and the comment is always negative: pop culture is trash. I don't do that," she told Nick Hornby. Nor was she interested, she claimed, in exposing the superficiality or shallowness of those who consumed mass cultural goods in the 1980s: "The fact that the culture may be shallow doesn't mean that the characters are shallow, or that they are stupid for enjoying it."[81]

Rather, in Mason's novel, the mass-produced, brand name goods that Sam and her family and friends use and consume are filled with meanings, partial and unsatisfactory as those meanings may be. "Everything means something," Sam insists to a veteran, articulating a perspective reflected throughout Mason's narrative.[82] At one point, for instance, Sam reflects on an image she has seen of soldiers marching through a field of corn in a made-for-TV Vietnam movie. She wonders whether corn really grows in Vietnam. "They certainly had corn in Mexico [where the film was shot]," she thinks, "because corn was an Indian plant. Maize. The woman in the Mazola commercial. It bothered her that it was so hard to find out the truth. Did corn actually grow in Vietnam?"[83] Her exposure to brand-named, mass-produced goods, the ordinary things she uses and consumes every day, does not simply inform, then, but has become inseparable from what some critics have described as her "quest" to discover the truth about Vietnam as her father and uncle experienced it.[84]

The way Mason has Sam generate these chains of signification from mass-produced objects, images, and brand names to the lingering cultural trauma of Vietnam illustrates not just the intensity of her curiosity but the way Vietnam and its legacies had not yet, by the mid-1980s, been properly consigned to history, remaining instead evident in the very surface textures of American cultural life. For veterans like Sam's uncle, for example, the defoliant Agent Orange is as discernible a cultural presence as mass-consumed sodas like Pepsi and Coke: "We'll never get anything out of the government for Agent Orange," Emmett said. "They're trying every way they know how to prove Agent Orange is good for you, like a big orange drink."[85] Agent Orange has become just another brand name. Sam suspects it is responsible for the pimples that encrust her uncle's face. Her mother disagrees, blaming them on the amount of Pepsi Emmett drinks. Encoded into the brand names, images, and goods that are consumed every day, inscribed onto the surface of Sam's uncle's skin, and, in the form of Maya Lin's recently erected Vietnam War Veterans' Memorial at which the novel ends, scored into the ground of the National Mall, material representations of the trauma of Vietnam proliferate throughout the novel. What might have been dismissed by other authors as signs of the superficial and meaningless—the brand name consumer good, a cooking oil advertisement—become in Mason's novel markers not just of a certain recognizable, late twentieth-century milieu, but of a profound individual, familial, and national scarring. Reading one of her father's letters, for example, Sam drops "a Dorito fragment" on it: "She picked it up with a moistened finger," Mason writes. "Atoms from the letter mixed with atoms of her saliva, across time."[86] There is a yearning here for a solid, material connection with her dead father that surpasses the merely linguistic or textual relationship represented by the words in the letter.

Thus did Mason "paint what we are" in the mid-1980s, transfiguring the repertoire of commonplace objects, brand names and all, into an index not of profit but of loss, and of forms of dispossession beyond the merely material. That was representative of the aesthetic value the most ordinary, despised, or disregarded things held for some producers of culture interested in pursuing through realism a humanist ethics and aesthetics that foreswore sweeping claims about the culture or civilization-at-large to focus on the local and particular textures of life lived in the United States in the opening phase of the age of neoliberalism. Distinct from the extensions of Pop Art's project inaugurated by Jeff Koons or the wry, anthropological bafflement assumed by artists like David Byrne or Don DeLillo, such realism re-presented a world lived in relation to real, material things in the teeth of critical resistance to the inclusion of *rhopographic* material details in the form of everyday goods and brand-named objects. That resistance was itself a culturally fascinating aspect of the argument about things that was gaining prominence in the era. For while the impulses that lay behind it might have been politically varied, from a poverty-denying Reaganism to a new leftist assault on the evils of "materialism," much of this criticism was analogous to the faux-anti-materialism of Jimmy Carter in the late 1970s. Just like Carter, many critics appeared to subscribe to a form of neo-Platonism, central to which was the belief that what ought to make life worth living lay beyond or beneath the merely material form of things, and that the art and culture of the period needed to acknowledge that. But few accounts of the culture of the United States of the "long 1980s" could be given without reference to the very particular things of that culture, and the widespread hostility to their inclusion in a realist aesthetics that sought to do what Raymond Carver described as "a bringing of the news from one world to another" begins in retrospect to look like either a major critical oversight or an over-determined resistance even to attempting to understand the "news" that realism can bring. "Maybe writing fiction about particular kinds of people living particular kinds of lives will allow certain areas of life to be understood a little better than they were understood before," Carver suggested.[87] Things, too, had their part to play in such understandings; perhaps we ought to have attended to them more carefully.

CHAPTER 4

Matter Unmoored

This book could easily have started with the trash of the 1980s. After all, trash, garbage, junk, pollution, and dirt were all conspicuous cultural presences in the United States in the "new Gilded Age" of that elongated decade.[1] Indeed, the more one looks at the "long 1980s," the more of such stuff one seems to see, oozing out of or into one aspect of American life after another and giving the lie to the various narratives of dematerialization that were already beginning to circulate in the opening phase of the era of neoliberalism. One of that era's signature literary styles, the "minimalism" discussed in the previous chapter, was in fact, according to one critic, a "dirty realism" that brought its news from a struggling, blue-collar world "cluttered with junk food and the oppressive details of modern consumerism."[2] On Wall Street, Michael Milken was recycling the toxic contents of the securitized debt markets and making an illegal fortune from "junk bonds" that eventually landed him in prison.[3] Such examples operate, of course, principally at the rather immaterial level of metaphor. The same was not true, however, of the March 1989 Exxon Valdez oil spill in Prince William Sound, Alaska, nor of the CFCs and carbon deposits that environmentalists like Bill McKibben showed were dirtying the air throughout the decade.[4] Nor was it true of the enormous mass of floating trash in the middle of the Pacific Ocean that we now know as the Great Pacific Garbage Patch, the existence of which was first postulated by government scientists in 1989, even while other researchers intensified efforts to reduce the amount of manmade debris that decades of space exploration had left spinning in continuous orbit around the earth.[5] Closer to home, there was nothing merely metaphorical, either, about the medical waste that washed up on New Jersey shores, closing beaches in the summers of 1987 and 1988.[6] Nor, again, about the more than three thousand tons of trash that the *Mobro 4000* garbage barge was unable to unload in the same year. This was all matter self-evidently out of place.[7]

Consider that garbage barge. In late March 1987, the *Mobro 4000* had originally left Islip, New York with the intention of dumping its load in Morehead City, North Carolina, where the waste it carried was to be put to use in the production of methane gas. The proposed deal fell through as the barge sailed South, amid rumors that it was carrying medical waste, including hypodermic syringes and bedpans. The *Mobro* was subsequently left searching for a port and a waste disposal facility that would accept its cargo. The owners approached ports in Alabama, Louisiana, Texas, Mexico, and Belize but none wanted the barge; the Governor of Louisiana even threatened to have National Guardsmen open fire on the vessel if it tried to dock. Given that a similar case—that of the *Khian Sea*—had ended with reports of that vessel's load having been dumped at sea, the barge's eventual return to New York, and the garbage's incineration in Brooklyn in October, months after it had departed, was cause for considerable local and national relief.[8]

However, that relief could hardly mask the cultural concerns such episodes brought into focus in the second half of the decade. For this trash was problematic. What did it mean that it could not be disposed of for so long? This chapter explores how such trash is important to our understanding of the culture of the United States in the long 1980s because it demanded—and still demands—that we see and understand such detritus as matter unmoored not just from spatial boundaries but also the temporal boundaries assigned by a culture of mass consumption. It demands, in other words, a materialist way of thinking about things as themselves mattering more, or at least differently, than much critical literature on consumer capitalism has typically intimated. For decades, those who had theorized such discarded matter had emphasized its ephemeral nature, whereas trash in the 1980s was asserting with increasing force both a characteristic resistance to being spatially contained and an alarming durability. Insofar as it was doing so, it invoked a certain "archaeological consciousness" that was also finding expression across diverse spheres of the nation's culture throughout the decade, with much art and culture of the era revealing that durable detritus was not just a pressing public policy issue but a marker of a number of cultural anxieties emerging out of the operations of archaeological consciousness. For time and again in cultural texts of the long 1980s, trash speaks to familiar concerns about the worthlessness and contingency of the mass-consuming culture of the late twentieth-century United States. But it also prompts reflections on its own epistemological complexity, with the kind of unmoored matter that featured in cultural texts mute and uncommunicative at least as often as it was eloquent and informative. And even when garbage did have much to say about the mortality of both the human subject and entire civilizations, it also frequently attested to the individual's obliviousness to such truths in a decade in which triumphalist political discourse figured the nation as back on the rise after the supposed confusion and inertia of the 1970s.

*

There can certainly be no doubt of the cultural impact of the ocean-worrying trash that made so much news in the late 1980s. National newspapers covered the garbage barge's journey. It featured on *The Tonight Show*, *The Phil Donahue Show*—on which its host called its load "the most famous 3,000 tons of garbage in the history of the universe"—and even in Steven Soderbergh's *sex, lies and videotape* (1989). In *See No Evil, Hear No Evil* (1989), when Richard Pryor and Gene Wilder drive a police car off a Manhattan wharf directly into "the 7,000 tons of garbage" hauled by a passing garbage barge, the audience may well have recalled media reports of the *Mobro*'s journey. Even political speech of the late 1980s drew directly on themes related to both the New Jersey medical waste and the *Mobro 4000*. "I am going to stop ocean dumping," George H. W. Bush promised the Republican National Convention in 1988. "Our beaches should not be garbage dumps and our harbors should not be cesspools."[9] The references were to the *Mobro 4000*, the *Khian Sea*, its highly controversial predecessor, and the medical waste that had polluted New Jersey shores for two consecutive summers, as well as to Boston harbor. One of the less remembered negative television ads of the infamously dirty 1988 Bush–Quayle campaign featured images of garbage afloat upon the water in the harbor and a voiceover accusing Massachusetts governor and Democratic presidential candidate, Michael Dukakis, of being responsible for its presence.[10]

A whole complex of cultural anxieties pulsed through such highly mediated events as the voyage of the *Mobro 4000*. In the midst of a criminally misunderstood AIDS crisis, in which many tens of thousands of hearts were supposedly, like Prior Walter's in Tony Kushner's *Angels in America* (1990), "pumping polluted blood," or else being treated like so much toxic waste themselves, medical waste was a particular cause of concern.[11] Broadcasting his weekly "Letter from America" for BBC Radio on July 29th, 1988, during what he called the "atrocious, burning summer" that followed that of the voyage of the garbage barge, Alistair Cooke told his British audience of the beach closures necessitated by the discovery of "hospital waste of every gruesome sort from syringes and bandages and decayed organs to the corpses of laboratory rats."[12] Subsequent studies may have proven that such waste constituted only a small proportion of the garbage washing ashore during those summers, but public health fears at this time were perfectly understandable.[13] After all, the revelations from the Love Canal scandal that had emerged in the late 1970s confirmed that the American way of life in the late twentieth century might well entail living on top of several tens of thousands of tons of toxic industrial waste. Why would Americans of the late 1980s *not* fear the unknowable consequences of (sun)bathing amid the kind of detritus so evocatively catalogued by correspondents like Cooke?

Such health concerns aside, no other set of cultural anxieties were more obvious in the cultural response to the garbage panics of the 1980s than those related to space. "SPACE," Charles Olson's "central fact to man born in America," was precisely what Americans were running low on, according to some media sources.[14] "Buried Alive!: The Garbage Glut" ran the headline of a *Newsweek* cover on the alleged crisis in November 1989, introducing a story that gave voice to an apparently earnest fear that the discarded matter of the late twentieth-century United States, of which the load of the *Mobro 4000* was but a representative fraction, would, as one Cape Cod newspaper put it, "come back to haunt, and bury, its inhabitants."[15] As Patricia Poore has argued, for all their rhetorical and symbolic force, such fears had little empirical basis on the national level.[16] As recently as the beginning of the twenty-first century, writers on garbage were citing studies that suggested that even "if the current rate of generation were maintained, all of America's garbage for the next one thousand years would fit into a landfill space 120 feet deep and forty-four miles square—a patch of land representing less than 0.1 percent of the surface area of the United States."[17]

Yet what the unbidden glimpse into both the national and international commerce in trash afforded by the garbage barge did make obvious was that the routes taken by garbage mapped onto (geo)political inequities in population and wealth, and that trash itself would thus prove just another globalized commodity in the age of neoliberalism. Populous states like New York and New Jersey, for example, used contractors to truck their garbage as far afield as New Mexico in the West or to Southern states like North Carolina or Louisiana, while the voyage of the *Khian Sea* entailed the dumping of a full 4,000 tons of its 14,000-ton load on Haiti before the remainder disappeared into the Indian and Atlantic Oceans.[18] Prompted in part by the *Khian Sea* affair, the 1989 Basel Convention on the Control of Transboundary Movements of Hazardous Waste and their Disposal was signed but not ratified by the United States; by 1992, Larry Summers, then Chief Economist for the World Bank and later Secretary of the Treasury in the second Clinton administration, was asserting in a memo subsequently leaked to Greenpeace that "the economic logic behind dumping a load of toxic waste in the lowest-wage country is impeccable."[19] Space, then, was an issue, but not quite in the way that the mainstream media portrayed. It was less a case of the United States being in danger of burying itself alive and more one of how the trajectories traced by trash disclosed to view the uneven development on which the maximization of profit (or the limitation of loss) might hinge in the already thoroughly globalized, trans-national systems of production, consumption, and disposal that have characterized the post-Bretton Woods age.

However, this was never only a question of space, or of the revelatory geographies inscribed by the solid waste streams pouring forth out of the United States in the 1980s. Since the early 1970s, the University of Arizona's Garbage Project had been investigating the "archaeology" of domestic waste: from 1987 onwards, prompted in part by the publicity surrounding the garbage crisis supposedly emblematized by the plight of the *Mobro 4000*, the Project's founder, William Rathje, expanded the scope of his research into what has been called "the archaeology of us" to begin excavating landfill sites.[20] Rathje and his team discovered that conditions inside landfills were such that the biodegradation supposedly occurring therein was, in many cases, absent, and that what was being buried at such sites was in fact "durable beyond precedent."[21] This coincided with a spate of legislation aimed at the synthetic plastics that appeared to many the principal cause of rubbish's unwanted durability. As early as 1988, the legislature of Suffolk County, New York, approved a bill banning plastic bags.[22] In 1990 alone, twenty-two states debated laws concerning disposable diapers. The state of New York even considered mandating environmental warnings on diaper packets informing consumers that the items contained within "may take over one hundred years to degrade in a landfill."[23]

This growing awareness of the surprising durability of the matter Americans were discarding in ever-greater volumes contributed to the distinctive character of the "garbage panics" of the decade. The discarded matter produced by a mass consuming, "throwaway" society had previously been characterized not in terms of its durability but its ephemerality. As early as 1930, Stuart Chase was sardonically insisting in a *Harper's* essay that it was "a duty partaking of the sacred to keep millions of tons of motor cars, radios, phonographs, furniture, clothing, toys, printed matter moving briskly towards the junk pile with a minimum of stoppage in the hands of the user."[24] Nearly twenty years later, Hannah Arendt argued in *The Human Condition* (1958) that while it was "durability which gives the things of the world their relative independence from men who produced and use them," this durability did not apply to waste.[25] When Arendt wrote that "our whole economy has become a waste economy, in which things must be almost as quickly devoured as they have appeared in the world," she neglected how things might not be "devoured" in their entirety, nor necessarily disappear from "the world" once whatever was left of them had been discarded.[26] Similarly, in *The System of Objects* (1968), Jean Baudrillard had claimed that "for centuries generations of people succeeded one another in an unchanging décor of objects which were longer-lived than they, whereas now many generations of objects will follow upon one another at an ever-accelerating pace during a single human lifetime."[27] There is a clear tendency in such commentary to underplay the lifespan of the discarded matter of the object world, as if things and what remains of things always moved briskly, barely pausing, barely being, as they lived and died, moved on, or disappeared.

In this light, the decidedly material news that William Rathje and his colleagues were bringing up from the depths of sanitary landfill sites from the late 1980s onwards was news precisely because it established that so much discarded matter survived, and was going to survive, far longer than anyone had previously hypothesized. The understanding that this might be true of some materials, such as the plastics that were themselves a by-product of the growth of the oil industry discussed in Chapter One, was what led to those local legislative responses aimed at plastic bags and disposable diapers. Indeed, plastics, the evocative by-product of the same fossil fuel-based economy that was such an important part of the network of conditions out of which the age of neoliberalism emerged, have in some sense been among the signature materials of the long neoliberal moment. The plastics industry itself claimed that "the United States entered the 'Plastics Age' in 1979, when the annual volume of plastic exceeded that of steel." If, as Jeffrey L. Meikle has argued, "most people" ignored the claim when it was made, by the end of the decade, it was precisely the durability of plastic products such as grocery bags and disposable diapers that prompted the kind of legislative attention described above.[28] This represented an important shift in understandings of the meaning of these materials: in the immediate post-war era, the emergence of ever-increasing numbers of plastic products had prompted fears "that what had been created was ephemeral or unreal," and Roland Barthes once wrote that plastic "hardly exists as substance."[29] By 1979, many Americans already understood that plastic not only existed but had a kind of immortality, and the sense of the emblematic, era-defining durability of plastic only intensified as the 1980s wore on. By 1989, for example, Bill McKibben was suggesting that plastic was representative of a shift in the ecological stance of Western societies that can be dated back to the flourishing of the synthetic plastics industry since the end of the Second World War, and Rathje, writing with Cullen Murphy, argued that plastic was "surrounded by a maelstrom of mythology; into the very word Americans seem to have distilled all of their guilt over the environmental degradation they have wrought and the culture of consumption they invented and inhabit."[30]

What Rathje was himself establishing was that none of this was simply a question of plastics alone. Accompanying the 1989 *Newsweek* story on "the garbage glut" was a photograph of an intact, well-preserved corncob and a newspaper dating back to 1952 that had been retrieved from a landfill. All manner of tossed-away things would live on long after what Arendt had called their "makers and users" passed away, regardless of the materials of which they were composed.[31] Hence the desire for the symbolic and material "reincarnation" of such objects enshrined in what were in the 1980s still nascent recycling schemes, which for some commentators represented a way out of the crisis of the moment. The deathlessness of such things made a change of material form, either by means of biodegradation or through some other transformative process, itself an object of desire.[32] Thus, a growing awareness of the temporally dislocated nature of the kind of late twentieth-century trash that made up the garbage barge's load, its recalcitrant refusal to go away after it had been thrown away, was of considerable historical and epistemological significance. So often conceptualized as ephemeral, this was not only matter out of place, it became clear. This was matter unmoored in both space and time, resistant to the ephemeral, here-today, gone-tomorrow lifespan assigned to it by a culture of mass consumption and planned obsolescence, reluctant to undergo the transformative processes so fervently wished upon it, and thus demonstrably capable of making what Michael Thompson had characterized in *Rubbish Theory* as "the seemingly impossible transfer" from "transience to durability."[33] This double dislocation of matter in time and space may inform many of our contemporary understandings of garbage, but it was still a relatively new notion in the 1980s. The period therefore represents an important watershed in our conceptualization of the nature of trash over recent decades. With American junk afloat on global tides, pooling on the surface of the Pacific in the form of the Great Pacific Garbage Patch, and even (as NASA had confirmed) orbiting the planet, the spatial extent of the problem posed by such matter was obvious for anyone willing to consider it. The news that much of the discarded matter already spatially contained in sanitary landfill sites was nevertheless evading death showed that the temporal extent of the material waste Americans were manufacturing ought to have been no less an object of wonder.

*

Rathje's work was both driven by and sought to invoke what one historian of archaeology, Alain Schapp, has called an "archaeological consciousness."[34] For Schapp, archaeological consciousness, varieties of which can be traced at least as far back as the sixth century BC cuneiform engravings on stone tablets uncovered in Larsa, modern-day Iraq, is a habit of mind "born more of confrontation with the future than with the past," in which one contemplates not just what has survived from other times but what will survive from ours. "We have to engage with the idea that other human beings, maybe tomorrow, maybe in a few hours' time, maybe a few years or centuries from now, will look upon our traces," Schapp writes.[35] For centuries, the survival through time of just such material traces has prompted a sense of contemplative wonder in those musing upon them, while scholars once conceived of the way such bits and pieces travel through time in metaphorical terms apt to describe the kind of ocean-borne detritus that plagued American shores and consciousnesses in the 1980s. For proto-archaeologists and early antiquarians had used the term "time's shipwreck" to describe the "jetsam on the shore of history," which "if properly interpreted, reveal[s] facts, practices and behaviour which could take us to the heart of past societies."[36] In a mass consuming society in which even the most ephemeral objects obtain a surprising durability, the sheer amount of such wreckage increases exponentially; and in Rathje's work and the antiplastic legislation of the late 1980s, we can surely detect an archaeological consciousness eager to reduce the exposure of the earth and future generations to the long-lived garbage of the late twentieth-century United States.

Such a consciousness, however, was by no means limited to archaeological research itself or to the public policy debates provoked by the growing awareness of the durability of even the most supposedly ephemeral things. Unmoored matter and archaeological consciousness teem across a range of the cultural production of the United States between the late 1970s and late 1980s. As early as 1979, in *Motel of the Mysteries*, the British-born illustrator, David Macaulay, previously known for educational books on the architecture and construction of the set-piece glories of Western European culture like *Cathedral* (1973) and *Castle* (1977), offered a satirical illustrated account of an archaeological excavation that takes place in the year 4022, more than two-thousand years after the supposed burial—in the middle of the 1980s—of the contemporary United States under the weight of its own junk. In keeping with the notion of plastic as the signature material of the age, in Macaulay's book, a plastic plant is named the "Plant That Would Not Die," while the archaeologists of the future classify the material used to produce the "Do Not Disturb" sign they mistake for a "Sacred Seal" as *plasticus eternicus.*[37] "Everywhere was the glint of plastic," Macaulay has the future discoverers of his motel observe, parodying Howard Carter's famous description of the sight of gold in Tutankhamun's tomb.[38]

In 1980, the artist Sam Weiner staged an installation called *Splendors of the Sohites* at New York's OK Harris gallery, a "sly parody of blockbuster museum loan shows, right down to the attached gift shop, [which] featured archaeological fragments of a supposedly vanished SoHo civilization—'funerary objects' that strangely resembled abandoned hubcaps, heavily patinated beer-can tabs labelled 'hermaphrodite symbols,' and other marvels."[39] Riffing on the success of the *Treasures of Tutankhamun* exhibition that had toured seven major cities in the United States and was seen by a million Americans between 1976 and 1979, the work of Weiner and Macaulay involved an ironic turn inwards. They speculated on what might remain of American civilization for archaeologists to marvel at in the future.[40] Both Macaulay and Weiner alighted on the most worthless refuse and part-objects as either the cause of civilizational collapse or as the remnants that would survive that civilization. More recent films like Mike Judge's *Idiocracy* (2006) and Pixar's *Wall-E* (2008), in which cultural apocalypses take the form of suffocating accumulations of trash, follow the contours of this satirical attack on the culture of the modern-day United States. Such versions of the apocalypse suggest that the United States might have nothing to offer posterity besides the worthless waste products of contemporary mass consumption and add to the same tradition of jeremiads about American materialism that had returned with such force at the beginning of the long 1980s. That the piles of goods conjured by the rhetoric of Jimmy Carter might ultimately result in civilizational death was certainly an intriguing possibility during a decade in which the atomic anxieties that had long been present in what Joseph Dewey has called the American "apocalyptic temper" continued to wax and wane. Americans were now confronted with the prospect that they and their civilization were existentially threatened not just by the nuclear-armed "evil empire" of the Soviet Union but by the sheer volume of disposable garbage that their own society produced.[41]

The plate paintings that the painter Julian Schnabel exhibited at the beginning of the 1980s present another interesting expression of archaeological consciousness. Works like "The Sea" (1981) and "The Mud in Mudanza" (1982), in which Schnabel used broken plates as the grounds of his painting, are artistic reifications of the notion of "time's shipwreck." "The Sea" communicates the idea most directly, with its partly clear, partly muddied, black and blue palette, its series of white horizontals foaming laterally across the painting like the spume that bubbles along the crests of waves, and its jumbled horde of pots and plates and hunk of actual charred wood fixed onto the canvas like something washed up on shore.[42] "The Mud in Mudanza" suggests not a sea but a river running dry to reveal a geological battleground: a violent gash of volcanic red runs through a panel dominated by a green-black hue reminiscent of petroleum deposits. Sandy shades turn muddier in patches or are streaked with a marine blue or ever-darker reds; a single swathe of plates retains a white china glaze, not yet subsumed into the slowly hardening geological gloop.[43] Thomas McEvilley has written of "The Mud in Mudanza":

> It is the loam of history that lies there among the gaping vessels that seem to come from another age. It is the dissolving and fertilizing ground of the past on which we raise our brief constructions, which are equally to be broken down into the death-and-life swamp of the archaeological rubbish dump [. . .] The fact that the shards are not really from ancient ceramic wares [. . .] but contemporary ones, usually brand new from the stores and sometimes still bearing labels or price tags, focuses the onslaught of ravaging time onto our own moment.[44]

McEvilley underscores the double vision inherent in such artistic works. Like Walter Benjamin's "angel of history," who "sees one single catastrophe which keeps piling wreckage upon wreckage and hurls it in front of his feet," they look backwards to the past as time serves to transport "the gaping vessels that seem to come from another age" into the present.[45] At the same time, such work looks forwards, as the objects that are part of the work raise the question of what amongst the endless mass of the material culture of the late twentieth-century United States might survive in times to come. Both perspectives contribute to a conceptual dialogue between the ephemeral and the durable as the paintings stage a tension between "the onslaught of ravaging time" and the things that survive, in one form or another, to tell the tale of that ravaging after individuals and civilizations have passed away.

Compare the archaeological tropes in the fiction of Don DeLillo. Archaeological consciousness had in fact characterized DeLillo's writing long before *White Noise* (1985), a novel steeped in a deeply ironic sense of the contingency of the culture of the late twentieth-century United States. As early as his first novel, *Americana* (1971), for example, his narrator meditates upon a car tire test track in Texas: "I looked at that huge circle of asphalt, nine-never-ending miles, something left behind by a crazed or childlike people."[46] A curious piece of Americana projected into the future, the test track is conceived as a monument or relic, with much to say about the culture that had produced it. By the time of his 1976 science fiction novel, *Ratner's Star*, DeLillo was having an archaeologist character discuss finding the material remains of civilizations "more advanced the deeper we dig," a comment on naïve faith in human progress but also a trope that echoes the famously apocalyptic movie *Planet of the Apes* (1968), which ends with Charlton Heston cursing the narrative and historical implications of a ruined Statue of Liberty, but not before he has discovered, as the first evidence of his worst fears, less spectacular remnants of his own civilization (eyeglasses, a child's doll) in a cave in the so-called "Forbidden Zone."[47]

By *The Names* (1982), DeLillo's fascination with material remnants leads not just another archaeologist but multiple characters to meditate on the meaning of things *qua* things. Thus, his half-mystified narrator, James Axton, on his wife's archaeological work:

> I was helpless, overwhelmed. The bare fact of it disheartened me. I couldn't see what the work signified or represented to her. Was it the struggle that counted, a sense of test of mission? What was the metaphor, exactly?
>
> I was compelled in the end to take her literally. She was digging to find things, to learn. Objects themselves. Tools, weapons, coins. Maybe objects are consoling. Old ones in particular, earth-textured, made by other-minded men. Objects are what we aren't, what we can't extend ourselves to be. Do people make things to define the boundaries of the self? Objects are the limits we desperately need. They show us where we end. They dispel our sadness, temporarily.[48]

In an inversion of the aesthetic logic of the still life touched on in the previous chapter, for Axton, the consolatory nature of objects, and especially of archaeological objects, stems from their resistance to human conditions of mortality and impermanence. For the same reason, elsewhere in *The Names*, a character involved in the murderous cult from which the novel takes its title speaks of the importance of finding what he calls "an external object" or "[s]omething to outlast us," a desire predicated on his sense that, as Barthes had once erroneously thought true of that material *bête noire* plastic, "[w]e barely exist."[49]

In *White Noise* itself, DeLillo's archaeological consciousness is hardly any less intense. Looking upon what he calls "the two-story world of an ordinary main street," the narrator finds that it reminds him "that Albert Speer wanted to build structures that would decay gloriously, impressively, like Roman ruins."[50] It is part of the humor of *White Noise* that Speer, of all architects, should be invoked here, given that Jack Gladney, DeLillo's narrator, is a professor of "Hitler Studies" who cannot speak German. The reference to an architecture responsive to the pathological death-drive of Hitler and the Third Reich captures DeLillo's preoccupation with the transience of human endeavors, the evanescence of the human subject, and the contingency of even the most powerful cultures and civilizations. "'We create beautiful and lasting things, build vast civilizations,'" Gladney observes to his colleague and sometime confidant, Murray Jay Siskind, who teaches in the department of "American environments." "'Gorgeous evasions,' he said. 'Great escapes.'"[51] Gladney is attempting to evade his own fear of death, but Siskind implies that the construction of "vast civilizations" is powered by the same impulse. Death cannot be evaded either on the cultural or individual level. "'The ruin is built into the creation,'" as Gladney says of the buildings he dwells upon on Main Street.[52] What stands in the present will collapse in the future, eroded into ruin and rubble: yet more wreckage on the tides of time.

At times, DeLillo's articulation of archaeological consciousness is even more explicit. When the Gladney family flee from their home in the face of looming ecological disaster and encounter a deserted gas station, DeLillo's narrator describes how the pumps "were not locked, which meant the attendants had fled suddenly, leaving things intriguingly as they were, like the tools and pottery of some pueblo civilization, bread in the oven, table set for three, a mystery to haunt the generations."[53] The metaphor of the vanished-civilization-to-be glimpses the present age as the past of a future still to come, and the everyday buildings and objects of the 1980s as what DeLillo would refer to in a later, post-9/11 essay as "the ruins of the future."[54] Such archaeological imagery is hardly out of place in literature of the 1980s. In *The Invention of Solitude* (1982), Paul Auster meditates upon the possessions his father left behind upon his death: "In themselves, the things mean nothing, like the cooking utensils of some vanished civilization."[55] In *In Country* (1985), Bobbie Ann Mason's narrator touches the name of her dead father engraved on the Vietnam Veterans' Memorial and discovers "[a] scratching on a rock. Writing. Something for future archaeologists to puzzle over."[56] What is distinctive about *White Noise*, however, is the way the novel incorporates such archaeological perspectives into its contemplation of everyday waste. For when, in another scene from the novel, Gladney observes the compacted trash his family generates, he describes himself feeling "like an archaeologist about to sift through a finding of tool fragments and assorted cave trash."[57]

And yet, if DeLillo's narrator turns to the family trash as an archaeologist turns to an archaeological find, in the hope that it might tell him something of the people and practices that left it behind, what defines this particular agglomeration of matter is its abiding epistemological elusiveness. One of the novel's earliest critics, Frank Lentricchia, argued that the rash of rhetorical questions that Gladney poses at the sight of his family's trash—"Is garbage so private? Does it glow at the core with personal heat, with signs of one's deepest nature, clues to secret yearnings, humiliating flaws? What habits, fetishes, addictions, inclinations? What solitary acts, behavioural ruts?"—mimics the questioning voice in John Keats's "Ode on a Grecian Urn."[58] If so, DeLillo emphasizes the impervious muteness of such things, for although Keats may have made his Grecian urn talk, saying "Beauty is truth, truth beauty,—that is all/Ye know on earth, and all ye need to know," the Gladney family trash is to a large extent unresponsive. As Bobbie Ann Mason's narrator suspects will be true of the Vietnam Veterans' Memorial unveiled in 1982, Gladney's trash remains something to puzzle over; in itself, as Auster claims of his father's banal legacy of abandoned things, it very often "mean[s] nothing." The point here is partly that trash, like any other future archaeological find, is difficult to understand. Shortly after the publication of *White Noise*, newspapers like the *New York Times* would publish details of William Rathje's interrogations of the much vaster accumulations of trash that had been collected in sanitary landfill sites. In such texts, Rathje spoke of the eloquence of trash, describing how reliably it informs archaeologists about human practices. *White Noise* illustrates that even as it prompts such interrogations, trash of all sorts is likely to refuse to answer many of the questions it raises, for sometimes trash is just meaningless trash, or what David Evans has called in relation to DeLillo's work a "stubbornly senseless" kind of matter.[59] If it says anything at all, it says, in a sense, nothing, and saying nothing speaks to nothing so much as the very idea of nothingness. Indeed, this cultural excrement is ultimately not so different from the pile of feces an earlier DeLillo narrator had found in the middle of the West

Texas desert, which with its "nullity" and "whisper of inexistence," had offered up yet another intimation of mortality.[60]

Eventually, however, such things are made to give up some of their meaning in *White Noise*. Consider, for example, the accumulated objects and common, everyday clutter that appears to gather in the narrator's family home, the kind of objects that, as we saw in the previous chapter, had frequently confounded Carver's characters. In the novel's opening pages, Gladney reflects on "Things, boxes. Why do these possessions carry such sorrowful weight? There is a darkness attached to them, a foreboding. They make me wary not of personal failure and defeat but of something more general, something large in scope and content."[61] Just what that "something" might be is clearer by the end of *White Noise*, as Gladney turns passionately against those possessions, and indulges in frequent mad spasms of domestic disposal and trash-making of his own. "I started throwing things away," he explains. "The more things I threw away, the more I found. The house was a sepia maze of old and tired things. There was an immensity of things, an overburdening weight, a connection, a mortality. I stalked the rooms, flinging things into cardboard boxes. Plastic electric fans, burnt-out toasters, *Star Trek* needlepoints."[62] There is DeLillo's usual comic seriousness at work here, while an uncanny process of accelerated ageing, if not decay, is deployed in the figurative transformation of a 1980s suburban home into a "sepia maze of old and tired things," as if every object in the house has somehow been transformed into a memento mori. The "mortality" of things pertains not to things themselves, which appear endless here, their recalcitrant materiality going on and on in time and space, proving impossible to get to the bottom of or finally free oneself from; rather, "mortality" pertains directly to Gladney, who has convinced himself that he is dying. Like Speer's specially designed buildings, he has had a "ruin worked out for" him "by the force or nonforce, the principle or power or chaos that determines such things."[63] He will die, he knows; indeed, he believes he is already dying. And it is objects themselves—things and boxes and the vast, endless accumulations of "stuff" that, as the comedian George Carlin reminded his audiences throughout the 1980s, littered many homes in a culture of mass consumption and consumerism—that, even without breaking their silence, appear eventually to whisper as much to someone as terrified of death as Gladney.

DeLillo has consistently been praised for the prescience of his work, and in seizing upon the apparent complexities of domestic trash in *White Noise*, he uncannily anticipated the cultural reception of the garbage panics that followed later in the decade. But other literary fiction produced after the voyage of the *Mobro 4000* exhibited equally clear signs of having been influenced by the intensification of the "garbage discourse" that followed in the barge's wake in ways that complicate the meaning of unmoored matter still further. For example, John Updike's *Rabbit at Rest* (1990), the final part of a tetralogy of novels that can also be read as a decade-by-decade social history of the United States from the 1950s to the 1980s, is uncommonly full of garbage. When Harry "Rabbit" Angstrom, by now the franchisee of a Toyota car dealership, anxiously awaits a visit from a company representative, he notices that the hedge bordering his lot "has collected a number of waxpaper pizza wrappers and Styrofoam coffee cups." Moved to remove this trash, Angstrom goes out into "the hot polluted air" and discovers that the "more wastepaper he gathers, the more it seems there is—candy wrappers, cigarette-pack cellophane, advertising fliers and whole pages of newspaper wrinkled by rain and browned by the sun, big soft-drink cups with the plastic lid still on and the straw still in and the dirty water from melted ice still sloshing around."[64] Updike's description of environmental pollution parallels Angstrom's own carefully documented physical decline and fall. Just as Angstrom clogs his arteries with snacks and junk food, so this particular "American environment" is choked with "crud."[65] There is a dramatic inevitability about the arrival of the Japanese executive, Mr. Shimida, at just the moment Angstrom realizes that there is more trash despoiling his lot than he can carry in his big, ex-basketball player's hands: more than just senseless, this rubbish serves as a symbol of both personal and national decline after a decade in which Japan's economic rise concerned so many American observers. But if the imagery of the trash-polluted hedge focuses above all on the *spatial* extent of the displaced matter littering the United States of the 1980s, it is the *temporal* endurance of matter that prompts intimations of Rabbit's own mortality. Contemplating the items of furniture that fill his Florida condominium, Rabbit observes first of his habit of touching the edge of the bureau in his and his wife's bedroom every time he gets up in the night to use the bathroom, that the "accumulated deposit of his groping touch [. . .] will still be there, a shadow on the varnish, a microscopic cloud of his body oils, when he is gone," and of the particular things he lives among, that they "all have a certain power, the ability to outlast him. He is flesh, they are inanimate things."[66] And so too, of course, are the items of trash that litter Rabbit's lot: they will outlast him even after they have been properly thrown away, for, as the decade had already revealed, garbage hardly dies.

Jay McInerney's *Brightness Falls* (1992) makes a related point through an image of accreted, layered burial. McInerney's narrator describes a character walking to work on mid-1980s Wall Street, and has her

> high-stepping over buried ceramic pipe bowls and wine jugs, bent nails, broken glass and brick fragments, partially fossilized pig, chicken and sheep bones, and other detritus that had been regularly tossed over the wall three centuries before, her route so familiar that she was as oblivious to it as she was to what was underneath the pavement, not really seeing the towering temples to Mammon as she walked toward the one in which she toiled, reading her paper in the available light that found its way to the canyon floor.[67]

Like Julian Schnabel's 1980s paintings, McInerney's prose moves two ways: down, towards the durable ephemera of the past; and up, towards the ephemeral durability of the present. He figures the investment banks and brokerage firms of 1980s Wall Street, the very beating heart of economic financialization, as anachronistic "towering temples to Mammon" and places those metaphorical temples in a context that implies they too will fall, like "the seventeenth-century log wall that had protected the Dutch settlers from the Indians and the British."[68] McInerney's pipe bowls and wine jugs, nails, glass, brick, and bone are of a piece with the family trash in DeLillo's *White Noise*, the hedge litter in *Rabbit at Rest*, and the three thousand tons of contemporary American detritus that formed the load of the *Mobro 4000*. All speak of cultures and individuals that once were but eventually will no longer be, even if they do not, as DeLillo's narrator implies, always speak with the clear-throated clarity an archaeologist might desire. Of course, McInerney's character, Corrine, knows nothing of what lies beneath her feet; her eyes are fixed on a mediated present, her newspaper commanding her attention even as she walks. In this way, McInerney emphasizes the obliviousness of the individual subject to the rising and falling motions of historical time, an obliviousness that found its counterpart in 1980s financial history, as well as in McInerney's novel, in the unexplained and to many still inexplicable Wall Street crash of October 1987. For if the United States' economy, and indeed the nation, was, as Ronald Reagan asserted in his successful reelection campaign, "back" and on the rise again after the stagflation of the 1970s, what the 1987 crash emphasized was the suddenness with which all rising bodies, as the Challenger disaster had already so spectacularly demonstrated the year before, can unexpectedly fall. McInerney's image thus offers an acerbic comment on the 1980s themselves: any tales the accumulated refuse of generations might have to tell about the contingency of all cultures and civilizations, and about the evanescence of all individual human practices, went pointedly unheeded in a decade in which the cultural air of the United States was at times as noisy with national self-congratulation as it had ever been. America was back; it was morning again. So why dwell on a national decline that had been predicted before without definitively materializing, or on a cultural death to which the United States might constitute an illimitable exception? Even when trash speaks, it is not necessarily heard.

*

To be clear, this was not just a case of culture warning against hubris on the national level. Nor were such engagements with unmoored matter the exclusive preserve of male writers. In the two books that Marilynne Robinson published in the 1980s, *Housekeeping* (1980) and *Mother Country* (1989), the ephemeral, the durable, and even trash itself are imagined on nothing less than a cosmological scale. *Housekeeping*, Robinson's debut novel, takes the form of a prolonged meditation on the part of the novel's narrator, Ruth, as she remembers her unconventional upbringing in the house referred to in the novel's title, which stands in Fingerbone, Idaho, a fictional town bordered by a lake that is the scene of repeated violent catastrophe: Ruth's grandfather has died when the train on which he was travelling came off its tracks while crossing the bridge that spans the lake; her mother has taken her own life by driving a car off a cliff into the same lake. The novel begins with a description of the disaster that had caused the death of Ruth's grandfather, after which local men and boys improvise harnesses and lower themselves down into the water to try and rescue survivors from the wreck of what she calls this "spectacular derailment."[69] "A suitcase, a seat cushion, and a lettuce were all they retrieved," Ruth relates. "[T]here was nothing to be saved, no relics but three," she adds.[70] Such objects are nothing remarkable in and of themselves, any more than the things reimagined in Sam Weiner's satirical installation, and yet they have survived where those with whom they are associated have not. One is reminded of the debt Robinson's fiction owes to Melville. "My name is Ruth," *Housekeeping* begins, in self-conscious echo of *Moby-Dick*.[71] And yet, no Ishmael survives the *Pequod*-like sinking of Ruth's grandfather's train; it is things, and things only, that escape to tell of the disaster to which Ruth explicitly emphasizes that no human subject was ever witness.

Elsewhere in *Housekeeping*, the notion of "time's shipwreck" is deployed as a metaphor for the experience of grief. When Ruth meditates upon the loss of both her mother and her grandmother during a night she spends in the local woods with her sister, Lucille, she asks, "[W]hy must we be left, the survivors picking among flotsam, among the small, unnoticed, unvalued clutter that was all that remained when they vanished, that only catastrophe made notable?"[72] Again, this is an expression of "time's shipwreck" on an individual scale; the arbitrary miscellany of things that survive an individual life become, like the objects left floating in the lake after the train's derailment, suddenly elevated to the status of relic once the subject living that life has vanished. By the end of the novel, when she and her unconventional Aunt Sylvie decide they must flee Fingerbone, Ruth wishes nothing less than complete destruction on the things that they are about to leave behind, which she fears will survive them:

> For even things lost in a house abide, like forgotten sorrows and incipient dreams, and many household things are of purely sentimental value, like the dim coil of thick hair, saved from my grandmother's girlhood, which was kept in a hatbox on top of the wardrobe, along with my mother's gray purse. In the equal light of disinterested scrutiny such things are not themselves. They are transformed into pure object, and are horrible, and must be burned.[73]

It is the very thought of things lasting and passing through time into other lives, and being "pawed and sorted and parceled out among the needy and the parsimonious of Fingerbone," which serves to explain Sylvie and Ruth's attempts to set fire to the objects inside the house and eventually to the house itself.[74] As she leaves, Ruth imagines "the spirit of the house breaking out the windows and knocking down the doors, and all the neighbors astonished at the sovereign ease with which it burst its tomb, broke up its grave [. . .] Every last thing would turn to flame and ascend, so cleanly would the soul of the house escape, and all Fingerbone would come marveling to see the smoldering place where its foot had last rested."[75]

If such a longing for the death and disappearance of things was remarkable enough on the local level, compare the sentiment expressed in *Mother Country* (1989), a polemical study of the British nuclear industry and the only other book-length work that Robinson published in the 1980s. Robinson concludes that book by reflecting back from Britain to the United States, and asserting, in a tone not dissimilar to that of Ruth in *Housekeeping*:

Of course the United States has been smirched by history. But in the larger scheme, the United States is an invention, like Constantinople, which, if life could be imagined going on, would drift and evolve into other shapes and things in the way of species, clouds, and continents. If I could dream that the world would live so long that our books were lost and our name forgotten, I could feel we had been a good and successful civilization, after all.[76]

The longing for oblivion might be equally reminiscent of aspects of Ruth's narrative in *Housekeeping*, but Robinson's essential point here is about the durability of poisonous things, and specifically radioactive waste, a form of late twentieth-century trash which is to all intents and purposes immortal in its toxicity. Her "dream" of the world living "so long" that the United States would leave no trace of itself on the face of the earth is an expression of "archaeological consciousness" that paradoxically longs for the effacement of contemporary American civilization rather than fears for its survival. Instead of polluting the cosmos and all of historical time with endlessly lethal materials, would it not in the end be better to be expunged from the archaeological record altogether, Robinson asked.

*

While the garbage panics of the 1980s thus clearly intensified the cultural expression of archaeological consciousness, bringing into renewed focus concerns about the values and contingency of late twentieth-century US civilization, a question remains whether such moments of wider cultural visibility are themselves fated to a frustrating transience. For all the uptick in recycling rates and the emergence of bags that proclaim "I am not a plastic bag" and cups that say "I am not a plastic cup," subsequent decades have proved just as durably trash-filled as the 1980s. Waste-generating carries on apace, with the stagnant wages and purchasing power of the US middle class partially compensated for by low-cost, overseas production and the expanding consumer power the ongoing reconfiguration of capitalism has brought to countries like China. Writers and artists continue to draw our attention to the material facts such processes leave behind. In the 1990s, works like A. R. Ammons's National Book Award-winning poem, "Garbage" (1993), or DeLillo's magnum opus, *Underworld* (1997), which includes repeated references to a *Khian Sea* or *Mobro*-like ship carrying a reportedly toxic cargo and rumored to have been "sailing port to port" for years, showed as much.[77] But one wonders to what effect. For even today, a phenomenon like the Great Pacific Garbage Patch occupies a position in the cultural consciousness of the United States akin to that of the domestic trash in *White Noise*, of which DeLillo's narrator asks, "Was this the dark underside of consumer consciousness?"[78] The Pacific's plastic floats miles offshore, open to the elements but culturally unseen and disregarded, an obscene testament to the durability of the most ephemeral things and the paths they trace across a globalized world. Scientists and photographers have already brought back news from that place, just as Rathje carried his up from the nation's subterranean garbage dumps.[79] Chris Jordan's images, for example, illustrate the durability of contemporary trash in the starkest possible terms: plastic bottle tops and cigarette lighters left exposed on the Pacific atoll of Midway as the flesh of the immature albatrosses that had the misfortune to swallow them rots away, framing each contingent mess of litter against small sad mounds of feather, beak, and bone. Still, for most of the wider public, the masses of floating trash may as well be buried deep beneath their feet (like that in McInerney's *Brightness Falls*), or carried imperceptibly through the air, like carbon emissions, so little attention have they commanded, even in an age we have taken to calling the "Anthropocene," in which manmade, durable plastics are "near-ubiquitous," forming "stratigraphic markers" of the present for generations of archaeologists still to come.[80]

In this sense, the foregoing discussion surely has important implications for our understanding of the argument about things in the 1980s, with the anxieties around trash and what it might say about the sustainability of the civilization that was producing it in such widespread and durable quantities serving to deepen a sense of the present era as having witnessed the dawning of a "new Gilded Age" in more ways than one. For what lay beneath the glister of late twentieth-century consumer culture, or was being produced alongside it, episodes like the voyage of the garbage barge disclosed, were not just inequalities of wealth and class touched on in previous chapters, but, at the same time, far-flung reliquaries of potentially deadly, durable detritus. The surface sheen of so many of our lives, in other words, is just that: a superficial gloss over sordid and troubling material realities. And if the "Gilded Age" that began somewhere around the late 1970s has in fact never ended, and we are instead truly stuck in a "long 1980s" that has continued to witness the global expansion of the ecologically disastrous systems of capitalist production, consumption, and disposal out of which the garbage discourse of the 1980s emerged, we can surely expect the further evanescent flaring of archaeological consciousness as producers of culture dwell, however transiently, on the implications for posterity of a truth acknowledged by Edward Abbey as early as 1968 but never before realized to the same extent as it is today. "Nature's polluted/There's man in every secret corner of her," observed Abbey, quoting Thomas Lovell Beddoes, in *Desert Solitaire*.[81] And in every such corner, many US citizens were first beginning to understand in the 1980s, the parings and refuse of even the most insignificant aspects of their civilization's material culture are likely to stay, in one form of another, long after those who made and all too briefly used them are gone. This, it seems to me, might be a kind of "1980s materialism" most worth thinking and talking about, and yet, to the extent that it is a materialism that is hard to see and harder still to comprehend, discourse on it, let alone anything befitting the name of action, has proven nearly impossible to sustain.

CHAPTER 5

At Peace with Things?

If garbage discourse and its attendant forms of cultural consciousness have flickered in and out of prominence over the course of the age of neoliberalism, by the second half of the 1980s themselves, as the Cold War approached its remarkable conclusion amid a reinvigoration of US–Soviet summit diplomacy, the more general argument about things remained an important characteristic of mainstream US political discourse. "Has the mindless materialism of the '80s left in its wake a values vacuum?" former Carter speechwriter Walter Shapiro asked in May 1987, going on to answer his question in the affirmative.[1] As we have already seen, in late 1988 and early 1989, Vice President George H. W. Bush was moved to address the question of "materialism" in both his nomination acceptance at the Republican National Convention and his January 1989 inaugural speech. For while the garbage panics of the late 1980s had evidently left their mark on political rhetoric, so too had the Iran-Contra affair (in which Bush himself was deeply implicated), as well as the kind of insider trading scandals that saw the prosecution of Ivan Boesky and others. Indeed, the prevailing public mood, or what passed for it in rhetorical arenas such as the Republican National Convention, seemed to have soured on the supposed "spirit" of the age, and while the promise to address the pollution of marine environments that Bush made in 1988 had the quality of a national purification rite, it was not just garbage but the consequences of Americans' attachments to material things *en masse* that found themselves vulnerable to rebuke from Reagan's own vice president. "Some people who are enjoying our prosperity, are forgetting, have forgotten [sic] what it's for," Bush told his fellow Republicans in 1988. "But they diminish our triumph when they act as if wealth is an end in itself." "We were practical," he argued, of some nostalgically remembered American populace of the past, "but we didn't live only for material things."[2]

In other discursive spheres, Americans already appeared more at peace, at least with certain things, than such rhetoric implied. In 1989, for example, Henry Petroski, a professor of civil engineering at Duke, published *The Pencil: A History of Design and Circumstance*. Aimed at a general readership, Petroski's book set out to explore the cultural history of an object that "is so common that it is virtually [. . .] invisible and ignored."[3] Petroski devoted some four-hundred pages, including appendices, notes, and bibliography, to rescuing the pencil from such phenomenological and epistemological invisibility, his book's own material heft providing ample supporting evidence for his point that the pencil is actually "a product of immense complexity and sophistication."[4] This was one of the first significant contributions to what has now become a burgeoning genre of books about the history of single objects or types of object aimed at a popular audience that by the early years of the twenty-first century was being satirized in the literary fiction of a new generation of American writers. In Keith Gessen's *All The Sad Young Literary Men* (2008), for example, one of its narrators deplores "the collapse of the discipline of history into *Antiques Roadshow*," which now produces graduate students researching such topics "as the cultural history of the coffee mug."[5]

It is a version of a criticism that some have fairly aimed at parts of the material turn in the humanities. See, for example, Andrew Cole's bracing critiques of neo-materialist philosophy and object-oriented ontologies as "commodity fetishism in academic form," incapable of recognizing either their own "idealism and mysticism" or the "cognitive limits that will never be breached by colorful, and sometimes only purple, prose."[6] For Cole, the risk for philosophers is that these ontologies not only fall prey to the kind of Logocentric ventriloquism by means of which, as we saw in the previous chapter, things are said to "speak" or withdraw at the ultimate behest of the subject (meaning object-orientation is itself anthropocentric), but that they also end up indicating not "much of anything but a philosopher's love of language, consumer goods, and entertaining thing-examples like hailstones and tar, aardvarks and baseball."[7]

In this context, and especially since Cole has pointed out how much the new philosophical materialisms themselves owe to traditions stretching all the way back to medieval mysticism, it becomes all the more important to understand that the renewed epistemological respectability that material things appear to have gained since the 1980s did not itself emerge *ex nihilo* as far as the United States is concerned. The fascination with the archaeological object discussed in the previous chapter, for example, had itself long been present in American cultural life and can be traced in the writings of Jefferson, himself an amateur archaeologist, or Thoreau—the scion of a small pencil manufacturing concern, as Petroski reminded his readers—who also had a habit of collecting Indian arrowheads, which he termed "fossil thoughts, forever reminding me of the mind that shaped them."[8] However, the specific tradition out of which Petroski emerges is that which turns its epistemological gaze not on the things of culturally distinct civilizations but, like much of the culture of archaeological consciousness examined in the previous chapter, on things that speak to the history and indeed contemporary realities of twentieth century American civilization, a later iteration of what Thoreau had called "relics of a more recent man."[9] Lewis Mumford's monumental *Technics and Civilization* (1934), for example, which had detailed the influence of technology on Western civilization up to and including the era in which Mumford was writing, is one of the foundational texts of this tradition, and while Petroski's book, alongside academic work by anthropologists, social psychologists, and others, certainly helped to prepare the ground for the "material turn" that many other scholars have taken since the 1980s, it was also part of a well-established, although not particularly well-known, stream of inquiry into everyday technologies, designed objects, and material culture that had long treated such things as legitimate objects of study instead of (or as well as) mere instances of the commodity form, ripe for critique.[10]

An intriguing series of contemporaneous analogues to Petroski's book was also emerging in the late 1980s in the sphere of literary and narrative culture in the work of the writer Nicholson Baker, whose first two novels, *The Mezzanine* (1988) and *Room Temperature* (1990), were filled not only with a sprawling mass of carefully detailed descriptions of everyday objects, from drinking straws to ballpoint pens, but also with descriptions of their narrators' thoughts about and interactions with those objects; and those thoughts and interactions were no less significant as far as the argument about things was concerned than the things themselves.[11] For in both *The Mezzanine* (1988) and *Room Temperature* (1990), any kind of social critique of the "mindless" acquisition of "consumer goods" is eschewed in favor of a much less disapproving representation of individuals' physical and psychological interactions with the things Americans were living among in the late 1980s, and in particular with the often disregarded paraphernalia of daily life. Indeed, Baker's writing of material culture was in fact part of a broader and aesthetically distinctive effort on his part to use language to articulate thought; and for Baker, the realm of thought, far from being (as materialism's critics have so often avowed) hollowed out or attenuated by the supposedly homogenizing mindlessness of consumption and consumerism, was instead unashamedly shaped by the multi-faceted engagements with material things that his extraordinarily detailed prose represented. In Baker's work, it appeared, thought and thing, subject and object, stood in equal and interdependent relation, interacting in his texts to construct a clear sense of a material individual self that made no apology for dismantling the Cartesian division between subject and object and locating itself, at least in part, within the external world of things. Yet in stark contrast to accounts of the culture of the 1980s as characterized by various forms of selfishness and solipsism, thoughts and things—or thoughts about things—also serve in Baker's work to construct a surprisingly expansive sense of intellectual community, underwritten by a faith that the design and manufacture of material things was in fact and should remain central to what the United States ought to be as a nation.

For this reason, Baker's books provide an indication of just how finely poised the argument about things was as far as American culture was concerned as the United States stood on the brink of the end of the Cold War. For Bush may ultimately have been reassuring, absolving his fellow citizens from the supposed sin of materialism ("we are not the sum of our possessions. . . . In our hearts we know what matters"), while the emerging scholarly and popular literature on "things" had already proven itself ready to turn away from the empty denunciations of materialism that had long characterized much mainstream political rhetoric, as well as even more avowedly anti-capitalist forms of cultural critique, such as that of Herbert Marcuse in the 1960s. As we will see, however, even Baker's partially object-oriented ontology incorporated concerns of a more than banally "anti-materialist" form. Among these were the first inklings, articulated somewhat inchoately in Baker's earliest works, that what had happened to the United States since the 1970s was not, in fact, all to the good, the optimistic meliorism of his stolidly liberal characters notwithstanding. This was an easily overlooked detail of a literary aesthetic that itself thrived on detail and one that exposes as somewhat uneasy the sense of being at peace with things that might otherwise have appeared to pervade aspects of American culture as the end of the Cold War approached and a new decade dawned. And what was haunting Baker's optimism, to be clear, were some of the consequences of the same reconfiguration of global capitalism discussed in Chapter One.

*

The Mezzanine documents a single lunch hour in the life of its narrator, Howie, a young office worker who does nothing so much over the course of that lunch hour as buy, consume, and relate his thoughts about and physical interactions with a vast array of manmade, material things: from escalators, shoelaces, and paper bags to drinking straws, staplers, doorknobs, milk cartons, and electric hand-driers. Baker's second novel, *Room Temperature* (1990), published two years after *The Mezzanine*, would extend the objective repertoire of his fiction still further as its young, male narrator reflected on peanut butter jars and plastic sandwich bags, the latches on airplane tray tables, and Bic ballpoint pens, all in the time taken to feed his infant child one afternoon. In a cultural climate in which ritualistic denunciations of Americans' supposed over-investment in material things were as prominent and widespread as they had ever been, it was not immediately clear how critics, scholars, and readers of Baker's fiction were to respond to the engagements with objects presented in his work. He was not, he once told an interviewer, "oppressed" by objects, in what he called a "French sense," and yet several literary critics assumed that an ironic intent on Baker's part lay behind his writing of material things.[12]

The uncertainty was only compounded by the style with which a writer like Baker depicted those things. By 1988, the high profile disputes about "minimalism" in the arena of literary fiction discussed in Chapter Three were reaching their highest pitch. Parataxis, linguistic economy, and the invocation of little more than a brand name to represent the all-too-familiar material objects of the external world appeared *de rigeur* as far as the prose style of much of the fiction being published in the United States was concerned. In this context, it would not necessarily have been entirely clear what was to be made of depictions of objects—and, indeed, whole novels, no matter how brief and condensed their narrative time span—rendered in a prose that, far from merely invoking a brand name to represent its material referents, honed in on the physical minutiae of things in the way Baker's does. Nor would it have been clear what to make of the fact that it was the seemingly inconsequential things of everyday life that were being rendered with all the attention to detail and metaphorical resourcefulness found in the work of John Updike—Baker's most obvious and openly acknowledged influence—and the "Prousto-Nabokovian" literary tradition out of which Baker would later intimate both he and Updike had emerged.[13]

The Mezzanine, for example, is replete with prolix descriptions of the objects on which its narrator dwells, including a long and involved footnote on the changes in design of drinking straws that extends along the bottom of two pages, speculating on such microscopic considerations as the manner in which "bubbles of carbonation attach themselves to invisible asperities on the straw's surface," or on the often-overlooked paraphernalia of daily office life.[14] Here is how Howie recalls a typical interaction with a piece of office technology on his colleague's desk:

> I picked up her heavy chrome date-stamper. It was a self-inking model: at rest, the internal dating element, looped with six belts of rubber, held its current numerology pressed upside down against the moist black roof of the armature. To use it, you set the square base of the machine down on the piece of paper you wished to date and pressed on the wooden knob (a true knob!) — then the internal element, guided by S curves cut out of the gantry-like superstructure, began its graceful rotational descent, uprighting itself just in time for landing like a lunar excursion module, touching the paper for an instant, depositing today's date, and then springing back up to its bat-repose.[15]

The chrome date-stamper is a far cry from the designer labels and sought-after status symbols that litter the work of some other writers of the 1980s. It is not an artifact prized for its exchange value or for any sense of social prestige that might be attached to it. It has a use value but that value is only part of its appeal to Baker's narrator. Analogous to Petroski's pencil, or to the approximately twenty- to thirty-thousand "everyday objects" that cognitive scientist Donald Norman estimated, at the time of writing *The Psychology of Everyday Things* (1988), were by the end of the 1980s embellishing the quotidian lives of Americans, it is an often overlooked, unexpectedly complex feat of engineering and industrial design, for which the term "consumer good" hardly seems appropriate.[16] Indeed, very often the things in Baker's writing were not even owned by consumers, or when they were, came to signify something other than ownership. The narrator of *Room Temperature*, for example, refers when speaking of repairing a broken lamp to a bond between subject and object "stronger than mere possession," suggesting a view of subject–object relations and consumption that extends beyond the simple acquisition or ownership of goods.[17] The chrome date-stamper is just a thing upon a colleague's desk and most likely the property of the corporation for whom both she and Howie work. These are, in short, things that Baker's narrators use rather than own, and even when they do own them, the fact of possession seems almost beside the point; they are material curiosities with which ordinary daily life causes them to interact in homes, offices, stores and shopping malls, the paraphernalia of daily life, yet no less important to the narrators of Baker's fiction for not being particularly widely esteemed.

The lingering, microscopic, almost erotic way in which the date-stamper is described is representative of Baker's aesthetic approach to things in both *The Mezzanine* and *Room Temperature*. The sustained contemplation of material details enforces a subordination of any sense of narrative drive or eventfulness. Plot, events, story, are not the issue here; the rendering of designed objects is. Ross Chambers refers to Baker's aesthetic as influenced by "descriptivitis," while Arthur Saltzman has characterized it as an "erotics of attentiveness."[18] Baker himself expounded on his technique in his quirky, book-length essay on the influence of John Updike on his work, *U and I* (1991), reflecting on his disagreement with a comment Updike once made in a review of another writer's journals to the effect that one of the writer's descriptions "couldn't be used in fiction" because "it would 'clog any narrative.'"[19] Baker disagreed: "The only thing I *like* are the clogs [. . .] I wanted my first novel to be a veritable infarct of narrative cloggers."[20] Those "clogs" are rendered with a commitment to detail that in *The Mezzanine*, Baker has Howie refer to as central to what he calls "microscopy."[21]

The question remains as to what broader end such depictions were being put in narratives like *The Mezzanine* and *Room Temperature*. Contemporaneous works such as Petroski's *The Pencil*, after all, sought to elucidate the surprisingly complex history of a common object in an epistemological project that had a better public understanding of that history as its end. While Baker's writing certainly featured what he had Howie call the "microhistory" of similar objects, setting out the changes in their design to which he, their narrator, had over the course of his life been a witness, these books were nevertheless works of fiction.[22] What, then, were these scrupulously detailed, frequently footnoted depictions of objects *for* in such a context? Did they amount to anything other than moments of considerable aesthetic and linguistic pleasure in a pair of otherwise slight, light, insubstantial, and humorous novels of little or no consequence as far as the cultural history of the decade is concerned? Did they have anything other than such moments of aesthetic pleasure to contribute to the argument about things? Or were they, in fact, merely reflective of the emerging tendency within the immediate historical context outlined above to grant such often disregarded things more sustained epistemological attention?

One way to answer those questions is to say that for all these narratives' focus on material things, neither *The Mezzanine* nor *Room Temperature* is principally "about" material things at all. Rather, both novels are primarily narratives of and about thought. Thinking, rather than things, might in fact usefully be understood as the essential concern of much if not all of Baker's writing throughout the 1980s. At the beginning of the decade, Baker had published essays entitled "Changes of Mind" (1982) and "The Size of Thoughts" (1983) in *The Atlantic*, which both took for their subject questions of thought and thinking. The first of these deals, in characteristically humorous fashion, with how gradually and imperceptibly one's thoughts upon a given subject might change, without conscious realization of the fact until the change has been effected: "Our opinions," Baker writes, "gently nudged by circumstance, revise themselves under cover of inattention."[23] In "The Size of Thoughts," meanwhile, Baker claims that "[e]ach thought has a size, and most are about three feet tall, with the level of complexity of a lawnmower engine, or a cigarette lighter, or those tubes of toothpaste that, by mingling several hidden pastes and gels, create a pleasantly striped product."[24] The focus on thought goes hand in hand with a focus on things; or, rather the former precedes the latter in the sense that, in this instance, it is not so much that a thing in the world has prompted a thought, as that the things of the world are used as the metaphorical vehicles for thought.

Indeed, in "Changes of Mind," what principally interests Baker, he claims, is the detail of the cognitive processes by means of which opinions change, of which he wants to know as much as is possible: "I want each sequential change of mind in its true, knotted, clotted, viny multifariousness, with all of the colorful streamers of intelligence still taped on and flapping in the wind," he writes.[25] The figure of the material thing with which Baker renders the series of psychological events that go into making "a change of mind" is, in one sense, peculiar. What, after all, is the thing being described? Manmade and handmade; improvised, idiosyncratic, and unfamiliar; the cognitive phenomenon of a change of mind has been rendered as a complex but unrecognizable object, an artifact as much as a thought or a series of thoughts. Here, then, is one of the first indications in Baker's oeuvre of one aspect of his characteristic conceptual and aesthetic interest not just in things, nor in thoughts alone, but in the inter-relationship between thought and thing. Similarly, in "The Size of Thoughts," the inner realm of thought is reconceived, with no small degree of the kind of comic—and in this case surrealist—detail that would be deployed in Baker's novels later in the decade. Once again, it is figured in relation to material objects, in this instance precisely the kinds of paraphernalia that would later be drawn upon so extensively in *The Mezzanine* and *Room Temperature*: lawnmower engines, cigarette lighters, tubes of toothpaste. There is an almost provocative metaphorical daring about such comparisons. It would not necessarily have been clear, for example, whether Baker's readers were to understand from his use of metaphors like these that the average thought lacked complexity; or that lawnmower engines, cigarette lighters, and tubes of toothpaste had, as Petroski would illustrate of the pencil, considerably more complexity than they were usually granted.

As *The Mezzanine* shows, as a novelist, Baker was seeking to illustrate just how complex and absorbing the design of everyday things could be. His point was never simply to belittle the kinds of thoughts thought by either himself or his narrators, only averagely complex as they may be. However, what both *The Mezzanine* and *Room Temperature* would also confirm is the consistency of Baker's interest in the rendering of thought as he moved from the essay form of some of his earliest work to the novel. In a 1994 interview, for example, Baker noted how as a reader he enjoyed "witnessing" the "thinking" of fictional characters, which is the position in which he placed his own readers in novels like *The Mezzanine* and *Room Temperature*.[26] They find themselves reading first-person narratives that recollect the tangle of thoughts thought in a condensed period of time in the past. In *The Mezzanine*, that period of time lasts the duration of a single escalator ride; in *Room Temperature*, the time it takes the narrator to feed his infant daughter. And just as Baker had intimated in both "Changes of Mind" and "The Size of Thoughts" that thought could be rendered as if it were metaphorically analogous to material things (the improvised and streamer-bedecked change of mind; the cigarette lighter or lawnmower engine of middling complexity), Baker's narrators in both *The Mezzanine* and *Room Temperature* deploy a series of implicit and explicit versions of what he calls "materialist analogies for cognition," in which things themselves become metaphors for thoughts and thought processes.[27]

This may have to do less with the radical object-oriented ontologies that Cole has critiqued (with their interest in not just human psyches but "the primitive psyches of rocks and electrons") than with the material basis of the mind itself.[28] Howie, for example, recalls his mother offering him reassurance over his typically idiosyncratic concern about the manner in which human brain cells inevitably die; she had told him, he remembers, that "your individual brain cells are dying, but the ones that stay grow more and more connections, and those connections keep branching out over the years."[29] But the mind is also in some sense present in the object world. There are frequent references throughout *The Mezzanine* to thoughts going round and round in a kind of cyclical motion. Thus, in a footnote in Chapter Fourteen, Howie describes how a thought that his partner had disclosed to him had "taken a place" on his "carousel," and how a thought he had read in Marcus Aurelius's *Meditations* "cycled around" in his mind.[30] The suggestion is that those systems of local transport of which Howie describes himself as particularly fond—such as the escalator itself, or indeed luggage carousels—are partly dwelled on in the novel precisely because they provide still more "materialist analogies" for the way thoughts occur to those who have thought them, as if the mind had been turned inside out and reconstituted within the world of things, recalling Walter Benjamin's observation at the end of "Unpacking My Library" that it is in fact in things that one "lives," or the claim made by Mihalyi Csikszentmihalyi and Eugene Rochberg-Halton that "the things one uses are in fact part of one's self; not in any mystical or metaphorical sense but in cold, concrete actuality."[31]

There is thus nothing "mindless" about Baker's materialism. On the contrary, it is inherently mind*ful*. Throughout *The Mezzanine* and *Room Temperature*, things and interactions with things, and the very fact of living and being among the paraphernalia of daily life, constantly prompt thoughts, shape thoughts, and send thoughts off into unusual directions. Mindlessness, in short, hardly comes into it. Instead, Baker shows how what Herbert Marcuse had called the "private space in which man may become and remain 'himself'" may, in fact, fare reasonably well in an era of mass consumption.[32] Indeed, by using the intertwined narration of thought and thing in *The Mezzanine* and *Room Temperature*, Baker emphasizes how certain aspects of such claims about the relationship between thought and thing made by thinkers like Marcuse were in fact remarkably old staples of the argument about things in American life. See, for instance, the somewhat unexpected influence of William James on Baker's narratives. In *U and I*, Baker describes himself as having read James's *Principles of Psychology* (1890) in a New York City McDonald's, while the narrator of *Room Temperature* also refers to James directly.[33] "Thoughts connected as we feel them to be connected are *what we mean* by personal selves," James had argued.[34] The total effect of novels like *The Mezzanine* and *Room Temperature*, with their rendering of one thought connected to another, is thus ultimately towards a form of intellectual biography, a rendering of the self, and thus a detailed answering of the question, "Who am I?", which Ross Chambers has described as central to much meditative writing from Descartes onwards.[35] In *The Mezzanine*, for example, having imagined what it would be like to tabulate the subjects of his own thoughts and the varying frequencies with which he thinks them, Howie asserts:

People seemed so alike when you imagined their daily schedules, or
watched them walk toward the revolving door (as Dave, Sue, and Steve,
not noticing me, were doing now), yet if you imagined a detailed
thought-frequency chart compiled for each of them, and you tried comparing one chart with another, you would feel suddenly as if you were
comparing beings as different from each other as an extension cord and a
grape-leaf roll.[36]

In such passages, there is little sense that what Marcuse had called
"technological reality" had really threatened the ability of people to be
"themselves." Indeed, Howie abjures anything like the Marxist notion of
commodity fetishism transforming human relations into "the fantastic form
of a relation between things," because the "extension cord" and "grape-leaf
roll" of his metaphor are not, in fact, commodities here. Instead, Howie is
articulating in somewhat peculiar circumstances a Jamesian conception of the
self as the experience of a continuous connection of thoughts, arguing against
the grain of much anti-materialist and some radically materialist rhetoric for
the ongoing primacy, residual humanity, and innate variability of the "inner"
life of thought, even in a world filled with revolving doors, extension cords,
multinational corporations, and plastic. After all, who *can* tell the difference
between Dave, Sue, and Steve, as they walk toward (and enter and exit) that
symbol of the expendability of the individual white-collar worker, the
revolving door? They seem not so much individuals as no more than a string
of names, bunched together in life as they are on the page: mundane,
monosyllabic, diminutive. But within each of their minds, Baker's narrator
suggests, both generously and democratically, there is still the true capacity
for individuality that the mere thinking of one's own idiosyncratic thoughts at
one's own idiosyncratic rhythms can create.[37]

Baker thus deployed a version of the Jamesian self to highlight the extent to
which what critics like Marcuse had claimed was true about the relationship
between individual selves and material things need not necessarily form the
basis of social critique or ethical despair. It had been James, after all, who had
argued in *The Principles of Psychology* that "*a man's Self is the sum total of all
that he* CAN *call his*," including within that definition "not only his body and
his psychic powers, but his clothes and his house, his wife and children, his
ancestors and friends, his reputation and works, his lands and horses, and
yacht and bank-account."[38] Material things, for James—lands and horses,
yachts and bank accounts—thus had, like thoughts, their own role to play in

the construction of the self, or at least, in this case, of the unapologetically bourgeois, patriarchal self. The paraphernalia of consumer capitalist daily life plays a similar role in *The Mezzanine* and *Room Temperature*. Marcuse had deplored the way in which people "recognize themselves in their commodities" and "find their soul in their automobile, hi-fi set, split-level home, kitchen equipment."[39] In his novels of the 1980s, in the way his narrator's self-constructing thoughts are so frequently thoughts about things, Baker effectively extends the sense of self deep into the object world of the paraphernalia of mass-consuming capitalist life but does so without any sense of implied critique. Howie's self, in other words, incorporates not just the thoughts he thinks, but the shoelaces and straws and escalators he thinks about, while the relationship between the narrator of *Room Temperature* and the peanut butter jars, airplane tray-table latches, and Bic ballpoint pens about which he thinks can be conceived of in much the same way. His self is somehow present in those things; the expression of them and his thoughts about them are a form of nothing less than self-expression, regardless of how Marcuse or Christopher Lasch—or Jimmy Carter, for that matter—felt about the moral desirability of that fact. As James had argued, "[e]ach of us dichotomizes the Kosmos in a different place":

One great splitting of the whole universe into two halves is made by each of us; and for each of us almost all of the interest attaches to one of the halves; but we all draw the line of division between them in a different place. When I say that we all call the two halves by the same names, and that those names are *"me" and "not-me"* respectively, it will at once be seen what I mean.[40]

The material things about which Baker's narrators think belong to that part of the "Kosmos" they define as "theirs," which as far as the construction of the self goes, is part of "them." That the consciousnesses that narrate *The Mezzanine* and *Room Temperature* locate their selves in odd miscellanies of easily overlooked, often undervalued things surely only reinforces James's point that the "altogether unique kind of interest which each human mind feels in those parts of creation which it can call *me* or *mine*" is both "a moral riddle" and a "psychological fact."[41]

*

But such an interest in the nature of what James called "the material self" does not mean that Baker's narrators merely conformed to simplistic characterizations of the 1980s as a decade defined by selfishness and self-absorption. For the thoughtful engagements with things that he and his narrators narrate are, in fact, productive not of mere self-absorption but of a surprisingly expansive sense of intellectual community. Take, for example, the fact that both *The Mezzanine* and *Room Temperature* are narrated by characters who find themselves more or less solitary for the bulk of their narratives. In a 1994 interview, Baker is reported as emphasizing the fact that in all his novels, his narrators "just happen to be solitary at the moment."[42] It is emphatically not that, as Arthur Saltzman has argued, "other people, if they do intrude at all, occupy roughly the same shelf in his consciousness as the replacement staples," or that "[r]egular and availing human contact is either an ambition that most of Baker's population cannot achieve or one they do not even aspire to."[43] For when Howie is alone thinking his thoughts about things, those things and his thoughts about them never leave him entirely isolated. For example, in the footnote in which Howie notes how unsatisfactorily plastic drinking straws tended to float in one's drink if not held in place, Baker's narrator's first response is to ask rhetorically, "How could the straw engineers have made so elementary a mistake, designing a straw that weighed less than the sugar-water in which it was intended to stand? Madness!"[44] Soon, however, he avers that "though the straw engineers were probably blameworthy for failing to foresee the straw's buoyancy, the problem was more complex than I had first imagined." Indeed, the combined effect of such changes in the design of the straw, Howie good-naturedly concludes, was that "the quality of life, through nobody's fault, went down an eighth of a notch."[45] One of the most striking aspects of such passages, beyond the intriguing fact that such thoughts occur to Howie at all, is the sense of imaginative sympathy they evince between the consumer of a product and its designers, and Howie's acknowledgement of the kind of thought and effort that goes into the design processes of even the most apparently trifling artifacts.[46] He sees himself in a mutually beneficial relationship with such unknown, presumably kindred spirits; indeed, the drinking straw footnote assumes at all times the good faith of the designers behind the products Howie uses and concludes with his observation that the slight diminution in quality of life that he had lamented lasted only "until just last year, I think, when one day I noticed that a plastic straw, made of some subtler polymer, with a colored stripe in it, stood anchored to the bottom of my can!"[47]

It is tempting, of course, to read into such wide-eyed responses to his interactions with the paraphernalia of consumer capitalist daily life the naivety of a dupe, and thus infer ironical or satirical intent on Baker's part, with the narrators' lack of either any evident class consciousness or sense of the nature and extent of capitalism's latest global reconfiguration one of the objects of the author's subtle critique. However, there runs throughout both *The Mezzanine* and *Room Temperature* a strong streak of genuine technological meliorism, if not techno-utopianism, a faith that things and the design of things are really getting better all the time. In "Changes of Mind," Baker cites as evidence in support of that possibility signs of technological progress such as "Teflon II. Reflective street signs. The wah-wah pedal," picturing the product engineers behind such things as like-minded individuals working towards the improvement of daily life for the pleasure and benefit of people like Nicholson Baker.[48] Their thoughts, labors, occasional missteps, and subsequent corrections are, as is the case with the drinking straw, bound up in the objects they "produce," waiting to be unpackaged and enjoyed by the deductive nous of such thoughtful consumers as Baker's narrators. Far from a dupe, then, Howie is—or, at least, sees himself as—an equal partner in an ongoing project of technological progress, happy to praise his counterparts' successes whilst constructively criticizing their relatively infrequent blunders, content (for the time being, at least) to assume that all are working together for the general betterment of the experience of everyday life. Consuming and thinking about things thus does not, in this sense, distance himself from other people so much as bring them intellectually and imaginatively closer to him, even if at the expense of any serious thought about the conditions under which the things he loves were actually being produced, rather than just designed, by the late 1980s.

This is why, in the final footnote of *The Mezzanine*, Howie reveals that he has discovered evidence, in a 1984 edition of a Polish journal of technology, of efforts made by a certain Z. Czaplicki to investigate "the abrasion resistance and knot slippage performance of shoelaces."[49] This otherwise unlikely discovery is of significance in the context of the rest of the novel because the shoelaces that Howie carries in the CVS bag described in the opening sentence of his narrative are bought as a replacement for a lace he later describes as having snapped before his lunch break starts.[50] Howie repeatedly wonders throughout *The Mezzanine* just why this has occurred, testing out various theories before finally footnoting his subsequent discovery of the research of his Polish counterpart with a comic encomium in which he expresses his certainty that Czaplicki must have been moved by the same sense of curiosity that he himself had experienced, and that therefore here was someone, many miles distant both culturally and geographically, who had thought some of the same thoughts about the same object as he had. "He was not going to abandon the problem with some sigh about complexity and human limitation after a minute's thought, as I had, and go to lunch—*he was going to make the problem his life's work*," Howie imagines.[51] There is humor in such assertions, of course, and a characteristic attentiveness to the detail of apparently small, trivial things, but the sense of connectedness that Howie forges by means of his thoughts about shoelaces ought to be taken seriously. Baker's 1984 essay, "Rarity," begins by asking whether anyone has "yet said publicly how nice it is to write on rubber with a ballpoint pen."[52] Baker worries whether the articulation of such pleasures is best kept to oneself or shared with a wider constituency. Having just articulated the pleasure, he imagines a "few readers, remembering that they did once enjoy taking down a toll-free number on the blade of a clean Rubbermaid spatula, react[ing] with guarded agreement: 'Yes, I guess I am one of those not-so-uncommon people who have that sort of rare experience.'"[53] Just as such things as shoelaces would bring into a kind of hypothesized intellectual communion two disparate individuals on opposite sides of the Iron Curtain in the concluding footnote of *The Mezzanine*, here Baker is imagining the forging of another community based on a shared experience of one of the pleasures to be had from interacting with the paraphernalia of late capitalist daily life.

There is a peculiar (and almost post-fetishistic) intimacy about such writing, which is quite at odds with the way materially mediated relations have so often found themselves the object of critique in the argument about things in American life. That intimacy may anticipate aspects of later, sexually explicit novels by Baker like *Vox* (1992) or *The Fermata* (1994), but it recurs in Baker's earliest novels too. One of the most unexpectedly poignant moments in *Room Temperature*, for example, is struck on, of all things, another ballpoint pen, in relation to the narrator's relationship with the infant child, or "the Bug," he has spent the course of his narrative feeding. The novel ends with its narrator thinking about the objects he has stored in an old Skippy peanut butter jar on his desk, including a Bic pen he has chewed:

> And if in ten years Bic pens were still around, and the Bug, inconceivably long-limbed, were to chew on one as she sat in class writing about birds or airplanes or the virtues of garbagemen, making large careful commas, she might taste the same quizzical six-sided plastic taste and wonder why

it tasted so good and so awful at the same time—so addictively sickening—and why the sound of her saliva fizzing through the tiny airhole in the side of the pen's barrel was such a peculiarly satisfying, calming, thought-provoking sound, and if she brought the chewed pen home, I could explain that it might have something to do with the hint of plastic in the warm evaporated milk that Patty and I had fed her from a six-sided bottle on magnificent fall afternoons when she was a tiny baby, only six months old.[54]

The cliché of the alienated individual absorbed in things to the exclusion of emotional or intellectual connections with other people is replaced by an alternative imaginative relationship within which it is things themselves and the individual's most intimate interactions with them that assist such connections. The child's sensory experience of the taste of a pen is fondly imagined as a sensual and sentimental connection between father and daughter, plastic taste and all. Indeed, his attempt to rescue reviled, long-lived plastics from their status as despised, abject materials is one of Baker's quirkiest contributions to the argument about things in the "long 1980s." Of the Bic pen in question, for example, Baker's narrator has already declared: "I would have had only to chew it for three or four minutes now for my cuspids to reawaken that nice almost chocolatey or anise-like headache-inducing taste of resinous clear plastic."[55]

Once again, then, objects are conceived of not as things that alienate individuals from one another, but as the often-surprising material means by which individuals might be able to form a sense of connection with one another. At a time when large numbers of Americans were paying to be told by Allan Bloom in *The Closing of the American Mind* (1987) that their younger generations were "turning in on themselves" with "a new degree of isolation," and that "[c]ountry, religion, family, ideas of civilization, all the sentimental and historical forces that stood between cosmic infinity and the individual [. . .] have been rationalized and have lost their compelling force" so that "America is experienced not as a common project but as a framework within which people are only individuals, where they are left alone," the way Baker casts everything from a Rubbermaid spatula to a snapped shoelace or a ballpoint pen as the grounds for a form of connection between such supposedly increasingly isolated individuals appears as another intriguing intervention into the argument about things in American life on his part.[56] In 1950, Georg Lukács characterized the relationship between "man as a private individual and man as a social being" as "the most difficult question" that fiction had to answer, and the critical literature on neoliberalism makes it clear which answer to that question we might expect to find in a thing-filled novel of the neoliberal age.[57] And yet, in his novels of the 1980s, Baker suggests that a far-reaching engagement with, and interest in, the paraphernalia of daily life does not necessarily preclude an individual's "social being." Indeed, there is a sense that this was happening, not in spite of such things but because of them. Take the peculiar way he wrote about friendship. Friends, Baker would argue in *U and I*, his book on John Updike, "are the only real means for foreign ideas to enter your brain."[58] Indeed, in that book, Baker would claim: "I *am* friends with Updike—that's what I really feel—I have, as I never had when I was a child, this imaginary friend I have constructed out of sodden crisscrossing strips of rivalry and gratefulness over an armature of misquotation."[59] Updike's "ideas," of course, entered Baker's head by means of that most ingenious of technologies, the book, just as Marcus Aurelius's thoughts on philosophy and on transience are seen as having entered Howie's in the penultimate chapter of *The Mezzanine* by way of what Howie stipulates is a Penguin Classics edition of his *Meditations*. Thought becomes text, text becomes thing (the book), and some sense of intellectual communion is achieved. Baker's object-mediated ontologies thus appear almost utopian in their reimagining of the social relations the world of neoliberalism might make possible. The overlooked paraphernalia of everyday life would not be without its consolations, Baker implies, even in the endless, expanding market(s) of the present, so perhaps we should all have long ago learned to stop worrying and just start liking things?

*

If anything, such intimations seem all the more significant in retrospect. In May of the same year that Baker's first novel was published, and as part of the summit diplomacy that characterized much of the sitting president's second term, President Reagan gave a speech at Moscow State University extoling the wonders of the coming revolution in information technology, the "emblem" of which was the "tiny silicon chip" that, although itself produced from sand, stood, Reagan claimed, for an emerging "new economy" that would make "physical resources obsolete." "We're breaking through the material conditions of existence," the retiring president of a purportedly "materialist" age and nation claimed, preparing the ground for the following decades' rhetorical paeans to the new global "knowledge economy" and notions of immaterial labor.[60] Setting the premature triumphalism of such predictions aside, we know now that what Reagan was in a sense hailing was the dawn of a new, digitally networked age. All the more significant, then, that Baker should have noted that we were, even Howie and Czaplicki and Updike and Aurelius, already part of prototypical "social networks" in which we could "friend" one another without knowing one another, networks formed of nothing more than thoughts and things and unbound, to borrow a phrase from another of Reagan's expertly delivered speeches, by the "surly bonds" of time and space because they could already unite Poles and Americans, writers and their readers, ancients and (post)moderns. And if such a network seems in one sense little more than a flight of neoliberal fantasy, perhaps this aspect of Baker's work is best understood as an unexpected harbinger of the deeply problematic ways neoliberalism has developed since the end of the Cold War, with the ever-thickening web of what Jodi Dean has called the "communicative capitalism" that information technology has offered us spinning (im)material connections across space and time that appear somehow both to bring us together and hold us apart—or "together alone," as Sherry Turkle has put it.[61] For if, as per Lukács, the relationship between "man as a private individual and man as a social being" was "the most difficult question" that fiction had to answer in 1950, it is a question that still evidently troubles us today, as so much of ourselves is now dispersed both materially and digitally throughout networks dominated by corporations and a peculiarly intrusive neoliberal state.

Baker's early work was in fact already indirectly registering the possibility that such a problematic development would occur as a later phase of the same reconfiguration of global capitalism that had already, by the late 1980s, had such a pronounced effect on the ways Americans spoke about, wrote about, and pictured things. For by so consistently thinking of things as designed rather than produced, Baker's narrators were close to intuiting the topography of a global capitalist structure that would increasingly, in the "new economy" heralded by Reagan, see things (including the silicon chip-bearing hardware we now use to stay connected with others almost every minute of almost every day) designed in one nation but produced in many others, and in resolutely material conditions. The key distinction, however, is that Baker's narrators were oblivious to the possibility of design and manufacture as two separable phenomena, such that although his work of the period evinced an uncharacteristically despondent strain of the kind of economic nationalism that had flourished earlier in the decade, that nationalism was expressed as a fear for the present and future of what the narrator of *Room Temperature* calls "the US tradition of industrial design," rather than manufacture.[62] Thus, in *The Mezzanine*, Howie praises (what may well have been by then) US-made "Toyota turn-signal switches" while also complaining that "[f]ew American products recently have been able to capture that same knuckly, orthopedic quality."[63] By *Room Temperature*, Baker's narrator's tone is even more plangent when he reflects on another latch, that which serves to stow the tray tables away on the backs of aircraft seats, and insists that all the recent "refinements" in their design were "almost entirely of Asian origin."[64] His narration of the episode eventually ends: "I painstakingly clutched the top of the seat ahead of me and, thus stably based, used that thumb to squeeze the table under the fastener before I allowed it to slide into place, imagining as I did so that I was closing the coffin on the US tradition of industrial design."[65]

The analogy of the coffin is amusing, but neither the force nor the implications of the genteel polemic buried within it ought to be underestimated. In one of Baker's later, far more controversial novels, he has a character insist that Japan had, in fact, won rather than lost the Second World War, simply because after the war "their best people spent their days and nights thinking about how to make beautiful things, tools, machines that just felt good to hold. Which they did with such artistry. They couldn't make fighter planes, we didn't let them. And so they won the war."[66] The United States, by contrast, the same character insists, "lost" because it now no longer makes anything but what he calls "[p]ills, pick-up trucks, and war."[67] This, then, is the direction that Baker's mild critique is headed: nostalgic materialism, for sure, but nostalgic materialism with a difference. For while they show signs of grasping how the world had already been transformed by the late 1980s, for Baker's enthusiastically and unashamedly "materialist" narrators, it was not so much economic deprivation or class inequality that would take the benign tint off the world of neoliberalism. Rather, it was the long, lingering consequences on the nation's industrial structure of that second great transformation that gave them cause to express an initially mild concern that would later evolve into a full-throated critique of American military imperialism. In this respect, Baker's work is representative of how, as the nation prepared to enter a post-Cold War world, and despite years of attempts to ensure this would not be the case, certain niches of the national culture were apt to communicate a sense of being weighed down not so much by the "mindless materialism" denounced or denied in an almost ritualistic fashion as far as the argument about things was concerned, but by the same peculiar form of imperialism that had played such a significant role in ushering in the era of neoliberalism more than a decade previously. The precise form that sense took in several examples of the narrative culture of the "long 1980s" provides the focus for the chapter that follows, which considers, through culture, the weight American imperialism was still exerting as the nation stumbled out of the end of one long war and almost immediately into another.

CHAPTER 6

All that Fall

In the previous chapter, we saw how Nicholson Baker's inchoate lament for the American tradition of industrial design harked back to the reconfiguration of global capitalism that occurred in the 1970s and that was so vital to the triumph of neoliberalism as the hegemonic ideology of our age. Baker's lament did so, however, in ways that necessitate more than a further reflection on the cultural phenomenon of a nostalgic materialism precipitated by capital's spatial reconfiguration and increased mobility. For the sticking point for Baker and his peace-loving characters was to become not so much the erosion of the United States' industrial base, but the retention, deep in the heart of its economic structure, of the kind of military Keynesianism that has seen, up to and including the time of writing, no effective demilitarization since the start of the Korean War in the early 1950s. It is an interesting detail of the passage in *Room Temperature* in which he complains about the design of American airlines' tray table latches, for example, that Baker's narrator fears for the economic future of Boeing, the airline manufacturer. That company is still with us, of course, operating the largest manufacturing plant anywhere in the world and deriving $30 billion of its $96 billion 2015 revenue not from civilian aircraft but from its "defense, space and security" activities.[1] Such figures make Boeing only the second biggest arms dealer on the planet, outperformed by its compatriot Lockheed Martin by several billion dollars. Thus, in one sense, Baker's narrator really need not have feared. To this day, seven of the ten largest arms manufacturers in the world are American, and the nation still makes and designs plenty of deadly, and readily exportable, weaponry.[2]

Although the plangent sentiment that war is one of the few remaining things the United States makes anymore was not expressed in Baker's work until the post-9/11 period, the earliest roots of it are clear enough in the material anxieties his narrators were expressing as the end of the Cold War approached. This was an economic nationalism that would evolve in later decades into the kind of anti-imperialist despair articulated in intensely controversial works like *Checkpoint* (2004), a dialogic novel in which two friends discuss the wisdom or otherwise of attempting to assassinate President George W. Bush, and *Human Smoke* (2008), Baker's pacifist counter-history of the Second World War. Reference to the material basis from which such critiques ultimately derived can also be glimpsed in some rather unexpected places elsewhere in the culture of the "long 1980s," even as US–Soviet relations thawed and peace approached. At the end of the romantic comedy *Pretty Woman* (1990), for example, as Ralph Bellamy's and Gere's characters revealed their hitherto illicit agreement to build "great big ships" together, few moviegoers of the time were likely to have dwelled on the military Keynesian premise that underlay the proposition, namely a lucrative set of production orders from the navy. Perhaps that is not surprising. The Elvis Costello/Robert Wyatt track "Shipbuilding" (1982), which pondered whether the deaths arising from British involvement in the Falklands War were "worth" the goods they enabled those working in the nation's newly reopened shipyards to buy, had never been released as a single in the United States, a casualty, perhaps, of Costello's having angered television producers by disobediently performing "Radio, Radio," a critique of commercialized media culture, on *Saturday Night Live* in the late 1970s. Indeed, in *Pretty Woman*, any sentiment similar to Costello's critique of the imbrication of manufacturing and militarism is conspicuous by its absence: the repentant financier played by Gere finds personal and material redemption by investing in the production of military matériel, with barely a thought to the ethical implications of his own apparent salvation.

To be sure, any detailed reflection on the taken-for-granted ethics of simply "making things" over and against the deindustrialization and financialization of the nation's economy may well have looked jarringly out of place in a heart-warming romantic comedy like *Pretty Woman*. Yet such only apparently abstruse details, hidden in plain sight in something like the manner described by Michael Rogin in his analysis of spectacle and amnesia in the "imperial politics" of the period, do suggest something of an uncomfortable truth about the self-sustaining momentum that the military-industrial complex had exhibited since the early Cold War era.[3] Eisenhower had famously highlighted the dangers of the nexus of a powerful armaments industry and a warfare state in his Farewell Address of 1961, and even certain Pop artists of the 1960s had felt moved to explore the relationship between industrial and military production. See Roy Lichtenstein's still disturbingly exhilarating "Whaam!" (1963), based on D.C. Comics' *All American Men of War*, or perhaps more critically, the way James Rosenquist's "F-111" (1964–65) had incorporated panels depicting contemporary American consumer life into his enormous collage representing a fighter jet. By the mid-1980s, Fredric Jameson was asserting that if what he termed "postmodern" culture was "the internal and superstructural expression of a whole new wave of American military and economic domination throughout the world," then "the underside" of that culture was "blood, torture, death, and terror."[4]

That possibility also bears thinking about in relation to the long post-Cold War era in which, as the decades-long conflict between two mighty superpowers ended, military spending fell from a mid-1980s zenith of 6 percent of GDP to a nadir of 2.9 percent on the eve of the 9/11 attacks.[5] Given the size of the economy in question, even the lowest of those figures constituted a massive boost to domestic demand in an economy supposedly now governed by the small-state doctrines of neoliberalism. Indeed, for military spending to begin to retreat, with the advent of Cold War peace, towards an eventual "low" of approximately $275 billion in annual appropriations hardly looks like any retreat at all, especially given the concomitant erosion of the corporate tax base and hollowing out of so many other forms of discretionary spending that went along with a headline decline in military expenditures that nevertheless never lost sight of Pentagon planners' unapologetically hegemonic goal of "full spectrum dominance."[6] This, after all, is precisely the kind of budgetary structure a nexus of neoliberalism and imperialism might be expected to produce, as the myth of the shrinking state is exposed as a truth only as far as certain functions and expenditures of government are concerned. Even in recent years, when it comes to the design, development, and purchase of weapons of war, the corrupt realities of contemporary electoral politics have increasingly determined that the Pentagon is literally bequeathed more money than it knows what to do with. Thus the material largesse, even in times of supposed austerity, of Congress funding programs that in the words of one US Senator from West Virginia, "force stuff on [the military] that we know you don't want."[7]

The apparently permanent militarization of the nation's economy since the start of the Korean War has certainly had some peculiar effects on the landscape of things, constantly shaping and adding to the range of products among which Americans live and thus inflecting the argument about things in interesting ways. Henry Petroski, for example, has demonstrated the role that the military played in the design and development of such staples of American life as WD-40 and duct tape, the latter a must-have, according to Petroski, on every manned NASA space mission from at least *Apollo 13* onwards.[8] The economist Mariana Mazzucato, meanwhile, in her work debunking the neoliberal myth of a private sector for whom government is always "the problem," has recently shown just how heavily some of today's most ubiquitous consumer goods relied on state support, including the products of military research and development programs. Apple's iPads, iPods, and iPhones, for example, bristle with innovations and technologies originally developed by agencies like the Defense Advanced Procurements Agency (DARPA). Even the Internet itself has its origins in the ARPANET, another DARPA-derived technological innovation.[9] In such a context, in which so much of our materially mediated civilian lives have been influenced by such military industrialism, it is surely worth dwelling on the relationship between militarism and materialism and how they sat in relation to the phenomenon of United States' imperialism as the long 1980s unfolded. For if the Cold War peace was partly won and also almost lost as a result of military manufacturing and design, including the as-yet still unrealized Strategic Defense Initiative, which seriously threatened the peacemaking and arms-reduction talks that Gorbachev and Reagan engaged in as the Cold War drew to a close, few issues up to that point had characterized the era's engagement with militarism more than the evidently material question of how the nation ought to remember the long and horrific war the United States had waged on Vietnam. And as we will see, the inauguration in 1982 of Maya Lin's Vietnam Veterans' Memorial did not so much settle that question as help to reanimate a cultural and political argument about that war that has to this day never been resolved.

Yet, if the Veterans' Memorial stands as the most obvious embodiment of the materialist-militarist nexus that had so profoundly shaped American life for so long, this chapter also considers another no less material remembering object from the realm of literary culture, Tim O'Brien's *The Things They Carried* (1990), which looks in juxtaposition to Lin's memorial like a significant intervention into both the argument about Vietnam and the argument about things in American life. For once considered in relation to a historical context that we now know saw the Cold War ending even as US militarism was about to find, in the Persian Gulf War of 1991, a form of expression that was itself both new and very old, *The Things They Carried* offered an invaluable, if unheeded, commentary on the military-industrialization that had in many respects characterized the American economy since the beginning of the Korean War. At the same time, through O'Brien's emphasis on the weight of the things carried through the Vietnamese jungle by US servicemen, and in its consistent framing of that carrying in relation to metaphors of rising and falling objects and bodies, O'Brien's book presented a portrait of war in which both men and objects were subject to forces beyond their control. They could resist gravity and the impulse to fall under the weight of their amassed burdens. They could dream of ascending, of being themselves the thing that was carried away and out of the war on a helicopter or airplane. And yet, the men's freedom to act was at all times limited by both the endless futility of their mission and their own material status as objects at the mercy of the physical laws of the universe. It is out of this emphasis on the weight of the things carried in the text that there emerges, in retrospect, a revelatory sense of the tremendous cultural weight that the Vietnam conflict and, by extension, the American mode of imperialism continued to exert even as the Cold War ended.

*

Throughout the "long 1980s," arguments about United States militarism had been much more prominent than in some of the easily overlooked details of the nation's narrative culture cited above. This was partly a result of the vast increases in defense spending and more aggressive foreign policy positions ushered in by the Reagan administration and partly a result of the enduring legacy of the Vietnam War. As early as 1981, for example, Michael T. Clare published a study of what had come to be known as the "Vietnam syndrome," which Clare characterized as the "American public's disinclination to engage in further military interventions in internal Third World conflicts."[10] Clare shared that disinclination, but his study was published in the same year the newly elected President Reagan announced that $25 million in arms and ammunition were to be supplied to the repressive leadership of El Salvador, then engaged in putting down a popular left-wing uprising, the horrific consequences of which would be detailed by writers like Joan Didion and Mark Danner.[11] As Clare notes, this latest involvement in a national liberation struggle, which was followed by the Reagan administration's end-run around the 1984 Boland Amendment in the Iran-contra affair, came just five years after the fall of Saigon.[12]

At the policy level, this supposed syndrome, which as we have already seen, had previously been challenged by Jimmy Carter's vociferous 1980 announcement that the United States would be willing to use force in defense of its interests in the Persian Gulf, appeared to have been shaken off surprisingly quickly. The Reagan administration reversed some of the reductions in defense spending witnessed during Carter's presidency, and the 1980s saw the United States adopt an increasingly aggressive posture on certain corners of the world stage, particularly in the American hemisphere. This was a period, after all, that witnessed the provision of military aid to despotic regimes throughout Central and Latin America, as well as the invasions of Grenada in 1983 and Panama in 1989, the former a tiny Caribbean island that had previously been a colonial possession of first France and then the United Kingdom, the latter a state that owed its existence to an earlier phase of American imperialism. Indeed, the state of Panama had fallen out of favor with Washington barely a decade after the United States had formally relinquished imperial sovereignty over its Canal Zone in 1979. And it is perhaps of more than passing interest to the argument about things that while Grenada had for centuries been prized for its spices, one of the *casus belli* of the invasion of Panama was the involvement of its president and former CIA asset Manuel Noriega in an illegal drugs trade that had seen ever-greater quantities of cocaine smuggled into the United States, where they ended up on the streets and in the pages and images of so much of the era's "narco-culture," from Oliver Stone's remake of *Scarface* (1983) to Grandmaster Flash's "White Lines (Don't Do It)" (1983), and the "bratpack" fiction of Ellis and McInerney.

Developments in foreign and military policy only added impetus to an unfolding debate about how best to remember and understand American involvement in the Vietnam War. In 1982, Maya Lin's Vietnam Veterans Memorial was unveiled in Washington, DC, an event that more than one account credits with marking a reanimation of both popular and scholarly discussions about Vietnam after a period in the mid to late 1970s in which, or so William Gibson claimed, "no one wanted to talk about the war."[13] That was an overstatement, but it was certainly the case that from 1982 onwards, there was plenty of talk about the war, including a litany of by-now almost canonical books, films, and other cultural reinterpretations of the conflict. By 1989, in a brilliant study in which she linked the cultural representation of the conflict with a project of national remasculinization, Susan Jeffords was describing an ongoing debate about Vietnam conducted through memoirs, novels, films, television series, cultural events, and political and scholarly discourse. The war, as Jeffords put it, "still seems in some ways to be going on," suggesting how the debate about Vietnam in the 1980s was every bit as intense as the argument about things itself.[14]

In the Veterans' Memorial, the nation had found suitable material in a suitable place to rally around and have this debate. For on the National Mall, as the philosopher Charles L. Griswold argued in 1986, "[m]atter is put to rhetorical use . . . the Mall says a great deal, in what it portrays and in what it omits to portray, about how Americans wish to think of themselves."[15] Griswold may have erred in intimating that Americans could agree on such a profound question, but the issue of precisely what Lin's monument said and did not say about both Vietnam and the United States was key to the debates that swirled around this controversial piece of public art. "The names," the veteran Jan Scruggs, who initiated the construction of the memorial, is reported to have thought the night he resolved to see the memorial built. "No one remembers their names."[16] But once those names were unveiled, on the black surface of the Vietnam Veterans memorial itself, they became a point of contention, for one of the most common criticisms leveled at the memorial after its unveiling was its apparent absence of narrative, a result of the fact that the rules of the design competition that Lin won explicitly sought to avoid the material expression of any statements about the war that might be deemed political, thus "virtually ensur[ing . . .] a lack of narrative content" in its eventual manifestation.[17] The location, relatively tucked away in the northwest corner of the mall; the form, scarred into the earth itself; and even the memorial's reflective black granite surface, led critics to deplore what Griswold called the "chthonic" nature of the memorial, its associations with death and gravesites in stark contrast to the heliocentric confidence of the Washington Monument's obelisk, visible from the Veterans Memorial, rising toward the sun as Lin's work cuts into the earth. This was material, it transpired, that required further embellishment, whether in the form of the figurative statuary honoring the men and women who served in the conflict that was later added to the memorial, or that of Reagan's dedication of the first of those pieces of statuary, Frederick Hart's "Three Fightingmen," at which the president had waxed metaphorical, addressing the calls for national "healing" in relation to Vietnam and saying, somewhat ominously in the light of the military adventurism that would follow, that "sometimes when a bone is broken, if it's knit together well, it will in the end be stronger than if it had not been broken." Needless to relate, nothing was said by Reagan of the Vietnamese bones that had been broken or of the millions of North and South Vietnamese lost in a war the president complained had "threatened to tear our society apart."[18]

Lin's memorial was just part of the wider cultural argument about Vietnam, which had seen early, facile glorifications of the United States' intervention into the conflict like John Wayne's *The Green Berets* (1968) give way to a mass of cultural expression shaped by both the counter-culture and the conservative backlash to that counter-culture, all leavened with the eye-witness testimony of soldiers, journalists, and even the viewers of photographs and television reports that had pictured the war in unusually graphic terms. Cultural representations of the war and its aftermath, like Michael Herr's *Dispatches* (1977), Michael Cimino's *The Deer Hunter* (1978), and Francis Ford Coppola's *Apocalypse Now* (1979), as well as novels such as *In Country*, discussed in an earlier chapter, contributed to the evolving argument about Vietnam, adding to a picture of the conflict as a Conradian "heart of darkness" on the bloodiest frontier of the Cold War's simultaneously material and ideological imperialisms that had indeed rent the socio-political fabric of the nation. Even Sylvester Stallone's "hard bodied" saga of Rambo movies, which Jeffords has argued were central to the project of national remasculinization after the emasculating experience of the war at least began, before tailing off into high-grossing, gratuitously violent macho fantasies, with the social truth of veteran dislocation, the nation's former soldiers having been over-represented in homeless statistics throughout the decade.

A veteran himself, Tim O'Brien was already a significant contributor to the ongoing arguments about Vietnam by the time that *The Things They Carried* (1990) was published. He had published a memoir, *If I Die in a Combat Zone, Box Me Up and Ship Me Home* (1973), and the National Book Award-winning novel, *Going After Cacciato* (1978), both of which drew upon his own experiences in the war. He was also an attendee at a May 1985 Asia Society conference on "The Vietnam Experience in American Literature" that was held in New York, at which his fellow veteran Ron Kovic, the author of *Born on the Fourth of July* (1976), sharply criticized a keynote address given by Jim Webb, the author of *Fields of Fire* (1978) and, by then, Secretary of the Navy in the Reagan administration. At a conference at which, as Timothy Lomperis has noted, such disagreements were far from unusual, and during which the prospect of further US involvement in Central America, and in particular Nicaragua, was referred to on more than one occasion, O'Brien is reported as having played a noticeably conciliatory role.[19]

With the publication of *The Things They Carried*, it became apparent that O'Brien had still more to say about the conflict, and with its focus on the eponymous things carried by a single company of men fighting in Vietnam, *The Things They Carried* is not just a narrative that explicitly remembers—or stages the remembrance of—the war through material objects at the end of a decade in which arguments both about Vietnam and about things were particularly intense. For the book was also a remembering, memorializing object in and of itself. In its pages were a series of interlinked stories that recollected and reflected upon the time spent by the narrator, who may or may not be O'Brien, in Vietnam. The book, which was neither a novel nor a memoir nor a short story collection but simultaneously all and none of these, appeared to have come into being out of a compulsion to narrate the experience of the war, still strong long after that war had ended: "Telling stories seemed a natural, inevitable process, like clearing the throat. Partly catharsis, partly communication, it was a way of grabbing people by the shirt and explaining exactly what had happened to me," O'Brien's narrator explains.[20] "By telling stories, you objectify your own experience. You separate it from yourself."[21] The book itself, then, was nothing less than a reification of the wartime experience of O'Brien (or his narrator of the same name), while its dedication, centered towards the top of the book's first facing page after the title page, made its memorializing function explicit:

> This book is lovingly dedicated to
> the men of Alpha Company, and in particular
> to Jimmy Cross, Norman Bowker,
> Rat Kiley, Mitchell Sanders, Henry Dobbins,
> and Kiowa

There is a kind of poetry simply in this arrangement of the names of some of the soldiers of Alpha company in lines, comparable to those written into the Memorial itself. While Griswold had argued that Lin's memorial "represents a book" whose "pages are covered with writing, and [. . . are] open partway through," the way *The Things They Carried* begins reversed the terms of the metaphor, such that the emphasis falls not on the book-like nature of the thing but on the thing-like nature of O'Brien's book.[22] In this sense, the dedication aspires not so much to the quality of writing, which might be effaced, but to that of something hewn into the remembering object that is his text.

Of course, that object was also, and primarily, a text; and within that text, things, and lists of things, are as central to O'Brien's effects as lists of men's names. Indeed, it is initially through things that O'Brien remembers the men listed in the dedication and his own experience of serving in the war. Very early on in the book, O'Brien has his narrator begin a series of lists of the things the soldiers of the company of which he was a part carried: "P-38 can openers, pocket knives, heat tabs, wristwatches, dog tags, mosquito repellent, chewing gum, candy, cigarettes, salt tablets, packets of Kool-Aid, lighters, matches, sewing kits, Military Payment Certificates, C rations, and two or three canteens of water."[23] In their 1987 essay on the Vietnam memorial, Karal Ann Marling and Robert Silberman reflected on the practice popularized shortly after the Vietnam memorial was unveiled of leaving objects next to the memorial in memory of the fallen soldiers: "the battered can of C-ration cinnamon nut rolls, the birthday cards, the single flowers stuck in the drainage channel below the Wall reify memories dematerialized and depersonalized despite the litany of names above the offerings." For Marling and Silberman, these offerings were "so many small, populist memorials to Vietnam, so many tangible specifics fleshing out the abstracted iconography of remembrance."[24] In *The Things They Carried*, depictions of objects themselves flesh out that "fleshing out" by performing not one but a series of functions in relation to the book's role as a means of remembering Vietnam.

First, there is the question of "the real," of the idea of truth and authenticity, which several critics have argued is central to O'Brien's examination of the relationship between what his narrator calls "happening-truth" and "story-truth."[25] Consider the epigraph O'Brien uses after his dedication:

> This book is essentially different from any other that has been published concerning the "late war" or any of its incidents. Those who have had any such experience as the author will see its truthfulness at once, and to all other readers it is commended as a statement of actual things by one who experienced them to the fullest.

The epigraph comes from John Ransom's *Andersonville Diary* (1881). While Ransom's invocation of "actual things" does not specifically allude to the kind of material objects with which this book is concerned, the epigraph takes on an altered complexion in the light of the proliferation of artifacts with which O'Brien's narrative is filled. As Robin Silbergleid has put it, depictions of such things are used in *The Things They Carried* "in order to define the 'real' parameters of Vietnam as experienced personally by the narrative's soldier-characters."[26] Willa Cather once characterized as "a popular superstition" the idea that "'realism' asserts itself in the cataloguing of a great number of material objects," and yet the listing of objects by O'Brien is surely in part intended as evidence of the "truthfulness" of the experiences narrated within the book, a fact that "[t]hose who have had any such experience as the author will see [. . .] at once," and of which those who have not will be convinced through the simple act of listing itself.[27] These are things that were there, O'Brien's narrator is insisting; these are the things that I saw these men carry and myself carried. More than just the Barthesian "reality effects" discussed in an earlier chapter, like the Vietnam-era Zippo cigarette lighter engraved with the plea, "PLEASE

DON'T TRY TO TELL ME ABOUT VIET NAM I'VE BEEN THERE," these objects serve in the first instance as evidence of the first-hand authenticity of the experience related.[28]

As with O'Brien's dedication, and as with the memorial, the effect achieved here is partly a question of naming. If one had not been in Vietnam oneself, one would not necessarily need to know what "P-38 can openers" or "heat tabs" or "C rations" were, any more than one would need to know who Jimmy Cross, Norman Bowker, Rat Kiley, Mitchell Sanders, Henry Dobbins, Kiowa—or indeed, any of the men whose names are engraved in their tens of thousands on the Vietnam war memorial—were in order to be convinced, by the mere invocation of those names in their given context, that they had been there. However, if naming and listing serve here as evidence of the veracity of the experiences narrated, there is considerably more to such a list of things than the part it plays in O'Brien's examination of the relationship between documentary and fictional truth. Consider, for example, the way Vietnam was consistently cast throughout the 1980s as a war that somehow eluded satisfactory or comprehensive narration. At the same time, of course, the sheer volume of cultural responses and references to Vietnam that continued to emerge throughout the 1980s suggests that if the conflict in some ways evaded the articulation of what theorists of the postmodern might characterize as "grand narratives" relating to the war and its place in the history of the nation, Vietnam simultaneously remained remarkably, even endlessly, generative of smaller, more personal narratives.

The question, then, is whether the objects depicted in *The Things They Carried* are merely material testaments to the experience of Vietnam or whether they too generate the kind of narratives about the conflict that were themselves proliferating throughout the 1980s. In a way, this is a question about O'Brien's distinctive use of the list throughout the opening section of his text. After the initial list of things that O'Brien's men carried, several of the men named in his initial dedication are themselves listed:

Henry Dobbins, who was a big man, carried extra rations; he was especially fond of canned peaches in heavy syrup over pound cake. Dave Jensen, who practiced field hygiene, carried a toothbrush, dental floss, and several hotel-sized bars of soap he'd stolen on R&R in Sydney, Australia. Ted Lavender, who was scared, carried tranquillizers until he was shot in the head outside the village of Than Khe in mid-April.[29]

Here the men are doubly enlisted, both in the army and in the naming, lists, and parallelisms of O'Brien's prose, with the things they carry serving as markers of identities formed in and by war, functions not only of the necessary matériel and equipment they are forced by their service roles to lug through the jungle, but by their individual characteristics, whatever they happen to be: their size, their cleanliness, their fear. And it is from out of this generation of character through an entangled list of men and the things they carried that part of the main narrative interest of the opening narrative in the book, itself called "The Things They Carried," eventually bursts forth. The things that Henry Dobbins and Dave Jensen carry, for example, are detailed and expounded upon; those carried by Ted Lavender (his tranquillizers) are not dwelt upon at all. Instead, the sentence conveys the circumstances of his death, which will be related in more detail later in the narrative, along with further lists after lists of the things the soldiers carried, including those things carried by Cross, sent by the girl he loves back home, his thinking thoughts about whom at the wrong moment he will later blame for Lavender's death. In this sense, objects do not clog, weigh down, or render O'Brien's narrative static and stationary as much as they provide the conditions out of which it emerges, for out of the lists of men and things arise many, if not all, of the stories that O'Brien will tell over the course of the book as a whole.

The idea of the list is also deployed elsewhere in *The Things They Carried* as a means of articulating a commentary upon the nation which had fought the Vietnam War but was nevertheless continuing throughout the 1980s to organize its industrial structure around the fighting of other such wars, for all neoliberalism's claims about the desirability of a small state. The manner in which O'Brien's lists of things address such concerns may frequently be oblique, but it is nonetheless traceable throughout his text. One of the lists that O'Brien uses, for example, picks up on the theme of waste that I argued in an earlier chapter remained an abiding concern throughout the 1980s:

> They would often discard things along the route of the march. Purely for comfort, they would throw away rations, blow their Claymores and grenades, no matter, because by nightfall the resupply choppers would arrive with more of the same, then a day or two later still more, fresh watermelons and crates of ammunition and sunglasses and woolen sweaters—the resources were stunning—sparklers for the Fourth of July, colored eggs for Easter—it was the great American war chest—the fruits of science, the smokestacks, the canneries, the arsenals at Hartford, the Minnesota

forests, the machine shops, the vast fields of corn and wheat—they carried like freight trains; they carried it on their backs and shoulders—and for all the ambiguities of Vietnam, all the mysteries and unknowns, there was at least the single abiding certainty that they would never be at a loss for things to carry.[30]

If the lists DeLillo had included in *White Noise*, among them lists of goods and lists of garbage, communicated a sense of the spatial and temporal endlessness both of American abundance and of hoarded junk in contemporary American life in the 1980s, here O'Brien offers a sense of the replenishable endlessness of things that had been supplied to men in the field in Vietnam. In *Going After Cacciato*, O'Brien had soldiers self-consciously debate the importance of industrial production to the successful waging of war, as if in deliberate echo of the kind of technological managerialism that James William Gibson argued in *The Perfect War* had characterized American military strategy in Vietnam, whereby the most well-resourced side in a conflict was believed to be assured of victory.[31] But there is also something else at work here. For as in O'Brien's previous list, the objects listed in this case are not all military things. There are certainly Claymores, grenades, and ammunition; but there are also watermelons, sunglasses, sweaters, sparklers and Easter eggs. Indeed, O'Brien even at one point has his narrator relate that the men carried chess sets and basketballs through the jungle.

Such a jumble of military and civilian objects makes a series of important points about the war itself and the systems of industrial production and consumption it was purportedly defending, or else attempting to impose upon the people and the land that the men end up "carrying." Tina Chen has argued of the pebble sent to Jimmy Cross from the New Jersey shore that it functions "as a metonym for the Jersey shoreline (and, by extension, America)."[32] Similarly, what O'Brien calls "the great American war chest" metonymically carries within it not just things representative of the United States but the United States itself. Place and state names (Hartford, Minnesota) emerge out of a list that is, in effect, a sketch of the industrial and agricultural landscape of the United States at the time of the Vietnam War. What the men are thus attempting to import—literally carry into—Vietnam (as if on "freight trains") is, along with their weaponry, mementos and good-luck charms, a system of industrial capitalism that the political architects of the war had claimed was the most effective bulwark against the spread of communism throughout Southeast Asia. In this sense, no less than the "alarm clock" invoked in O. Henry's

Cabbages and Kings, the things the men carry, the things they use and waste and replace, confident in the knowledge that there will be no end to them, are in fact representative of an imperialist (or, perhaps in the eyes of some of the war's planners, counter-imperialist) project embarked upon in the wake of the decisive military defeat of the forces of an older, European imperialism at Dien Bien Phu. It is not just American things that the soldiers carry, then, but the system of steadily globalizing capitalism that the United States of America has increasingly come to represent throughout the post-Second World War era.

Of course, in a novel published at the end of the 1980s, the sketch of the industrial landscape of the United States that emerges out of this list-within-a-list, with its view of fields and freight trains, smokestacks and canneries, might have seemed like a pointed backward glance in light of the ongoing deindustrialization that had already been brought to parts of the American economy. As production capital continued to move away from the traditional industrial heartlands of the Northeast, increasingly crossing national borders, the view of still-operating smokestacks and booming industrial production invoked by O'Brien was becoming less familiar in many regions of the United States than the decaying cityscapes glimpsed in the mid-1980s songs of Springsteen, with their non-hiring plants and closed-down textile mills.[33] Ironically enough, the dip in effective demand caused by falling military expenditures as the United States withdrew from Vietnam also itself contributed to the "stagflation" of the 1970s, which as we have seen provided the proximate context for the triumph of the neoliberal consensus discussed earlier in this book.[34] In this sense, the industrial landscape evoked by the things in O'Brien's list illustrates both the weakening economic position of American manufacturing and the ultimate impotence that such industrial and military power had had when it attempted to exercise itself, through the figures of the men and the things in O'Brien's stories, in pursuit of victory in an unwinnable war.

Moreover, if O'Brien's list of infinitely expendable civilian and military objects, produced and published at the end of the 1980s, thus reflects the apparently irrevocable military-industrialization of the American economy by the time of the Vietnam War, it also simultaneously speaks to how militarism and military production had become ever more central to that economy by the end of the 1980s. The large increases in military spending under Reagan may have at least served the function of both increasing demand in one sector of an otherwise declining manufacturing base and, by some accounts, contributed significantly to the eventual demise of the Soviet Union and victory in the Cold War. In either case, much of that spending was, as it remains today, inherently wasteful; the thrown-away rations, the set-off Claymores and grenades are versions of enterprises such as Reagan's missile defense system writ small, a way of commenting on an American economy that amid the deindustrialization and financialization of the 1980s risked growing increasingly dependent on its own continued militarization.[35]

*

One further significant way *The Things They Carried* contributed to arguments about things, Vietnam, and the 1980s themselves at the end of the Cold War is in relation to the text's representations of and meditations upon what might be termed "the weight of things." For of all the things the soldiers in O'Brien's text are said to have carried, perhaps none is more surprising than "gravity." "[T] hey carried gravity," O'Brien's narrator asserts, at the end of one of his characteristic lists of the things carried by the men he fought alongside.[36] Such an assertion is part of a broader series of metaphors of rising and falling related to gravity that can be traced throughout the text as a whole and which relates to the weight that the conflict in Vietnam had itself assumed in the cultural discourse of the United States. See, for example, how O'Brien's narrator repeatedly details the weight of things. Of the original list of things the men carry, he has his narrator estimate that "[t]ogether, these items weighed between 15 and 20 pounds, depending upon a man's habits or rate of metabolism."[37] "On their feet they carried jungle boots—2.1 pounds," he later remarks, and "a steel-centered, nylon-covered flak jacket, which weighed 6.7 pounds, but which on hot days seemed much heavier."[38] "Every third or fourth man carried a Claymore antipersonnel mine—3.5 pounds with its firing device. They all carried fragmentation grenades—14 ounces each. They carried at least one M-18 colored smoke grenade—24 ounces."[39]

While Silbergleid argues that "[t]he literal heaviness of these objects stands in metaphorically for the weight of war," which he characterizes as "an enormous emotional burden O'Brien's narrator shares with the reader," such an assessment does not quite do justice to the extent to which that "literal heaviness" is dwelled on in the text.[40] For, if as O'Brien's narrator puts it, to "carry something was to hump it," and in "its intransitive form, to hump meant to walk, or to march," then the war itself, before it is anything else, is just one long "hump" in the context of *The Things They Carried*: "the war was entirely a matter of posture and carriage, the hump was everything, a kind of inertia, a kind of emptiness, a dullness of desire and intellect and conscience and hope

and human sensibility."[41] The idea of the endless weary trudge of soldiers phys-
ically weighed down, first and foremost, by the things they carried as being the
essence of the war, even before those things take on any metaphorical significance, is articulated in the book's opening section:

> They endured. They kept humping. They did not submit to the obvious
> alternative, which was simply to close their eyes and fall. So easy, really.
> Go limp and tumble to the ground and let the muscles unwind and not
> speak and not budge until your buddies picked you up and lifted you into
> the chopper that would roar and dip its nose and carry you off to the
> world. A mere matter of falling, yet no one ever fell.[42]

The passage puts into context the narrator's claim that the men "carried gravity." For what is gravity but the tendency of all matter downwards, a tendency
that is seen here to characterize not just the inanimate objects the men carry
but what Tina Chen, in her discussion of O'Brien's text, has called "the materiality of the body"?[43] Gravity *is* the "mere matter of falling," or rather, the mere
falling of matter. Thus, when O'Brien's narrator claims that the men he served
with carried gravity, he is suggesting that they resisted on a daily basis the urge
to cease carrying themselves and their things in the aimless, endless trudge
that was the war; that they refused as they marched to give in to the natural
inclination of all things to fall down towards the center of the earth.

And yet many, of course, did fall. Consider, in this light, the emphasis placed
throughout the text not just on the matter of falling but on falling matter,
human bodies and all. Here, for example, is how the death of Ted Lavender, the
central event of the story that emerges out of O'Brien's narrator's list of things
the men carried, is framed:

> Ted Lavender, who was scared, carried 34 rounds when he was shot and
> killed outside Than Ke, and he went down under an exceptional burden,
> more than 20 pounds of ammunition, plus the flak jacket and helmet and
> rations and water and toilet paper and tranquilizers and all the rest, plus
> the unweighed fear. He was a dead weight. There was no twitching or
> flopping. Kiowa, who saw it happen, said it was like watching a rock fall,
> or a big sandbag or something—just boom, then down—not like the
> movies where the dead guy rolls around and does fancy spins and goes
> ass over teakettle—not like that, Kiowa said, the poor bastard just flat-
> fuck fell.[44]

In *If I Die in a Combat Zone, Box Me Up and Ship Me Home* (1973), his first, ostensibly non-fiction account of his time in Vietnam, O'Brien relates, in a list that reads as a summation of the lessons he learned from his experience, that "[d]ead human beings are heavy and awkward to carry," an observation repeated in *Going After Cacciato*.[45] The heaviness of the things carried by Lavender, tangible and intangible, only adds to and complements the heaviness of his own body once rendered instantaneously dead. Inanimate, and no longer able to carry or support the burden that is gravity, which it has been humping through the jungle of Vietnam, his body is transformed not in a metaphorical but in a literal sense to "a dead weight." The emphasis is placed, via the perspective of the observing Kiowa (who will himself become one of the fallen) on the way Lavender's body becomes nothing more than a falling object, as too will Lee Strunk, who "fell hard," there being "nothing left to run on" once his leg has been blown off; and as will the water buffalo—like the soldiers themselves, a mere bearer of burdens—which Rat Kiley shoots in perverse, anguished response to the death of Curt Lemon.[46] After all, the terminology used to describe the falling animal, which "went down hard, then got up again [. . .] fell hard and tried to get up," is of a piece with that used to depict the death and the dying of the men.[47] All are falling physical objects, surrendering finally not to a largely unseen enemy but to the inexorable, inevitable pull of gravity. Compare the fantastical scene in *Going After Cacciato* in which Paul Berlin imagines himself, and much of the war, falling: "Something came plunging by—a peculiar living object, a man—and as it descended he saw it was the old lieutenant spread out full-eagle like a sky diver. Then a flurry of falling objects: weapons and ammunition and canteens and helmets, rucksacks and grenades, all of it falling."[48]

This writing of gravity in the context of death reaches a climax in *The Things They Carried* in the episode in which O'Brien relates the death of Kiowa. For Kiowa's body does not merely fall to the ground but sinks into it, disappearing into the mud and sewage of a field used by Vietnamese villagers as an open latrine, as if being pulled ever deeper into the earth itself: "Kiowa was gone. He was under the mud and water, folded in with the war."[49] Where the conflict in Vietnam had acquired the metaphorical soubriquet of a "quagmire" to capture how the United States became bogged down in an unwinnable war, here the quagmire is literal, laced with excrement, and as O'Brien's narrator himself will later point out on his return to Vietnam years later, all the more symbolic as a result of the waste that was the war itself: "For twenty years this field has embodied all the waste that was Vietnam, all the vulgarity and horror."[50] But again, it is also the tendency of matter downwards upon which O'Brien's narrator meditates when he imagines how Jimmy Cross would communicate Kiowa's death to his next-of-kin:

> He would explain this to Kiowa's father. Carefully, not covering up his own guilt, he would tell how the mortar rounds made craters in the slush, spraying up great showers of filth, and how the craters then collapsed on themselves and filled up with mud and water, sucking things down, swallowing things, weapons and entrenching tools and belts of ammunition, and how in this way his son Kiowa had been combined with the waste and the war.[51]

The process here, again, is that which acts on all bodies, human and non-human, forcing them down into the collapsing craters created in the wet earth by the war itself. The heaviness, working in concert with gravity, is once again that of death. Later in the book, O'Brien's narrator recalls the death of Linda, a childhood friend. He remembers, for example, watching with her as a body is thrown from an airplane in a movie, and "the awful splash as that corpse fell into the sea [. . .] I kept seeing the soldier's body tumbling toward the water, splashing down hard, how inert and heavy it was, how completely dead."[52] The death on screen foreshadows the early death of Linda herself, of a brain tumor; and the narrator relates how, seeing her, "[s]he looked heavy and totally dead."[53] To be heavy, to fall, to sink, is to die; it can only be resisted, in the day-to-day monotony of the seemingly endless "hump" that is the war, so long as the burden of gravity itself can be shouldered.

Different versions of a metaphorical counterforce, an alternative to the ceaseless carrying of things, of oneself and of gravity, are also present throughout *The Things They Carried*. For some of the things depicted in the text are not so much carried by the soldiers as carry them, like their standard issue, waterproof ponchos:

> Because the nights were cold, and because the monsoons were wet, each carried a green plastic poncho that could be used as a raincoat or groundsheet or makeshift tent. With its quilted liner, the poncho weighed almost two pounds, but it was worth every ounce. In April, for instance, when Ted Lavender was shot, they used his poncho to wrap him up, then to carry him away across the paddy, then to lift him into the chopper that took him away.[54]

The grim irony in the narration, of course, is that what makes the poncho worth its weight is not the fact that it is waterproof, but that it serves as an initial stretcher-cum-coffin for the thing that once was Ted Lavender. Moreover, such things as Lavender's body are carried to yet another object that carries men throughout the war, "the chopper that took him away." The helicopter, anthropologist Ian Walters and others have argued, "is the object that has come to symbolize and characterize the Vietnam War"; it is the "master vehicle, emblem, image of the war."[55] Indeed, in Michael Herr's *Dispatches* (1977), helicopters themselves are conceived in part as just more falling objects: "choppers fell out of the sky like fat poisoned birds a hundred times a day. After a while I couldn't get on one without thinking that I must be out of my fucking mind."[56] At the same time, however, for Herr the helicopter was "the sexiest thing going; saver-destroyer, provider-waster, right hand-left hand, nimble, fluent, canny and human."[57] In *The Things They Carried*, helicopters are what "carry you off to the world," a formulation that suggests not just a longing on the part of the men to be for once the thing carried, but a sense that Vietnam itself is somehow removed from whatever is meant by "the world," as if it were some other realm, beyond and apart.

Of course, for those that fall like Ted Lavender, that carriage comes too late to alleviate the heaviness of the body in death. On the other hand, for the more fortunate, the helicopter surely represents something similar to the "freedom birds" about which O'Brien's narrator claims the men dream:

> At night, on guard, staring into the dark, they were carried away by jumbo jets. They felt the rush of takeoff. *Gone!* They yelled. And then velocity—wings and engines—a smiling stewardess—but it was more than a plane, it was a real bird, a big sleek silver bird with feathers and talons and high screeching. They were flying. The weights fell off; there was nothing to bear . . . they were baked, they were light and free—it was all lightness, bright and fast and buoyant, light as light, a helium buzz in the brain, a giddy bubbling in the lungs as they were taken up over the clouds and the war, beyond duty, beyond gravity and mortification and global entanglements [. . .] just riding the light waves, sailing that big silver freedom bird over the mountains and oceans, over America, over the farms and great sleeping cities and cemeteries and highways and the golden arches of McDonald's, it was flight, a kind of fleeing, a kind of falling, falling higher and higher, spinning off the edge of the earth and beyond the sun and through the vast, silent vacuum where there were no

burdens and where everything weighed exactly nothing [. . .] and so at night, not quite dreaming, they gave themselves over to lightness, they were carried, they were purely borne.[58]

Here the day-to-day heaviness of the soldier's being, which is a precursor to the further heaviness that is death, is imagined being thrown off in the act of flight. Indeed, O'Brien's narrator is explicit that this is precisely what is happening: "The weights fell off; there was nothing to bear," he pictures, and the emphasis on lightness ("all lightness, bright and fast and buoyant, light as light"), offers a metaphorical counterpoint to the emphasis on heaviness that will otherwise predominate O'Brien's depictions of things. Similarly, flight itself is conceived in such imaginings as commensurate with falling; it is "a kind of falling, falling higher and higher." This is nothing less than an ascension, but one that will take the soldiers not out of "the world," but back to it. The world, of course, is in this case, the United States. The American landscape ("farms and great sleeping cities and cemeteries and highways and the golden arches of McDonald's"), that same aerially glimpsed landscape so disdained in Talking Heads' "The Big Country," once again impinges itself upon things and the thought of things. To be taken back to the world, then, in an illusion of weightlessness, is to be carried or to be "purely borne," which suggests not just an alleviation of burdens but a rebirth, a return to the world of the living from that other realm that is Vietnam.

Such dreams of flight pick up on a trope that had been in circulation in the wider literary culture of the United States since at least the late 1970s. In *Song of Solomon* (1978), for example, Toni Morrison bookended the story of Macon "Milkman" Dead with two episodes of human flight. The first is a suicidal leap off a city hospital building in an unnamed city in Michigan that results in the death of a local insurance agent, teaching him "that only birds and airplanes could fly."[59] The second is the unaided one Macon learns his great-grandfather allegedly took when he literally "flew back to Africa" to escape a life of cotton-picking slavery in Virginia: he "[j]ust stood up in the fields one day, ran up some hill, spun around a couple of times, and was lifted up in the air."[60] This unexpectedly magical-realist casting off of a weight of oppression is foreshadowed in Morrison's novel by the figure of a peacock glimpsed in a city street, unable to fly because of the weight of its own tail: "Can't nobody fly with all that shit. Wanna fly, you got to give up the shit that weighs you down," Macon learns.[61] Such were the historical burdens of slavery and its role in the history of capitalism, Morrison intimates. In Jayne Anne Phillips's *Machine Dreams*

(1984), it was, as in O'Brien's writing, Vietnam and the burdens it forced the foot soldiers of Cold War capitalist imperialism to bear that leads the draftee Billy Hampson, who loved airplanes as a boy, to insist to his sister Danner that he will "stay off the ground if they send me, get into an air crew."[62] The full details of Billy's bitterly ironic reasoning are later revealed in a letter he sends home from basic training to Danner in West Virginia: "If I go down in a chopper there will be another chopper in fast, to get me and to protect the machine."[63] Billy's approximation of his own relative value is all the more poignant because he never returns, and the novel ends with a dream of Danner's in which she hears her still missing-in-action brother "imitating with a careful and private energy the engine sounds of a plane that is going down . . . So gentle it sounds like a song, and the song goes on softly as the plane falls, year after year, to earth."[64]

In all these cases, to fly was to escape, or at least free oneself from the awful burden of systems of oppression and war in which the human body is just another laboring asset or piece of military matériel. It is in anticipation of an ascension away from such burdens that flight itself is so repeatedly figured throughout *The Things They Carried*. The soldiers believe, for example, that like the mythical Solomon in Morrison's novel, their enemy "could levitate," "could fly."[65] O'Brien's narrator even claims to have experienced the sensation of flight while about to exact revenge on Bobby Jorgenson, a medic who had wronged him by failing to treat a wound effectively: "Eyes closed, I seemed to rise up out of my own body and float through the dark down to Jorgenson's position. I was invisible; I had no shape, no substance; I weighed less than nothing."[66] If one of his sensations after having first been wounded was "a sinking sensation," O'Brien's narrator's experience upon receiving his second wound is quite distinct: "I was drifting upward out of my own body."[67] At times in O'Brien's text, these images of bodies and men not falling but rising are in fact images of brutal violence. The death of Curt Lemon, for example, is related by the narrator recalling, in bald terms and the historic present tense, how "Curt Lemon steps from the shade into bright sunlight, his face brown and shining, and then he soars into a tree."[68] Later he will reflect, of Lemon's death, that "when he died it was almost beautiful, the way the sunlight came around him and lifted him up and sucked him high into a tree full of moss and vines and white blossoms," a sucking upwards to contrast with the later sucking downwards of Kiowa and things in the quagmire.[69] Finally, of an enemy fighter he claims at one point in the text to have killed, O'Brien's narrator relates how "the young man seemed to jerk upward as if pulled by invisible wires. He fell on his back," a description that encapsulates the twin tendencies that characterize so much of the writing of things and bodies throughout the work: to fall and to rise; or in this case, to rise and to fall, like stock markets, empires, flying machines.[70]

Taken together, the key point illustrated by such images of the weight of things, and of the rising and falling of objects and bodies, is that the depiction of material things throughout O'Brien's book is in fact at all times framed and informed by the abiding sense that in war, soldiers and things alike are subject to—and subjected to—forces which, like the physical laws of the universe, are by definition beyond their control. The men can "carry" gravity, resisting the urge to simply fall under the burden of the weight of things as they hump from one day to the next through the Vietnamese jungle; and if helicopters and airplanes are afforded privileged mystique within accounts such as Herr's, Phillips's and O'Brien's, it is surely partly because they can, through flight, defy for a time some of the burdens of gravity. However, for the most part, what O'Brien presents is a picture of a conflict in which the limits of human agency in war are consistently highlighted.[71] Things happen to the men; they can act, but their freedom to act is forever compromised by the sense that they and the things they carry are in constant danger of being pulled down into the earth or blown up into the air. If they rise, they will eventually fall; and if they fall, they will be lucky to rise again.

*

This writing of weight, of gravity, encountered in O'Brien's work is itself related to the notion of Vietnam as a kind of cultural weight with which veterans, the bereaved, and policymakers were having to deal in the 1980s. Senator Ted Kennedy insisted that "the lesson [of Vietnam] is that we must throw off the cumbersome mantle of world policeman," a figure in which it is not Vietnam but an object symbolizing the foreign policy posture that led to American involvement in Vietnam that must be "thrown off."[72] In the early years of the 1990s, however, President George H. W. Bush quite deliberately objectified Vietnam in a radio address to US forces serving in the Gulf on March 2, 1991, in the wake of a comprehensive five-week victory in the Gulf War: "We promised this would not be another Vietnam. And we kept that promise. The specter of Vietnam has been buried forever in the desert sands of the Arabian Peninsula."[73] That such a claim could have been made was the fruit of more than five weeks work, of course. The interventions conducted throughout the 1980s had set the stage for a larger erasure from the cultural scene of images depicting the withdrawal—indeed, the literal, helicopter-led flight—of American power from South Vietnam in 1975, while a series of militaristic Hollywood blockbusters of the 1980s also played a part in projecting a resurgent militarism after the relatively muted tones of US foreign policy during the Carter presidency. Nevertheless, what is fascinating about Bush's rhetorical figure in relation to *The Things They Carried* is the way it simultaneously portrays "Vietnam" as both spectral and tangible, as both an apparition and a physical object that has not only been separated from the national body politic but has been buried for good, as if never to rise again, its reification providing the precondition for its disposal while its status as some kind of phantasm suggests its effect on the nation had always been more imagined than real anyway.

Such a figure recalls the visit to Vietnam O'Brien's narrator makes years after the war. When his friend Kiowa had been killed and had sunk into the filth of a literal quagmire, his body buried deep in mud, slime, and excrement, the first thing those looking for him found was his rucksack.[74] Returning to Vietnam years later with his daughter, O'Brien's narrator seeks out the site in the same marshy, waterlogged, river-flooded field "where Mitchell Sanders had found Kiowa's rucksack" and there proceeds to bury the moccasins Kiowa had kept in that rucksack and that the narrator had supposedly maintained in his possession: "Right here, I thought. Leaning forward, I reached in with the moccasins and wedged them into the soft bottom, letting them slide away [. . .] I tried to think of something decent to say, something meaningful and right, but nothing came to me."[75] The sense of contrast between the burial figured in Bush's speech and that written into O'Brien's text could hardly be sharper. Where the politician would rhetorically transform the conflict itself into a thing to be buried, thus drawing from the act of burial a parable of meaning and political significance, here O'Brien's narrator performs a burial characterized by a conspicuous lack of accompanying articulation, in which saying "something meaningful" proves beyond him. Where the burial recounted by the narrator represents an act of remembrance, the burial conjured by Bush represents a deliberate act of—or wish for—a kind of triumphalist cultural forgetting, desperate for what one military historian has called "the only true defeat for the United States in the long history of American wars" to be erased and supplanted in the minds of the American electorate.[76] Finally, where Bush's rhetorical burial takes place in the dry "desert sands of the Arabian Peninsula," O'Brien's fictional burial is enacted in the quagmire-like conditions with which Vietnam had long been associated. The point is not simply that these were two very different conflicts. Rather, it is that the experience of Vietnam, for O'Brien, defies the kind of neat, objectifying rhetorical reconfigurations that Bush proposes. Kiowa's moccasins might be buried, but the war, and the memory of war and the so heavily harnessed men who fought in the war, cannot be so tidily packaged up and disposed of. War and the fractured memories of war endure, instead, in the thought of precisely the kind of objects that proliferate throughout the rest of *The Things They Carried*. For these latter are things, as O'Brien's narratives make clear, that for veterans like him must continue to be borne precisely because they rarely stay buried.

Conclusion

It is no accident that this book ends as it began: dwelling on the "desert sands of the Arabian Peninsula." If the preceding chapters had one overriding aim, it was to complicate the picture of the 1980s as a decade in which something called "materialism" held sway over the culture of the United States. Things, I wanted to argue, were somewhat more complicated than that. To that end, I proposed that what we often mistake for the "materialism" of the era might better be understood as an intensification, or at least a rendering more culturally and discursively prominent, of an argument about things that has long animated the cultural discourse of the nation. The reason that argument altered in intensity, prominence, or both as the 1970s gave way to the 1980s was a reconfiguration effected by global capitalism that was necessarily both material and ideological, and that had at least some of its roots in places many thousands of miles distant from the homeland of the United States.

The Arabian Peninsula was one of those places. In the early 1970s, in an introduction to a previously unpublished book he had written more than a decade earlier for the oil conglomerate Aramco, Wallace Stegner had cast that corporation's involvement in the economic and social development of the Kingdom of Saudi Arabia as something rather nobler than an exercise in enlightened self-interest. The bottle of oil one executive kept on his desk was there, Stegner had claimed, to remind him that his real purpose was to help extract hydrocarbons (and from them, profit) from those sands beneath his feet, rather than to lose himself in projects of social and developmental uplift. Roughly two decades later, Tim O'Brien showed in *The Things They Carried* what it had been like to bear the material burdens of empire as a foot soldier on the bloodiest frontier of the Cold War, even as the first President Bush was about to claim that the "specter" of that earlier war had been buried forever in the Persian Gulf War. As if to attend that specter's peculiarly material grave, the United States has maintained its military presence in the region ever since. The military bases flooded with troops and military matériel in preparation for Operation Desert Storm, the mission to liberate Kuwait in 1991, only remained there until shortly after the attacks of 9/11, which is to say, more than a decade, more than enough time to provide the planners and perpetrators of those attacks with years of propaganda material against what they called the "far-away enemy," as opposed to the enemies "near at hand" of the supposedly insufficiently Islamist regimes of North Africa and the Gulf.[1] The Fifth Fleet of the United States Navy is still, of course, stationed in Bahrain, following invasions of and interventions in Afghanistan, Iraq, Libya, Syria, and Yemen. Other US military assets stud the region, evidence enough that the same strategic vision enunciated by President Carter just months after he deplored excessive attachments to material things remains very much in force. Andrew Bacevich has, in his turn, deplored the strategic dead-end of what he calls the United States' forty-year "war for the Greater Middle East," but the story is, in fact, much older than that.[2] In any case, one need not be a dyed-in-the-wool oil determinist to sense the material and ideological entanglements involved here; and if those entanglements remain relatively under-explored and potentially irresolvable, the political economist Helen Thompson is surely right to argue in reference to the post-2008 world that we need to give more thought to "oil's place in the underlying material basis of western civilisation without which ideological politics as we know it would not exist."[3]

By beginning and ending my own argument about the argument about things in the same part of the world, and in the same part of the American imaginary, I wanted not just to achieve a sense of narrative circularity but to stress that if the shift to neoliberalism has been, at least in part, both imperial in origin and imperialist in its effects, the fundamental global conditions out of which that shift emerged remain to most intents and purposes still in place. Indeed, with significant proportions of the federal budget now rigidly structured around maintaining global military dominance, while domestic infrastructure and other public goods are underfunded to the point of fatal decay; with capital now, in the post-Cold War era, more globalized than perhaps ever before; and with the finance, insurance, and real estate sectors now accounting for a full twenty percent of the United States GDP, the political and economic trend lines of history that emerged out of the crisis-best 1970s appear to have been followed in remorselessly linear fashion.[4] It is for that reason that I maintain that if the 1980s began sometime in the 1970s, there is no definitive evidence as yet that we have ever actually left them. Today *is* the 1980s, only more so. Some radical voices on both sides of the Atlantic may hope that neoliberalism is running out of steam, but for the time being, despite challenges from the anti-globalization left and the nationalist right, it remains the dominant ideology. Perhaps we will one day look back on the present as part of the transition to another "great transformation," one of those moments in which, as the Italian Marxist Antonio Gramsci wrote when reflecting on a much earlier "wave of materialism," "the old is dying and the new cannot be born."[5]

Be that as it may, any assessment of American culture's engagement with material things in the era will have to engage, as I have sought to engage, with a complex, globally dispersed, and militarily policed network of matter, ideas, inequity, and culture to which mainstream political and historiographical incarnations of aspects of the argument about things, such as that instantiated in Carter's infamous speech of 1979, have rarely been able to do justice. Indeed, once pursued across multiple different discursive, aesthetic, and epistemological arenas, through an examination of the decidedly nuanced and varied ways in which Americans wrote about, spoke about, thought about, and pictured some of the things they have lived among in the age of neoliberalism, the value of the heuristic tool of the argument about things itself becomes all the clearer, precisely because it offers us a way of conceptualizing the nation's cultural engagement with things in ways that move beyond, on the one hand, empty denunciations of materialism and, on the other, no less problematic celebrations of the nation's supposedly innate mastery over the material world. For the heterogeneity of the contributions to the argument about things examined in this book is striking, and suggests that while there has indeed been, and will continue to be, an argument about things conducted across American culture in the age of neoliberalism, it is one in which many different things were being put to many different ends by many different makers of culture for many different reasons. No less striking is how relatively few representations of things in the "long 1980s" themselves served as a means of either simply condemning or celebrating the "materialism" of the decade. Indeed, it is one of the ironies of the argument about things in the era that authors like Jay McInerney and Bret Easton Ellis, who most overtly sought to critique the vacuity of what Jimmy Carter might have called the "emptiness" of young lives structured around brand names, designer goods, and consumerism, were themselves criticized for producing a literature insufficiently oppositional to the purported dictates of the prevailing culture. For the most part, even such a writer as Don DeLillo, who has spoken of the vital importance of what he calls the "writer in opposition," used depictions of objects in his fiction to advance a view of things and Americans' relationships with them infinitely richer than that proposed in the political sphere or through more mainstream cultural sources.[6] In itself, this process of complication, this articulation of the heterogeneity of meanings that things had in American lives and culture, corresponds with evolving views of the age of neoliberalism as a period not of straightforward, binary polarizations but of ever-increasing dispersal, fracture, and fragmentation.[7]

But the nature of the contributions to the argument about things made by depictions of objects in the culture of the 1980s also pulls into focus the question of the relationship between the age of neoliberalism and earlier eras. For on the one hand, this book has focused on aspects of the argument about things in what look like the early years of our present age: with controversies surrounding the aesthetic worth of the representation of mass-produced, mass-consumed, often brand-named objects; with ideas of the increasing durability of ephemeral things; with the relationship between things, thinking, and the self; and with the entanglement of military and industrial production. On the other hand, the preceding chapters also show how this argument about things carried echoes of older, sometimes much older, discussions in American life and Western thought that predate the ascent of neoliberalism: discussions about Pop Art and the depiction of everyday objects; about the supposed transience of all things, including the human subject and the civilizations such subjects take pride in building; about the importance of the epistemological study of things and the role of industrial design and manufacturing in the United States' conception of itself as a nation; about American abundance and the experience of war.

But where, then, does that leave the present? The broader argument about things in American life evidently neither began nor ended in the 1980s. So how does one historicize arguments that consistently overspill the historical boundaries imposed upon them, methodologically expedient as those boundaries may be? How does one examine an argument when that argument began not just in the preceding decade or century, but millennia previously? Ultimately these questions speak not just to the issue of the historical intensity of a long-running cultural argument at any one moment or in any one period, but to the power of metaphor. For in this study, I have used the idea of an "argument" as a metaphor; and yet, there is a sense in which it offers a more rigorous hermeneutical model than might at first appear. Arguments are often complex and disorderly, full of imperfect echoes and discordant voices; lines of correspondence are dropped and then taken up again; the boundaries of the debate are variously challenged and reasserted; there is no guarantee that all voices will be heard, nor that those that are will speak directly to the point without their contributions inflecting towards particular concerns of their own. Much of the culture examined in this book contributes to the argument about things in their depictions of objects in similarly disorderly ways, dragging it into often far richer discursive territory as a result. The argument about things overspills its historical boundaries in the same way that it moves beyond straightforward denunciations or celebrations of materialism and simultaneously coheres and fails to cohere with the terms in which discussions about things were being conducted elsewhere in the cultural discourse of the nation. Historicizing the cultural production of the era involves recognizing this tendency towards complexity.

However, there are also dangers in over-emphasizing the heterogeneity of the debate that this book has examined. Infinitely complex as it was, the argument about things in the long 1980s was still frequently animated by underlying questions of value and cost. In his 1979 speech, Jimmy Carter was advancing the position that material things and people's use of and desire for them are of relatively little value or of no value at all, and that to value them at all came at a cost. Some of these settled notions of the limited value of material things were precisely what Mary Douglas and Baron Isherwood and the scholars who came after them sought to interrogate more carefully from the late 1970s onwards, showing the limits of kneejerk, neo-Platonic anti-materialism and the value of things in symbolizing, for example, participation in what Douglas and Isherwood called the "social process."[8] The culture discussed in this book contributed to the same discussion of value, whether to explore the aesthetic or epistemological worth of things, pronounce upon their transience, or otherwise. The idea of value is not pecuniary in this instance, of course; rather, it is related to the question of what material things might mean, or be made to mean. In an era in which the "materialism" of American culture was under attack, and in which figures like Carter were insisting that "things do not satisfy our longing for meaning," that question seems to me a vital one. For as Csikszentmihalyi and Rochberg-Halton put it in 1981, the "only weapon we have" against the kind of "terminal materialism" that was so roundly denounced in the era is "the human ability to create meaning."[9]

As I have already indicated, these questions, and the broader argument about things to which they pertain, remained pertinent to American culture as the long 1980s advanced deep into the post-Cold War 1990s. See, for example, how two major novels of the later decade were both brought to a close with extended meditations upon things. Here is an excerpt from the closing passage of Don DeLillo's *Underworld* (1997):

and you look at the things in the room, offscreen, unwebbed, the tissued grain of the deskwood alive in light, the thick lived tenor of things, the argument of things to be seen and eaten, the apple core going sepia in the lunch tray, and the dense measures of experience in a random glance, the monk's candle reflected in the slope of the phone, hours marked in Roman numerals, and the glaze of the wax, and the curl of the braided wick, and the chipped rim of the mug that holds your yellow pencils, skewed all crazy, and the plied lives of the simplest surface, the slabbed butter melting on the crumbled bun, and the yellow of the yellow of the pencils, and you try to imagine the word on the screen becoming a thing in the world.[10]

And here is part of a description of a disposable camera that features in the closing pages of Richard Powers's *Gain* (1998):

The camera jacket says: "Made in China With Film From Italy Or Germany." The film itself accretes from more places on the map than emulsion can cover. Silver halide, metal salts, dye couplers, bleach fixatives, ingredients gathered from Russia, Arizona, Brazil, and underwater seabeds, before being decanted in the former DDR. Camera in a pouch, the true multinational: trees from the Pacific Northwest and the southeastern coastal plain. Straw and recovered wood scrap from Canada. Synthetic adhesive from Korea. Bauxite from Australia, Jamaica, Guinea. Oil from the Gulf of Mexico or North Sea Brent Blend, turned to plastic in the Republic of China before being shipped to its mortal enemies on the Mainland for molding. Cinnabar from Spain. Nickel and titanium from South Africa.[11]

The way such passages can be set in dialogue with one another illustrates some of the continuities and new inflections that characterized the argument about things as the neoliberal age marched on. As he had in the 1980s, DeLillo dwells on issues of transience, deploying here the kind of *vanitas* symbols frequently seen in the still lifes of the Dutch masters. The "apple core going sepia" and "the monk's candle," for example, are iconographic markers of the passing of time, serving the same function in DeLillo's description that rotting fruit or extinguished lamps and candles had in the traditional painted still life. Ecclesiastes' pronouncements on the vanity of all things, among the oldest contributions to the arguments about things, speaks through these objects as late as the second half of the 1990s, once again illustrating the complex historical nature of the debate.

The passage from Powers is also in part a meditation upon human transience, but it is a meditation on that transience in the age of the multinational corporation. The camera is described sitting in a drawer beside the now vacant bed of a woman, Laura Bodey, dead from a cancer caused, the novel implies, by environmental pollution generated by the industrial processes of the Clare corporation, the history of which Powers has charted in a narrative intertwined with that of Laura's demise. The camera's disposability is heavily symbolic: Powers's narrator discloses that a "nurse's aide throws it out, prior to the next occupant"; it is, the narrator observes, a "disposable miracle, no less than the least of us."[12] For Powers, the camera barely outlasts its user; it and the human subject are as miraculous, and as miraculously ephemeral, apparently, as one another.

In unfolding the disposable miracle that is the thing, Powers is also engaged in an examination and a critique of the ever-increasingly globalized capitalism of the 1990s, as if to emphasize the always-historical nature of the argument about things. The triumph of neoliberalism and of globalized capital in the post-Cold War 1990s is embodied in the form of the disposable camera. This is no American thing. Its very existence straddles the globe, the processes of its manufacture dispersed throughout and traceable back to all the different earthly locations Powers invokes. In his own way, DeLillo is no less engaged with the historical nature of the argument about things. Bill Brown suggests in "Thing Theory" that "if the topic of things attained a new urgency in the closing decades of [the twentieth] century, this may have been a response to the digitization of our world."[13] The designation of the "things in the room" as "offscreen, unwebbed" by DeLillo speaks to the processes of this digitization, that same process heralded by Reagan in the 1988 speech at Moscow State University. The virtual realities to whose expansion that revolution gave impetus are what DeLillo's narrator is dwelling on here. The end of *Underworld* takes the form of a meditation upon a single word on a computer screen. This word, "peace," is what DeLillo's narrator imagines "becoming a thing in the world," vainly as it has turned out. Again the venerable trope of the transience of things inscribed into the iconography of DeLillo's still life arrangement is combined here with the more immediate historical influence wrought on the argument about things by advances in information technology.

And yet, within DeLillo's long, sustained sentence, it is not, in a sense, language that becomes a thing but things that take on some of the properties of language. Is the argument about things really an argument "of things," then, as

DeLillo's narrator has it? Shortly before the passage from *Gain* quoted above, Powers's narrator reflects on that always-symbolic substance, plastic, an important component of the disposable camera whose global complexity he unpacks: "Plastic happens; that is all we need to know on earth. History heads steadily for a place where things need not be grasped to be used."[14] The echo of Keats's "Ode on a Grecian Urn" ("that is all/Ye know on earth, and all ye need to know") recalls the traces of the same poem that Frank Lentricchia has found in Jack Gladney's interrogation of his family's compacted trash in DeLillo's *White Noise*. With its play on the meanings of "grasp," Powers's sentence emphasizes the limits of human knowledge about things. Keats's urn is an archetype of the mute, impassive artifact, unresponsive to the questions that are asked of it. Nevertheless, it too speaks to its interrogator, or is finally made to speak by him, if only once again to emphasize its own speechlessness, its own resistance to his desire for it to disclose its meanings. "It says less, as all things must," as the poet Frank O'Hara had put in "John Button Birthday," in contra-distinction to that quasi-mystical tendency in new materialist thought that is always listening out for the rustle and chatter of things, a tendency that, as Andrew Cole has shown, stretches all the way back to medieval mystics like Meister Eckhart.[15]

I want to end on such questions of speaking and meaning because they themselves speak to the role of the critic and the scholar in the age of neoliberalism. After all, there is a sense in which the argument of this book, and the tenor of this conclusion, risk defeating themselves precisely because I have tried to resist the temptation to ventriloquize on behalf of the culture of the period when it comes to the oft-cited phenomenon of "materialism." For the transformations ushered in by the age of neoliberalism have quite evidently been the target of some of my critique, and yet I fear I have been left at the end of this study with the kind of pile of disaggregated fragments that might make one nostalgic for the old certainties of binary thought. Earlier interpretations of the era have read American culture's engagement with goods and garbage in the early neoliberal era inaccurately, I believe, as a result of their desire either to squeeze critical analyses of culture into a pre-formed argument about the supposed materialism of the age, or to use criticism to take a stand against that perceived materialism. It was surely this latter tendency that led so much cultural criticism that emerged at the time of the initial shift towards neoliberalism to take the form of a sorting of producers of culture into those that colluded with the supposedly signature feature of the age and those that opposed it, through one aesthetic strategy or another, even while various forms of culture, from rap to literary realism, were being attacked for having the temerity to show what peoples' resolutely material lives were actually like on the internal frontiers of regional and class inequalities. The real picture, I have shown, was more complicated than that.

The question remains, however, of what value, in the end, have cultural critics' denunciations of materialism been to the dispossessed? In his recent memoir, retired Congressman Barney Frank, looking back over a political career that had begun in the Great Society era and ended in the early twenty-first century, spoke of his own frustration with an emerging political left whose anti-materialist, disdainful politics was encapsulated, he complained, in the critical aesthetic of the Malvina Reynolds song "Little Boxes" (1962), with its description of mid-century housing tracts. Although Reynolds's lyrics may have been more class conscious than Frank acknowledges, the problem, he argued, was that many of his constituents would very much like to be able to afford to live in such circumstances, banal, homogenous, and uninspiring as they may seem to a postmaterialist, critical left.[16] Perhaps, then, in an age in which capitalism has repeatedly proven its ability to take away what it may once, in the long postwar boom, have seem almost innately coded to provide, including the "little boxes" of the nation's housing stock, materialism per se was always the wrong target for critique, especially given the present formation's habit of presenting itself as a valorization of such supposedly immaterial phenomena as freedom and liberty. Inequality, and the redistribution of resources up the income scale, were another matter. Some of what now looks like the most vital culture of the period, from the photography of Mary Ellen Mark and William Eggleston to the fiction of the new realists, reveals as much, prefiguring lessons about inequality and degradation that had, in fact, been taught before and will need to be taught again.

And if other examples of culture that engaged with things in the early years of the "long 1980s" appeared less focused on merely echoing the empty denunciations of materialism modeled by Jimmy Carter in the late 1970s than at times has been assumed, that is not to say that some of the most interesting examples of that culture were not fascinated, or horrified, by the complex material effects in time and space of phenomena that appeared central to national life, from mass consumption to garbage disposal, especially in a world in which the power of the United States remained both deep-rooted and diffuse. Imperfect and at times unsatisfactory as it might feel, the task of cultural critique is surely to attempt to take the measure of such far-reaching complexity. For the phenomena we might mistake for materialism, such as the desire for a degree of wealth, security, and a better future, have a proven habit of taking the most nuanced and ironic forms. Let the record show, for example, that Representative Frank, whose name adorns the financial regulations passed in an attempt to avoid a repeat of the most epic crises associated with both the neoliberal model and the age of oil, namely the 2007–08 financial crash and the recession that followed, now sits on the board of a bank. As Helen Thompson has shown, the timing of that crash and recession was itself arguably determined by yet another, somewhat under-narrated oil shock that occurred in the run-up to 2008, when oil prices were thirty percent "higher in constant prices than the last peak they reached in 1980."[17] Donald Trump, meanwhile, who made his name in the 1980s as a notorious race-baiter, self-publicist, and "builder" of things, sits in the White House, having won the presidency on a remarkably statist ticket of economic nationalism, xenophobia, and law and order. Immediately following his unexpected victory, Trump, who would soon appoint the former CEO of ExxonMobil as his Secretary of State, held forth on the question of things, promising to "fix our inner cities and rebuild our highways, bridges, tunnels, airports, schools, hospitals." As for the nation itself, he declared, ever the real estate impresario, that it had "tremendous potential," and was "going to be a beautiful thing."[18]

We may or may not be stuck in history; we are certainly stuck *with* it.

Notes

INTRODUCTION

1. Qtd. in Brogan, *Penguin History*, 46.
2. Brogan, *Penguin History*, 48.
3. Tocqueville, *Democracy in America*, 623.
4. See, for example, James Gilbert's claim that "[w]hile American society is the most consumer-oriented in the world (in terms of the sheer number of material objects), it is also a society that quizzes itself endlessly about the effects of materialism, of inauthenticity, of defining oneself in terms of consumer objects." Qtd. in Glickman, *Consumer Society and American History*, 2.
5. Krugman, "Making Things in America"; Pelecanos, "Bad Dreams."
6. Hirschman, *Passions and Interests*, 9.
7. Columbus, "Letter to Luis de Santangel," 32.
8. Bercovitch, "Rites of Assent," 8.
9. Qtd. in Brogan, *Penguin History*, 47.
10. New, *Christian Fundamentalism*, 37.
11. See Macpherson, *Possessive Individualism*.
12. Emerson, "Ode Inscribed to W. H. Channing," in *The Portable Emerson*, 648.
13. Iyotake, "Behold, My Friends," 166.
14. Plato, *Republic*, 66–67.
15. See Jefferson's *Notes on the State of Virginia* (1787): "[W]e have an immensity of land courting the industry of the husbandmen. Is it best then that all our citizens should be employed in its improvement, or that one half should be called off from that to exercise manufactures and handicraft arts for the other? Those who labour [sic] in the earth are the chosen people of God, if ever he had a chosen people, whose breasts he has made the peculiar deposit for substantial and genuine virtue. . . . Corruption of morals in the mass of cultivators is a phaeneomenon [sic] of which no age nor nation has furnished an example. It is the mark set on those, who not looking up to heaven, to their own soil and

industry, as does the husbandman, for their subsistence, depend for it on the casualties and caprice of customers." *Selected Writings*, 135.

16. Brown, *Sense of Things*, 5. See also Marx's discussion of "primitive accumulation," land, and the United States, in *Capital*, 933–40.
17. Turner, *The Frontier*, 37.
18. Turner, *The Frontier*, 37.
19. Dario, "To Roosevelt," 504.
20. Roosevelt, "Citizenship in a Republic."
21. Benedict, *Chrysanthemum and the Sword*, 22.
22. Steinbeck, *A Life in Letters*, 652.
23. King's words in context read: "I am convinced that if we are to get on the right side of the world revolution, we as a nation must undergo a radical revolution of values. We must rapidly begin . . . the shift from a thing-oriented society to a person-oriented society. When machines and computers, profit motives and property rights, are considered more important than people, the giant triplets of racism, extreme materialism, and militarism are incapable of being conquered." King, Jr., "Beyond Vietnam: A Time to Break the Silence," 107.
24. Strait, "What is a Hippie?" 311.
25. Strait, "What is a Hippie?" 312.
26. Davies, "Reasons for Corbyn."
27. Qtd. in Adler, *Drawing Down the Moon*, 344.
28. Qtd. in Adler, *Drawing Down the Moon*, 341.
29. Kramer, *Normal Heart*, 17, 3, 35.
30. See, for example, Burgin, *Great Persuasion*, 204–205; Klein, *The Shock Doctrine*, 75–87; Mirowski and Plehwe, *Road From Mont Pèlerin*.
31. Mirowski, *A Serious Crisis*, 1.
32. Lewis, "The End."
33. "Greenspan Admits Flaw"; Althusser, "Ideology and Ideological State Apparatuses," 294.
34. La Berge, *Scandals and Abstractions*.
35. Fukuyama, "The End of History?"
36. Troy, *Morning in America*, 18.
37. Sewall, *The Eighties*, xv.
38. For less Reagan-centered accounts of the 1980s, see in particular Martin, *The Other Eighties* and Foley, *Front Porch Politics*.
39. Troy, *Morning in America*, 17.
40. "The Simple Life," *Time* 1991.
41. Gallup, "What is Your Religious Preference? [1948–2105]"

42. See, *inter alia*, Veblen, *Theory of the Leisure Class*; Packard, *The Waste Makers*; Cohen, *A Consumer's Republic*; Glickman, *Consumer Society and American History*; Potter, *People of Plenty*. This in itself is only a small sample of a vast literature.

43. Annual GDP growth 1981–1990: 1981: +2.594%; 1982: -1.911%; 1983: +4.632%; 1984: +7.259%; 1985: +4.239%; 1986 +3.512%; 1987 +3.462%; 1988: + 4.204% ; 1989: +3.681%; 1990: +1.919%. See World Bank, "GDP Growth (Annual %): United States 1981–1990."

44. Lasch, *Culture of Narcissism*, xv; McClay, "Where Have We Come Since the 1950s?" 52.

45. Collins, *Transforming America*, 158–59.

46. Ponce de Leon, "New Historiography," 303.

47. Blyth, *Great Transformations*, passim.

48. Italics mine. Collins, *Transforming America*, 153; Laswell, *Who Gets What, When, How*. passim.

49. Troy, *Morning in America*, 119.

50. Anderson, "Imperium."

51. Blyth, *Great Transformations*, 126.

52. Heidegger, "What is a Thing?" 11; Danto, *Transfiguration of the Commonplace*, vi.

53. DeLillo, *White Noise*, 3.

54. Pearlman, *Unpackaging Art*, 9.

55. Thompson, *American Culture in the 1980s*, 63.

56. Pearlman, *Unpackaging Art*, 20, 22.

57. Clune, *American Culture and the Free Market*, 7; Foster, "Future of an Illusion," 92.

58. Eagleton, *After Theory*, 3; Hendin, "Fictions of Acquisition," 225–26, 228.

59. Bawer, "Literary Brat Pack," 210–21; Miller, *Material Culture and Mass Consumption*, 11.

60. Csikszentmihalyi and Rochberg-Halton, *Meaning of Things*, 235.

61. Brown, "Thing Theory," 6. See also Brown, *Sense of Things*; Latour, "News from the Trenches" and *Reassembling the Social*; Law and Hassard, *Actor-Network Theory*; Bennett, *Vibrant Matter*.

62. Kouwenhoven, *Made in America*, 79–82; Carson, "Material Culture History," 403.

63. Brown, "Thing Theory," 2.

64. See, *inter alia*, Douglas and Isherwood, *The World of Goods*; Csikszentmihalyi and Rochberg-Halton, *Meaning of Things*; Deetz, *Small Things Forgotten*; Miller, *Material Culture and Mass Consumption*.

65. Cole, "The Call of Things"; "Obscure Objects."
66. Frost, *Stuff*, 20.
67. The 1980s and early 1990s generated a vast literature on the postmodern. See, for example, Lyotard, *The Postmodern Condition*; Harvey, *The Condition of Postmodernity*; Jameson, *Postmodernism, or, The Cultural Logic of Late Capitalism*; McHale, *Postmodernist Fiction*.
68. DeLillo, *Players*, 107.
69. Harvey, *Condition of Postmodernity*, 284.
70. Baudrillard, *America*, 30.
71. Stallybrass, "Marx's Coat," 184. Stallybrass' point is that commodity fetishism fetishizes not the material object, as was the case with the African tribes in which fetishes were first observed, but the exchange value of the object. Marx argued in *Capital* that "the commodity-form [. . . has] absolutely no connection with the physical nature of the commodity" (Marx, *Capital*, 165). Thus, as Stallybrass puts it, "[t]o fetishize commodities is [. . .] to reverse the whole history of fetishism. For it is to fetishize the invisible, the immaterial, the supra-sensible" (184). Baudrillard's hologram also recalls the observations of Debord, who in *Society of the Spectacle* (1967) insisted that "commodities are now *all* that there is to see; the world we see is the world of the commodity" (29). Like Baudrillard, Debord deployed a rhetoric that suggested the "world" inhabited by Western societies was already by the late 1960s more or less illusory, referring, for example, to what he called "the pseudo-concreteness of [the spectacle's] universe" (152).
72. Brown, "Thing Theory," 14.
73. Jameson, *Postmodernism*, 9. For a provocative account of the assimilation of the work of Baudrillard and other practitioners of what he calls "French theory" on the American academy, see Cusset, *French Theory*. Cusset's account of Baudrillard's later influence on American popular culture, from Oliver Stone's TV series *Wild Palms* (1993) to the Wachowskis' *The Matrix* (1998), is particularly interesting. The former, according to Cusset, "told the story of a virtual-reality magnate who seized power using 'holograms' he controlled," while the latter depicts a dystopian future in which human beings have been enslaved by computers and plugged into a program that projects "an exact sensory copy of the vanished late-twentieth-century world—that is, the complete fictional equivalent of the 'simulacrum'" (259).

74. Baudrillard, *Simulacra and Simulation*, 2. For an important critique of Baudrillard's rhetoric from within the debates surrounding postmodernism, see Harvey, *The Condition of Postmodernity*, 291, 300–301.
75. DeLillo, *Players*, 157; Michaels, "Meaning and Affect"; McCarthy, "Book of a Lifetime." Michaels cites McCarthy, who credits his own use of the term to the philosopher Simon Critchley.
76. See Bilton, "Matter and Mammon," 417–37.
77. Brown, "The Matter of Materialism," 68.
78. Brown, "The Matter of Materialism," 68.
79. Bennett, *Vibrant Matter*, 2, 21–22.
80. See, for example, Rodgers, *Age of Fracture*; Cowie *Stayin' Alive*; Blyth, *Great Transformations*; Brown, *Edgework*; Dean, *Neoliberal Fantasies*; Mirowski, *Never Let A Crisis*; Mirowski and Plehwe, *Road From Mont Pèlerin*.
81. Qtd. in Mirowski and Plehwe, *Road from Mont Pèlerin*, 8.
82. Foucault, *Birth of Biopolitics*, 10.
83. Mirowski, *A Serious Crisis*, 94.
84. Mirowski, *A Serious Crisis*, 39.
85. Mirowski, *A Serious Crisis*, 40.
86. Mirowski, *A Serious Crisis*, 42–43.
87. Mirowski, *A Serious Crisis*, 42, 50–67. Mirowski and Plehwe, *Road From Mont Pèlerin*.
88. See Fisher, *Capitalist Realism*; Shonkwiler and La Berge, *Reading Capitalist Realism*.
89. Shonkwiler and La Berge, *Reading Capitalist Realism*, 5.
90. See Michaels, "Going Boom" and *The Trouble With Diversity*; Reed, Jr, "Django Unchained, or *The Help*."
91. Dimock, *Through Other Continents*.
92. Carter, "Address on Energy and Goals."
93. Collins, *Transforming America*, 147.
94. Vidal, "American Plastic."
95. Michaels, "Going Boom."

1. THE TRIUMPH OF NEOLIBERALISM

1. Stegner, *Discovery!*, ix–xvii; Mitchell, *Carbon Democracy*, 115.
2. Stegner, *Discovery!*, xxv.
3. Twain, "To The Person Sitting in Darkness," in *Crossing the Equator*, 2–16: 2–3.

4. Stegner, *Discovery!*, xxxii.
5. Stegner, *Discovery!*, xxxiii.
6. Stegner, *Discovery!*, xxxii.
7. Stegner, *Discovery!*, xxxii.
8. Hobson, *Imperialism, passim*; Lenin, *Imperialism* (esp. Part IV and Part VII); Schumpeter, *Social Classes/Imperialism*, 64–98; Arendt, *Origins of Totalitarianism*, 121–57.
9. Henry, *Cabbages and Kings*, 10.
10. Henry, *Cabbages and Kings*, 9.
11. Stegner, *Discovery!*, 44.
12. Wilson, "Address to Salesmanship Congress."
13. Carter, "State of the Union Address."
14. Mitchell, *Carbon Democracy*, 105.
15. Mitchell, *Carbon Democracy*, 144–45.
16. Stegner, *Discovery!*, xxxiii.
17. Stegner, *Discovery!*, 5.
18. On the CIA presence in Aramco, see Mitchell, *Carbon Democracy*, 212, 213.
19. See, in particular, Schumpeter and Arendt, both of whom explain the phenomenon of late nineteenth-century imperialism in terms of what Arendt calls "the emancipation of the bourgeoisie" (123). While such a view sounds roughly consonant with that famously espoused by Lenin, who leaned heavily on the earlier work of the British liberal, Hobson, Schumpeter's aim in his analysis was actually to defend capitalism. His point was that a small minority of a particular class had effectively hoodwinked the state into the coercive perversion of what ought always to be the inherently peaceful business of free trade.
20. Mitchell, *Carbon Democracy*, 44.
21. Mitchell, *Carbon Democracy*, 207.
22. Mitchell, *Carbon Democracy*, 5, 29.
23. Mitchell, *Carbon Democracy*, 38, 200–30.
24. Mitchell, *Carbon Democracy*, 210.
25. Mitchell, *Carbon Democracy*, 107.
26. Mitchell, *Carbon Democracy*, 107.
27. Sargent, *Superpower Transformed*, 132, 139–40.
28. Stegner, *Discovery!*, xxv; Sargent, *Superpower Transformed*, 135.
29. Stegner, *Discovery!*, xxv.
30. Sargent, *Superpower Transformed*, 142.
31. Kiernan, *New Imperialism*, 176.

Notes

32. The "Nixon shock" may have smacked of self-interested protectionism but Nixon's actions were neither intended to nor capable of altering the already salient fact that by 1971, the United States was already sliding into the deep dependence on imported oil that would make the shocks that would follow later in the decade so consequential. Moreover, the fact that exposure to speculative raids on an overvalued dollar, vast quantities of which were by the early 1970s in circulation globally (far in excess of the nation's gold reserves), was a precipitating factor in bringing about the "Nixon shock" indicates just how vulnerable to economic wounds the already partly integrated Western system had left the nation that had been so central to its design. See Sargent, *Superpower Transformed*, 101–31.

33. See, in particular, Jacobs, *Panic at the Pump*, in which "imperialism" is only mentioned once, and then in relation to what the Arab oil states were doing in the 1970s, not the United States (41). "Empire" features in Jacobs's account, but only in metaphorical reference to "Big Oil" (19), the USSR (306), and, finally, once, to the United States . . . *of the McKinley era* (emphasis mine, 306). Incidentally, neither "neoliberal" nor "neoliberalism" feature at all in Jacobs's book, despite its central argument that the 1970s energy crisis "was an object lesson in the limitations of governmental power" (9).

34. Hardt and Negri, *Empire*.

35. Panitch and Gindin, *Global Capitalism*, 275–340.

36. Mitchell, *Carbon Democracy*, 215, 213.

37. Sargent, *Superpower Transformed*, 311; Johnson, *Blowback*.

38. Sargent, *Superpower Transformed*, 156.

39. Mitchell, *Carbon Democracy*, 155.

40. Stein, *Running Steel*, 197; Johnson, *Blowback*, 193.

41. Harvey, *Neoliberalism*, 27–31.

42. US Census Bureau, "Trade in Goods and Services 1960–2015."

43. Cowie, *Capital Moves*.

44. For a monetarist account of the great inflation of the 1970s, see Mayer, *Monetary Policy*. Challenges to the monetarist interpretation include Blyth, *Great Transformations*, 135–51, 158–90; Mosler, "Now Versus the 1970s" and *Seven Deadly Frauds*, 7–8.

45. Mosler, *Seven Deadly Frauds*, 7; Mosler, "Now Versus the 1970s."

46. Blyth, *Great Transformations*, 3–7.

47. Starting in the mid-2000s, Thomas Piketty and Emmanuel Saez compiled revelatory data sets that showed how "top incomes" have soared since the 1970s.

See, for example, Piketty and Saez, "Evolution of Top Incomes" and Piketty, *Capital in the Twenty-First Century*.

48. Brown, *Edgework*, 44; Polanyi, *The Great Transformation*, 3.

49. Hacker and Pierson, *Winner-Take-All*, 117–18.

50. Qtd. in Nichols and McChesney, *Dollarocracy*, 76.

51. The concept of "drift," or "the deliberate failure to adapt public policies to the shifting realities of a dynamic economy," has been vital to cementing the inequalities of the neoliberal era. See Hacker and Pierson, *Winner-Take-All*, 52. The extent of the success of the political organization of business can be measured in PACs, a creation of the Campaign Finance Reform Act of 1971: "In 1976, there were 224 labor PACs, a number that would increase modestly to 261 a decade later. Over the same period, corporate and trade PACs increased from 992 to 2,182. Both sides ramped up spending over the period, but throughout the decade, trade and corporate PACs were able to outspend labor two or three to one," Hacker and Pierson, *Winner-Take-All*, 171. See also Blyth, *Great Transformations*, 154–61.

52. Harvey, *A Brief History of Neoliberalism*, 11.

53. Mitchell, *Carbon Democracy*, 197–99

54. Carter, "Address to the Nation on Energy and National Goals."

55. Collins, *Transforming America*, 151, 161–62.

56. Byrne, *True Stories*, 18.

57. Qtd. in Troy, *Morning in America*, 229.

58. On the Boesky scandal, see James B. Stewart, *Den of Thieves*; Collins, *Transforming America*, 93–100.

59. Lewis, *Liar's Poker*, 79–80.

60. Bush, "Inaugural Address."

2. AFTER THE GREAT TRANSFORMATION

1. Oppen, *Collected Poems*, 147.

2. Lasch, *Culture of Narcissism*, 36.

3. See Zaretsky, *No Direction Home*, 214–21.

4. See Troy, *Morning in America*, 119.

5. For discussions of the prevailing economic conditions as they looked to historians, see Collins, *More*, 132–65; Collins, *Transforming America*, 7–11; Ehrman, *The Eighties*, 30–41. On Carter's speech itself, see Mattson, *What the Heck?*. For the transformations in private finance that emerged in the 1970s, see Schulman, *The Seventies*, 132, 136–40 and "Slouching Towards Supply Side."

6. Carter, "Address to the Nation on Energy and National Goals."
7. Cowie, *Stayin' Alive*, 304.
8. Sacvan Bercovitch has emphasized the extent to which the Puritan rhetorical tradition of the jeremiad was founded upon a sense of crisis. Crisis, according to Bercovitch, was the Puritans' "source of strength. They fastened upon it, gloried upon it, even invented it if necessary." Bercovitch, *The American Jeremiad*, 62.
9. Bercovitch, *The American Jeremiad*, 6–7.
10. Qtd. in Cowie, *Stayin' Alive*, 301.
11. Warren Mosler has claimed the Gas Policy Act was actually more effective in taming the inflation of the late 1970s than the radical monetarist policies that Volcker was pursuing at the Fed. See Mosler, *Seven Innocent Deadly Frauds*, 7–8.
12. Owen, "Deregulation in the Trucking Industry."
13. As Blyth points out, the idea that high budget deficits led to high inflation was comprehensively disproved by the co-existence of both massive deficits and low inflation throughout much of Reagan's term. See Blyth, *Great Transformations*, 189.
14. Halpern, "Arkansas and the Defeat of Labor Law Reform," 100.
15. Kiernan, *New Imperialism*, 240.
16. Reagan, "Address Accepting Nomination"; qtd. in Foley, *Front Porch Politics*, 110.
17. Reagan, "Address Accepting Nomination."
18. Steinberg, "The Mass Market Is Splitting Apart"; Reich, "A Culture of Paper Tigers," 95.
19. Reich, "A Culture of Paper Tigers," 99–100, qtd. in Collins, *Transforming America*, 99.
20. Crowdus and Georgakas, "Blue Collar," 35.
21. Crowdus and Georgakas, "Blue Collar," 36.
22. Douglas and Isherwood, *The World of Goods*, 50–51.
23. Mark, "Streets of the Lost," *Streetwise, Life*, "Sixty Pictures that Changed Us Forever."
24. Lewis, "Greed Never Left."
25. Lewis, "The End."
26. Ellis, *American Psycho*, 197
27. Munby, *Under A Bad Sign*, 20. The outrage against rap was expressed by some African Americans themselves. See the following complaint in a 1988 letter to a *Los Angeles Times* music reviewer: "It's horrible enough that as adults we stand by helplessly watching as our black youth become lost in the worst that Babylon

has to offer in the form of rap music. In addition to being loaded with messages of misogyny and terminal materialism, rap also is driving black children further away from their rich African history," Bridget Overton, "Too Much Misogyny For Comfort."

28. Nils Gilman, "The Twin Insurgency."
29. Baker, "Welcome to Fear City."
30. Masters, "Race and the Infernal City," 209.
31. Fisher, *Capitalist Realism, passim.*
32. Heale, "Anatomy of a Scare," 23. Both the scholarly and popular literature on Japan and the Japanese economic incursion into the 1980s is fascinating. In *Japan as Number One: Lessons for America* (1979), for example, Ezra Vogel sought to explain Japanese economic success to an American audience; in *MITI and the Japanese Miracle: The Growth of Industrial Policy, 1925–1975* (1982), Chalmers Johnson gave an in-depth, scholarly account of the key role of Japan's Ministry of International Trade and Industry in nurturing that success. Popular fictions like Michael Crichton's chauvinistic thriller *Rising Sun* (1992) played on American fears related to Japanese economic power, while Richard Katz's *Japan: The System That Soured: The Rise and Fall of the Japanese Economic Miracle* (1998) would later attempt to diagnose the reasons why those fears were never quite realized.
33. Fleeson, "Report from Sheffield," AO2.
34. Morris, *Japan-Bashing,* 46–47; Don Mecoy, "Equipment Damaged."
35. Heale, "Anatomy of a Scare," 28.

3. RHOPOGRAPHY AND REALISM

1. Burke, *Philosophy of Literary Form,* 1.
2. Burke, *Philosophy of Literary Form,* 1.
3. Michaels, "Going Boom," "Beauty of a Social Problem."
4. Michaels, "Beauty of a Social Problem."
5. Michaels, "Beauty of a Social Problem."
6. See Suplee, "Sayonara, Apple Pie"; Hillkirk, "Made in USA."
7. Qtd. in Manchester, "Three Ball Total Equilibrium Tank."
8. Danto, *Transfiguration of the Commonplace, passim.*
9. Brenson, "Shifting Image and Scale," C22.
10. See Foster, "Future of an Illusion"; Perl, "Koons Cult"; Pearlman, *Unpackaging Art,* 143.
11. Pearlman, *Unpackaging Art,* 143.

12. Sorrentino, "Kitsch Into Art," 48.

13. Qtd. in Swenson, "What is Pop Art?" 105.

14. Qtd. in Lippard, *Pop Art*, 10.

15. Bryson, *Looking at the Overlooked*, 61; Gallagher, *Still Life*, 6.

16. Solomon, "The New Art," 92.

17. Qtd. in Lethem, *Fear of Music*, 105.

18. Lethem, *Fear of Music*, 53; Schulman, *The Seventies*, 155.

19. David Byrne, *True Stories*, 15.

20. Qtd. in Phillips, "Crowding out Death"; DeLillo, *White Noise*, 7.

21. Gallagher, *Still Life*, 16.

22. Warhol, qtd. in Madoff, *Pop Art*, 103, 107. My emphasis.

23. DeLillo, *White Noise*, 20.

24. DiPietro, *Conversations*, 71.

25. Marx, *Capital*, 163.

26. For a reading of *White Noise* that foregrounds the "anthropological" aspect of DeLillo's literary aesthetic, see Packer, "At the Dead Center."

27. Danto, *Andy Warhol*, 16.

28. Danto, *Andy Warhol*, 57.

29. Foley, *Front Porch*, 265–66.

30. Cohen, *Consumers' Republic*, 395.

31. Qtd. in Schwenger, *Tears of Things*, 140n.1.

32. Welty, "Introduction," in Eggleston, *Democratic Forest*, 14–15.

33. Welty, "Introduction," in Eggleston, *Democratic Forest*, 15.

34. Foley, *Front Porch*, 266

35. Rebein, *Hicks, Tribes*, 6.

36. Rebein, *Hicks, Tribes*, 20.

37. Rebein, *Hicks, Tribes*, 22–32.

38. La Berge, *Scandals and Abstractions*, 5.

39. Annesley, *Blank Fictions*, 4.

40. Barth's full definition of "minimalism" is typically elaborate: "Minimalism (of one sort or another) is the principle (one of the principles, anyhow) underlying (what I and many another interested observer consider to be perhaps) the most impressive phenomenon on the current (North American, especially the United States) literary scene (the gringo equivalent to el boom in the Latin American novel): I mean the new flowering of the (North) American short story (in particular the kind of terse, oblique, realistic or hyperrealistic, slightly plotted, extrospective, cool-surfaced fiction associated in the last 5 to 10 years with such excellent writers as Frederick Barthelme, Ann Beattie, Raymond

Carver, Bobbie Ann Mason, James Robison, Mary Robison and Tobias Wolff, and both praised and damned under such labels as 'K-Mart realism,' 'hick chic,' 'Diet-Pepsi minimalism' and 'post-Vietnam, post-literary, postmodernist blue-collar neo-early-Hemingwayism.'" Qtd. in Rebein, *Hicks, Tribes*, 33–34.

41. Hoberek, "DeLillo, Minimalist," 103.
42. *New York Times*, "Noted With Pleasure."
43. Eichman, "Raymond Carver."
44. Gentry and Stull, *Conversations*, 212, 130.
45. Barthelme, "Convicted Minimalist."
46. Wilde, *Middle Grounds*, 104–30; Aldridge, *Talents and Technicians*.
47. Carver, "On Writing," in *Collected Stories*, 730.
48. McInerney, "Still, Small Voice."
49. LeClair, "Fiction Chronicle," 86; Saltzman *Understanding Raymond Carver*, 4.
50. Barthes, *Rustle of Language*, 142.
51. The story originally appeared under the title, 'What Is it?', but was subsequently retitled by Carver. I use the revised title here.
52. Carver, *Collected Stories*, 159–60.
53. Rebein, *Hicks, Tribes*, 23.
54. Gallagher, *Carver Country*, 10.
55. Rebein, *Hicks, Tribes*, 22.
56. Carver, *Collected Stories*, 741.
57. Lainsbury, *Carver Chronotope*, 9.
58. Carver, *Collected Stories*, 223.
59. Kaufmann, "Yuppie Postmodernism," 100.
60. Applefield, "Fiction & America: Raymond Carver," in Gentry and Stull, *Conversations with Raymond Carver*, 205.
61. Carver, *Collected Stories*, 292. For the earlier version of the story, see *Beginners*, Carver's original manuscript for *What We Talk About When We Talk About Love*, in *Collected Stories*, 901–908.
62. Carver, *Collected Stories*, 295.
63. Carver, *Collected Stories*, 296.
64. Carver, *Collected Stories*, 294.
65. Carver, *Collected Stories*, 296.
66. Gornick, *Men in My Life*, 147–72.
67. Carver, *Collected Stories*, 440.
68. Gornick, *Men in My Life*, 172.
69. Qtd. in Simmons, *Deep Surfaces*, 137.

70. For a reading of brand names and mass cultural references in Ellis's novel, see
    Annesley, *Blank Fictions*, 84–107. Ellis famously takes the invocation of brand
    names within a paratactic style to extremes in *American Psycho* (1991), in which
    the signature features of the "neo-Realist" aesthetic are used to communicate an
    individual and supposed cultural pathology nauseating in its commitment to
    repetitive surface detail: "I'm wearing a lightweight linen suit with pleated
    trousers, a cotton shirt, a dotted silk tie, all by Valentino Couture, and perfo-
    rated cap-toe leather shoes by Allen-Edmonds. Once inside Harry's we spot
    David Van Patten and Craig McDermott at a table up front. Van Patten is wear-
    ing a double-breasted wool and silk sport coat, button-fly wool and silk trouser
    with inverted pleats by Mario Valentino, a cotton shirt by Gitman Brothers, a
    polka-dot silk tie by Bill Blass and leather shoes from Brooks Brothers.
    McDermott is wearing a woven-linen suit with pleated trousers, a button-down
    cotton and linen shirt by Basile, a silk tie by Joseph Abboud and ostrich loafers
    from Susan Bennis Warren Edwards" (29). Such passages are just as unsettling
    in their own way as the novel's descriptions of extreme violence.
71. Kaufmann, "Yuppie Postmodernism," 95, 97.
72. McInerney, *Bright Lights*, 182.
73. Rilke, *Best*, 103.
74. Carver, *Collected Stories*, 7.
75. Kaufmann, "Yuppie Postmodernism," 101.
76. Hendin, "Fictions of Acquisition," 219; Qtd. in Annesley, *Blank Fictions*, 9.
77. Mason, *In Country*, 3.
78. Hornby, *Contemporary American*, 31.
79. Qtd. in Rebein, *Hicks, Tribes*, 67.
80. Leslie White, for example, has argued how, in Mason's *Shiloh and Other Stories*
    (1982), "the hallowed southern sense of place [is 'surrendered'] to a deadly
    blanketing of popular culture" (71). Although White argues that *In Country*
    represents a transformation in "Mason's fictional world" (76), Joanna Price
    maintains that "rural Kentucky has been largely subsumed" by mass culture in
    the novel (55).
81. Qtd. in Hornby, *Contemporary American Fiction*, 86.
82. Mason, *In Country*, 80.
83. Mason, *In Country*, 70.
84. See, for example, Booth, "Sam's Quest."
85. Mason, *In Country*, 59.
86. Mason, *In Country*, 180.
87. Gentry and Stull, *Conversations with Raymond Carver*, 52.

4. MATTER UNMOORED

1. Collins, *Transforming America*, 157.
2. Buford, "Dirty Realism," 4.
3. Milken, a trader with Drexel Burnham Lambert, was a controversial figure throughout the decade. For an account of his rise and fall, along with that of arbitrageur Ivan Boesky, the model for the era-defining Gordon "Greed is Good" Gekko in Oliver Stone's *Wall Street* (1986), see Stewart *Den of Thieves*.
4. McKibben, *The End of Nature*.
5. Day, Shaw and Ignell, "The Quantitative Distribution"; Inter-Agency Group (Space), "Report on Orbital Debris."
6. Hanley, "Many Beaches," 42.
7. Douglas, *Purity and Danger*, 35. Douglas claimed to have taken this well-known definition of dirt from Lord Chesterfield, but the attribution has been disputed. See Fardon, "Citations Out of Place."
8. McFadden, "Garbage Barge Returns," A1; Firstman et al., *Rush to Burn*; Goff, "The Old Disaster."
9. Bush, "Address Accepting."
10. Frankenberry, "Harbor."
11. Kushner, *Angels in America*, 40. See also Larry Kramer's play, *The Normal Heart* (1985), in which one character relates the harrowing aftermath of the AIDS-related death of his lover in an Arizona hospital: "The hospital doctors refused to examine him to put a cause of death on the death certificate, and without a death certificate, the undertakers wouldn't take him away, and neither would the police. Finally, some orderly comes in and stuffs Albert in a heavy-duty Glad Bag and motions us with his finger to follow and he puts him out in the back alley with the garbage"(60).
12. Cooke, "America's Polluted Waters."
13. See, for example, Wagner, "Medical Wastes."
14. Olson, *Call Me Ishmael*, 11.
15. Beck et al., "Buried Alive"; *Cape Cod Times*, "Editorial."
16. Poore, "America's 'Garbage Crisis.'"
17. Rathje and Murphy, *Rubbish!*, 108.
18. Rathje and Murphy, *Rubbish!*, 108; Reeves, "The Way We Live Now."
19. Summers, "Let Them Eat Toxics."
20. Rathje, "The Garbage Project"; Gould and Schiffer, *Modern Material Culture*.
21. Rathje and Murphy, *Rubbish!*, 130.

22. New York Times, "Suffolk Votes A Bill."
23. Rathje and Murphy, *Rubbish!*, 165.
24. Chase, "Mad Hatter's Dirty Teacup," 585.
25. Arendt, *Human Condition*, 137.
26. Arendt, *Human Condition*, 134.
27. Baudrillard, *System of Objects*, 172.
28. Meikle, *American Plastic*, 8.
29. Meikle, *American Plastic*, 8; Barthes, *Mythologies*, 98.
30. See McKibben *The End of Nature*: "[T]ime is not uniform. The world as we really know it dates back perhaps to the Renaissance. The world as we really, *really* know it dates back to the Industrial Revolution. The world we actually feel comfortable in dates back to perhaps 1945. It was not until after World War II, for instance, that plastics came into widespread use" (5); Rathje and Murphy, *Rubbish!*, 99.
31. Arendt, *The Human Condition*, 137.
32. Beck et al., "Buried Alive," 68, 71–75.
33. Thompson, *Rubbish Theory*, 9.
34. Schapp, *Discovery of the Past*, 18.
35. Schapp, *Discovery of the Past*, 18.
36. Schapp, *Discovery of the Past*, 163.
37. Macaulay, *Motel of the Mysteries*, 90–91, 54.
38. Macauley, *Motel of the Mysteries*, 26.
39. Tomkins, "The Art World," 80.
40. Chase, "Museum Show Inspires Tutmania," C9.
41. Dewey, *In a Dark Time*, 10.
42. Schnabel, *The Sea* (1981), http://www.julianschnabel.com/category/paintings/plate-paintings/plate-paintings-group-2
43. Schnabel, *The Mud in Mudanza* (1982), http://www.julianschnabel.com/category/paintings/plate-paintings/plate-paintings-group-2
44. Schnabel, *Paintings*, 15.
45. Benjamin, *Illuminations*, 249.
46. DeLillo, *Americana*, 375.
47. DeLillo, *Ratner's Star*, 360.
48. DeLillo, *The Names*, 133.
49. DeLillo, *The Names*, 212.
50. DeLillo, *White Noise*, 257.
51. DeLillo, *White Noise*, 290.
52. DeLillo, *White Noise*, 258.

53. DeLillo, *White Noise*, 126–27.
54. DeLillo, "In the Ruins of the Future."
55. Auster, *Invention of Solitude*, 10–11.
56. Mason, *In Country*, 244.
57. DeLillo, *White Noise*, 258.
58. DeLillo, *White Noise*, 259; Lentricchia, "Tales of the Electronic Tribe," 106.
59. Evans, "Taking Out the Trash," 111.
60. DeLillo, *End Zone*, 85.
61. DeLillo, *White Noise*, 6.
62. DeLillo, *White Noise*, 262.
63. DeLillo, *White Noise*, 275.
64. Updike, *Rabbit at Rest*, 349–50.
65. Updike, *Rabbit at Rest*, 361, 349.
66. Updike, *Rabbit at Rest*, 449.
67. McInerney, *Brightness Falls*, 41.
68. McInerney, *Brightness Falls*, 41.
69. Robinson, *Housekeeping*, 5.
70. Robinson, *Housekeeping*, 6.
71. Robinson, *Housekeeping*, 3.
72. Robinson, *Housekeeping*, 116.
73. Robinson, *Housekeeping*, 209.
74. Robinson, *Housekeeping*, 209.
75. Robinson, *Housekeeping*, 211–12.
76. Robinson, *Mother Country*, 235–36. For a more detailed analysis of this work, see Jelfs, "Marilynne Robinson's Turn."
77. DeLillo, *Underworld*, 277–81.
78. DeLillo, *White Noise*, 259.
79. Moore, "Trashed'; Chris Jordan, *Midway: Message from the Gyre 2009–Present*, available at http://chrisjordan.com/gallery/midway/#CF000313%2018x24
80. Zalasiewicz et al., "Geological Cycle."
81. Qtd. in Abbey, *Desert Solitaire*, 165.

5. AT PEACE WITH THINGS?

1. Shapiro, "What's Wrong."
2. Bush, "Nomination Acceptance Address."
3. Petroski, *Pencil*, 55.
4. Petroski, *Pencil*, 11.

5. Gessen, *Literary Men*, 131.
6. Cole, "Call of Things," 107.
7. Cole, "Call of Things," 115.
8. Thoreau, *I to Myself*, 391.
9. Thoreau, *I to Myself*, 389
10. For an indispensable overview of the field and its development in its American context, see Schlereth, *Material Culture Studies*.
11. Other scholars have noted the affinities between Petroski and Baker. Arthur Saltzman cites Petroski's subsequent work, *The Evolution of Useful Things* (1994), as a way of introducing Baker's own interest in the everyday. Jeffrey L. Meikle has also commented on the affinities between Petroski's work and Baker's, noting in a review of Petroski's *Small Things Considered* (2003), for example, that *The Mezzanine* is "listed in Petroski's bibliography but not mentioned in the text." See Saltzman, *Understanding Nicholson Baker*, 3; Meikle, "Ghosts in the Machine," 389, n.3.
12. Laurence and Strauss, "Interview with Nicholson Baker."
13. Baker, *U and I*, 19.
14. Baker, *Mezzanine*, 4–5.
15. Baker, *Mezzanine*, 32
16. Norman, *Everyday Things*, 11–12.
17. Baker, *Room Temperature*, 29.
18. Chambers, "Escalator Principle," 772; Saltzman, *Understanding Nicholson Baker*, 181.
19. Baker, *U and I*, 72.
20. Baker, *U and I*, 73.
21. Baker, *The Mezzanine*, 8.
22. Baker, *The Mezzanine*, 47.
23. Baker, *The Size of Thoughts*, 4.
24. Baker, *The Size of Thoughts*, 10.
25. Baker, *The Size of Thoughts*, 9.
26. Laurence and Strauss, "Interview with Nicholson Baker."
27. Baker, *The Size of Thoughts*, 22.
28. Graham Harmon qtd in Cole, "Obscure Objects," 384.
29. Baker, *The Size of Thoughts*, 22.
30. Baker, *The Mezzanine*, 129, 131
31. Benjamin, "Unpacking My Library"; Csikszentmihalyi and Rochberg-Halton, *Meaning of Things*, 15.
32. Marcuse, *One-Dimensional Man*, 10.

33. Baker, *U and I*, 41–3; *Room Temperature*, 20.
34. James, *Writings*, 154.
35. Chambers, "Escalator Principle," 777.
36. Baker, *The Mezzanine*, 129.
37. For a discussion of *The Mezzanine* and Baker's later novel, *The Fermata*, in relation to what Graham Thompson has characterized as "a shift from the culture of the Organization Man to the culture of the Individualized Corporation" (134), see Thompson, *Male Sexuality*, 133–64.
38. James, *Psychology*, 291.
39. Marcuse, *One-Dimensional Man*, 9.
40. James, *Psychology*, 290, 289.
41. James, *Psychology*, 289.
42. Laurence and Strauss, "An Interview with Nicholson Baker."
43. Saltzman, *Understanding Nicholson Baker*, 79.
44. Baker, *The Mezzanine*, 4.
45. Baker, *The Mezzanine*, 4–5.
46. Jeffrey L. Meikle referred to this footnote when addressing the Design History Society on the occasion of its twentieth anniversary, praising it as a "*tour de force* of material deduction and the best writing on design I know." Meikle's larger point about *The Mezzanine* was that, in a time when there had been a general shift away from what Meikle calls the "Frankfurt School-inspired" view of consumption, Baker's novel provided an example of an alternative way of writing about design and consumption. Meikle, "Material Virtues," 197, 195.
47. Baker, *The Mezzanine*, 5.
48. Baker, *The Size of Thoughts*, 8. As Leo Marx shows in *The Machine In The Garden* (1964), the idea of "progress" through technology lies at the heart of a particularly long-running discussion in the argument about things in American life. See Marx, *Machine in the Garden*, 181–94.
49. Baker, *The Mezzanine*, 132.
50. Baker, *The Mezzanine*, 11
51. Baker, *The Mezzanine*, 132–33.
52. Baker, *Size of Thoughts*, 18.
53. Baker, *Size of Thoughts*, 18–19.
54. Baker, *Room Temperature*, 115–16.
55. Baker, *Room Temperature*, 115.
56. Bloom, *American Mind*, 84, 85.
57. Lukács, *European Realism*, 8–9.

58. Baker, *U and I*, 59.
59. Baker, *U and I*, 58–59.
60. Reagan, "Remarks and Question-and-Answer."
61. See Dean, *Democracy and other Neoliberal Fantasies*, passim.
62. Baker, *Room Temperature*, 47.
63. Baker, *The Mezzanine*, 27.
64. Baker, *Room Temperature*, 46.
65. Baker, *Room Temperature*, 46–47.
66. Baker, *Checkpoint*, 62.
67. Baker, *Checkpoint*, 74.

6. ALL THAT FALL

1. Boeing, "100 Years of Boeing."
2. SIPRI, "Arms Database."
3. Rogin, "Make My Day!"
4. Jameson, *Postmodernism*, 5.
5. Office of Management and Budget, *Historical Tables*, Table 3.1.
6. On the erosion of the corporate tax base, see, for example, the 2011 Congressional Research Service report quoted in a Memorandum from the US Senate's Permanent Subcommittee on Investigations during its 2013 hearings on "Offshore Profit Shifting and the US Tax Code," which showed how corporate tax revenues fell from a 1952 high of "32.1% of all federal tax revenue" to a meager "8.9% of federal tax revenue" at the time the CRS report was written. Qtd. in Levin and McCain, "Offshore Profit Shifting."
7. Cox, "Pentagon Tells Congress to Stop."
8. Petroski, *Small Things Considered*, 129–37.
9. Mazzucato, *Entrepreneurial State*, 73ff.
10. Clare, *Vietnam Syndrome*, 1.
11. See Didion, "Salvador"; Danner, *El Mozote*.
12. Clare, *Beyond the Vietnam Syndrome*, 95, 83.
13. Gibson, *Perfect War*, 3.
14. Jeffords, *Remasculinization of America*, 7.
15. Griswold, "Veterans Memorial," 691.
16. Marling and Silberman, "Statue Near the Wall," 8.
17. Marling and Silberman, "Statue Near the Wall," 10. Marita Sturken dissents from the idea that the memorial lacks narrative content, arguing that the arrangement of names in chronological order of death itself "provides" the

structure "with a narrative framework." See Sturken, "The Wall, the Screen," 127–28.

18. Reagan, "Remarks at Dedication Ceremonies."
19. Lomperis, *Reading the Wind*, 6–7, 32, 37.
20. O'Brien, *The Things They Carried*, 157.
21. O'Brien, *The Things They Carried*, 157.
22. Griswold, "Veterans Memorial," 708.
23. O' Brien, *The Things They Carried*, 3–4.
24. Marling and Silberman, "Statue Near the Wall," 14, 15.
25. O'Brien, *The Things They Carried*, 179–80.
26. Silbergleid, "Making Things Present," 133.
27. Cather, "The Novel," 834.
28. Buchanan, *Vietnam Zippos*, 118. See also Walters, "Vietnam Zippos," an anthropological study in which Walters likens the Zippos to "Pleistocene axes or Grecian urn shards" and notes that while hundreds of thousands of Zippos were available to buy from Saigon tourist markets when he was researching the phenomenon in the 1990s, most were "copies, or fakes" (65, 70).
29. O' Brien, *The Things They Carried*, 4.
30. O' Brien, *The Things They Carried*, 14.
31. O'Brien, *Cacciato*, 198.
32. Chen, "Unraveling," 85.
33. The references are to "Born in the USA" and "My Hometown," the opening and closing tracks on Springsteen's *Born in the USA*.
34. Harvey, *History of Neoliberalism*, xxv.
35. For a discussion of the Strategic Defense Initiative (SDI) and the role it played in Reagan's waging of the Cold War in the 1980s, see Collins, *Transforming America*, 197–204.
36. O'Brien, *The Things They Carried*, 13.
37. O'Brien, *The Things They Carried*, 4.
38. O'Brien, *The Things They Carried*, 4.
39. O'Brien, *The Things They Carried*, 7.
40. Silbergleid, "Making Things Present," 135.
41. O'Brien, *The Things They Carried*, 5, 13.
42. O'Brien, *The Things They Carried*, 18.
43. Chen, "Unraveling," 87.
44. O'Brien, *The Things They Carried*, 6–7.
45. O'Brien, *If I Die*, 29; *Cacciato*, 286.
46. O'Brien, *The Things They Carried*, 63.

47. O'Brien, *The Things They Carried*, 75–76.

48. O'Brien, *Cacciato*, 82–83.

49. O'Brien, *The Things They Carried*, 163.

50. O'Brien, *The Things They Carried*, 186.

51. O'Brien, *The Things They Carried*, 168.

52. O'Brien, *The Things They Carried*, 226.

53. O'Brien, *The Things They Carried*, 233.

54. O'Brien, *The Things They Carried*, 4–5.

55. Walters, "Vietnam Zippos," 62; Biedler, "Last Huey," 6.

56. Herr, *Dispatches*, 20.

57. Herr, *Dispatches*, 16.

58. Herr, *Dispatches*, 18–19.

59. Morrison, *Song of Solomon*, 15.

60. Morrison, *Song of Solomon*, 322.

61. Morrison, *Song of Solomon*, 180.

62. Phillips, *Machine Dreams*, 267.

63. Phillips, *Machine Dreams*, 286.

64. Phillips, *Machine Dreams*, 331.

65. O'Brien, *The Things They Carried*, 200.

66. O'Brien, *The Things They Carried*, 205. Like the metaphor of falling, the metaphor of flight is also deployed in *Going After Cacciato*. In the novel's opening chapter, in which Cacciato's supposed intent to leave the war and walk to Paris is revealed, Paul Berlin watches through binoculars as his fellow soldier stands on a hilltop and waves his arms: "Very slowly, deliberately, Cacciato was spreading his arms out as if to show them empty, opening them up like wings, palm down" (11); "the arms kept flapping, faster now and less deliberate, wide-spanning winging motions—flying, Paul Berlin suddenly realized. Awkward, unpracticed, but still flying (12)."

67. O' Brien, *The Things They Carried*, 191, 209.

68. O' Brien, *The Things They Carried*, 32.

69. O' Brien, *The Things They Carried*, 69.

70. O' Brien, *The Things They Carried*, 130.

71. This, of course, is why the flight of fancy—walking to Paris—supposedly pursued by Cacciato in *Going After Cacciato* is in its own way so emblematic of the soldier's predicament: it is not just that to travel so far is in itself fantastical, but that to follow personal whims of any sort out of and away from the brutality and senselessness of the war is impossible. One of the only other alternatives is that taken by Rat Kiley in *The Things They Carried*, when he literally shoots

himself in the foot as a way of ensuring his flight out of the war (218), an act that is as much an abdication as an exercise of agency.

72. Clare, "Beyond the Vietnam Syndrome," 2–3.
73. Bush, "Remarks to Armed Forces."
74. O' Brien, *The Things They Carried*, 166.
75. O' Brien, *The Things They Carried*, 187.
76. Kurth, "American Way of War," 71.

CONCLUSION

1. Kepel and Milelli, *Al-Qaeda*, 156.
2. Bacevich, *America's War*, passim.
3. Thompson, *Oil*, 4.
4. Witko, "How Wall Street."
5. Gramsci, *Prison Notebooks*, 556.
6. DiPietro, *Conversations*, 96–97.
7. Ponce de Leon, "The New Historiography," 310.
8. Douglas and Isherwood, *World of Goods*, 50–51.
9. Csikszentmihalyi and Rochberg-Halton, *Meaning of Things*, 235.
10. DeLillo, *Underworld*, 827.
11. Powers, *Gain*, 347–48.
12. Powers, *Gain*, 348.
13. Brown, "Thing Theory," 16.
14. Powers, *Gain*, 347.
15. Cole, "The Call of Things," 108–109.
16. Frank, *Frank*, 10–11.
17. Thompson, *Oil*, 4.
18. Trump, "Victory Rally."

Bibliography

Adams, William. "Vietnam Screen Wars." In *Culture in an Age of Money*, edited by Nicolaus Mills, 156–174. Chicago: Ivan R. Dee, 1990.

Adler, Margot. *Drawing Down the Moon: Witches, Druids, Goddess-Worshippers and Other Pagans in America Today*. Boston: Beacon Press, 1986.

Aldridge, John. *Talents and Technicians: Literary Chic and the New Assembly-Line Fiction*. New York: Scribner's, 1992.

Alter, Robert. *Pen of Iron: American Prose and the King James Bible*. Princeton: Princeton University Press, 2010.

Althusser, Louis "Ideology and Ideological State Apparatuses." In *Literary Theory: An Anthology*, edited by Julie Rivkin and Michael Ryan, 294–304. Malden and Oxford: Blackwell, 1998.

Anderson, Benedict. *Imagined Communities: Reflections on the Origin and Spread of Nationalism*. London and New York: Verso, 1989.

Anderson, Perry. "Imperium." *New Left Review* 83 (September–October 2013). https://newleftreview.org/II/83/perry-anderson-imperium.

Annesley, James. *Blank Fictions: Consumerism, Culture, and the Contemporary American Novel*. London: Pluto Press, 1998.

Appadurai, Arjun. *The Social Life of Things: Commodities in Cultural Perspective*. Cambridge and New York: Cambridge University Press, 1986.

Arendt, Hannah. *The Human Condition*. Chicago: University of Chicago Press, 1998.

Arendt, Hannah. *The Origins of Totalitarianism*. London: Andre Deutsch, 1986.

Auster, Paul. *The Invention of Solitude*. New York: SUN, 1982.

Bacevich, Andrew. *America's War For the Greater Middle East: A Military History*. New York: Random House, 2016.

Bacevich, Andrew, ed. *The Long War: A New History of U.S. National Security Policy Since World War II*. New York: Columbia University Press, 2007.

Baker, Kevin. "'Welcome to Fear City': The Inside Story of New York's Civil War, 40 Years On." *The Guardian*, May 18, 2015. https://www.theguardian.com

/cities/2015/may/18/welcome-to-fear-city-the-inside-story-of- new-yorks-civil -war-40-years-on.

Baker, Nicholson. *Checkpoint.* London: Chatto and Windus, 2004.

Baker, Nicholson. *The Fermata.* London: Vintage, 1994.

Baker, Nicholson. *Human Smoke: The Beginnings of World War II, the End of Civilization.* New York: Simon and Schuster, 2008.

Baker, Nicholson. *The Mezzanine.* London: Granta, 1998.

Baker, Nicholson. *Room Temperature.* London: Granta, 1998.

Baker, Nicholson. *The Size of Thoughts: Essays and Other Lumber.* London: Vintage, 1997.

Baker, Nicholson. *U and I.* London: Granta, 1998.

Baker, Nicholson. *Vox.* London: Granta, 1998.

Barth, John. *The Friday Book: Essays and Other Nonfiction.* Baltimore and London: The Johns Hopkins University Press, 1984.

Barthelme, Frederick. *Moon Deluxe.* London: Penguin, 1984.

Barthelme, Frederick. "On Being Wrong: Convicted Minimalist Spills The Beans." *New York Times,* April 3, 1988. http://www.nytimes.com/1988/04/03/books/ on-being-wrong-convicted-minimalist-spills-beans.html.

Barthes, Roland. *Mythologies.* Translated by Annette Lavers. London: Vintage, 2000.

Barthes, Roland. *The Rustle of Language.* Translated by Richard Howard. Oxford: Basil Blackwell, 1986.

Baudrillard, Jean. *America.* Translated by Chris Turner. London: Verso, 1988.

Baudrillard, Jean. *Simulacra and Simulation.* Translated by Sheila Glaser. Ann Arbor: University of Michigan Press, 1994.

Baudrillard, Jean. *The System of Objects.* Translated by James Benedict. London: Verso, 2005.

Bauman, Zygmunt. *Liquid Modernity.* Cambridge: Polity Press, 2000.

Bawer, Bruce. "The Literary Brat Pack." In *The Eighties: A Reader,* edited by Gilbert T. Sewall, 207–216. Reading, MA: Perseus., 1997.

Beck, Melinda, et al. "Buried Alive." *Newsweek,* November 27, 1989.

Bell, Martin, dir. *Streetwise.* Bear Creek, 1984.

Benedict, Ruth. *The Chrysanthemum and the Sword: Patterns of Japanese Culture.* Boston: Houghton Mifflin, 1989.

Benford, Gregory. *Artifact.* London: Orbit. 2001.

Bennett, Jane. *Vibrant Matter: A Political Ecology of Things.* Durham, NC and London: Duke University Press, 2010.

Benjamin, Walter. *Illuminations*. Translated by Harry Zorn. London: Pimlico, 1999.

Boeing. "100 Years of Boeing." http://www.boeing.com/resources/boeingdotcom/company/general_info/pdf/boeing_overview.pdf

Bercovitch, Sacvan. *The American Jeremiad*. Madison: University of Wisconsin Press, 1978.

Bercovitch, Sacvan. "The Rites of Assent: Rhetoric, Ritual, and the Ideology of American Consensus." In *The American Self: Myth, Ideology, and Popular Culture*, edited by Sam B. Girgus, 5–42. Albuquerque: University of New Mexico Press, 1981.

Berman, Marshall. *All That Is Solid Melts Into Air: The Experience of Modernity*. London: Penguin, 1988.

Bibby, Michael, ed. *The Vietnam War and Postmodernity*. Amherst: University of Massachusetts Press, 1999.

Biedler, Philip. "The Last Huey." In *The Vietnam War and Postmodernity*, edited by Michael Bibby, 3–16. Amherst, MA: University of Massachusetts Press, 1999.

Bilton, Alan. "Matter and Mammon: Fiction in the Age of Reagan." In *The 1980s: A Critical and Transitional Decade*, edited by Kimberly R. Moffitt and Duncan A. Campbell, 417–37. Lanham: Lexington, 2011.

Bloom, Allan. *The Closing of the American Mind: How Higher Education Has Failed Democracy and Impoverished the Souls of Today's Students*. New York: Simon & Schuster, 1987.

Blyth, Mark. *Great Transformations: Economic Ideas and Institutional Change in the Twentieth Century*. New York: Cambridge University Press, 2002.

Boddy, Kasia. "Companion-Souls of the Short Story: Anton Chekhov and Raymond Carver." *Scottish-Slavonic Review* 18 (1992): 105–12.

Bonn, Maria S. "Can Stories Save Us? Tim O'Brien and the Efficacy of the Text." *Critique* 36, no.1 (1994): 2–16.

Booth, David. "Sam's Quest, Emmett's Wound: Grail Motifs in Bobbie Ann Mason's Portrait of America After Vietnam." *The Southern Literary Journal* 23, no. 2 (1991): 98–109.

Boxall, Peter. *Don DeLillo: The Possibility of Fiction*. London: Routledge, 2006.

Brenson, Michael. "Shifting Image and Scale." *New York Times*, December 2, 1988: C22.

Brewer, Jan and Frank Trentmann. *Consuming Cultures, Global Perspectives: Historical Trajectories, Transnational Exchanges*. Oxford and New York: Berg, 2006.

Brogan, Hugh. *The Penguin History of the USA*. London: Penguin, 2001.

Brown, Bill. "How to Do Things with Things (A Toy Story)." *Critical Inquiry* 24, no.4 (1998): 935–64.

Brown, Bill. "The Matter of Materialism." In *Material Powers: Cultural Studies, History and the Material Turn*, edited by Tony Bennett and Patrick Joyce, 60–78. London and New York: Routledge, 2010.

Brown, Bill. "The Secret Life of Things: Virginia Woolf and the Matter of Modernism." *Modernism/Modernity* 6, no. 2 (1999): 1–28.

Brown, Bill. *A Sense of Things: The Object Matter of American Literature*. Chicago and London: University of Chicago Press, 2003.

Brown, Bill, ed. *Things*. Chicago and London: Chicago University Press, 2004.

Brown, Bill. "Thing Theory." *Critical Inquiry* 28, no. 1 (2001): 1–22.

Brown, Wendy. *Edgework: Critical Essays on Knowledge and Politics*. Princeton and Oxford, Princeton University Press, 2005.

Browne, Thomas. *The Major Works*. Harmondsworth: Penguin, 1977.

Bryson, Norman. *Looking at the Overlooked: Essays on Still Life Painting*. London: Reaktion, 1990.

Buchanan, Sherry. *Vietnam Zippos: American Soldiers' Engravings and Stories 1965–1973*. Chicago: The University of Chicago Press, 2007.

Buford, Bill. "Dirty Realism: New Writing from America." *Granta* 8 (1983): 4–5.

Burke, Kenneth. *Philosophy of Literary Form*. Berkeley: University of California Press, 1973.

Burgin, Angus. *The Great Persuasion: Reinventing Free Markets since the Depression.* Cambridge, MA and London: Harvard University Press, 2012.

Bush, George. "Address Accepting the Presidential Nomination at the Republican National Convention in New Orleans," August 18, 1988. http://www.presidency.ucsb.edu/ws/?pid=25955.

Bush, George. "Inaugural Address," January 10, 1989. http://www.presidency.ucsb.edu/ws/?pid=16610.

Bush, George. "Radio Address to United States Armed Forces Stationed in the Persian Gulf Region," March 2, 1991. http://www.presidency.ucsb.edu/ws/?pid=19355.

Butler, Robert Olen. *Countrymen of Bones*. London: Vintage, 1998.

Byrne, David. *True Stories*. New York: Viking Penguin, 1986.

Calloway, Catherine. "'How to Tell a True War Story': Metafiction in *The Things They Carried*." *Critique* 36 no. 4 (1995): 249–58.

Carlin, George. "Stuff" (1986), Recording of live performance https://www.youtube.com/watch?v=ryy_QgDXnX4

Carson, Cary. "Material Culture History: The Scholarship Nobody Knows." In *American Material Culture: The Shape of the Field*, edited by Anne Smart Martin and J. Ritchie Garrison, 401–428. Winterthur: Winterthur Museum, 1997.

Carter, Jimmy. "Address to the Nation on Energy and National Goals," July 15, 1979. http://www.presidency.ucsb.edu/ws/?pid=32596.

Carter, Jimmy. "State of the Union Address Delivered Before a Joint Session of the Congress." January 23, 1980. http://www.presidency.ucsb.edu/ws/?pid=33079.

Carter, Jimmy. *White House Diary*. New York: Picador, 2010.

Carver, Raymond. *Collected Stories*. New York: Library of America, 2009.

Castillo, Greg. "Domesticating the Cold War: Household Consumption as Propaganda in Marshall Plan Germany." *Journal of Contemporary History* 40, no.2 (2005): 261–88.

Castro, Janice. "The Simple Life: Goodbye to having it all." *Time*, April 8, 1991. http://content.time.com/time/magazine/article/0,9171,972670-7,00.html.

Cather, Willa. *Stories, Poems, and Other Writings*. New York: Library of America, 1992.

Chambers, Ross. "Meditation and the Escalator Principle (on Nicholson Baker's *The Mezzanine*)," *Modern Fiction Studies* 40, no. 4 (1994): 765-806.

Chase, Marilyn. "Museum Show Inspires Tutmania." *The New York Times* March 8, 1978, p. C9.

Chase, Stuart. "The Mad Hatter's Dirty Teacup." *Harper's* Apr 1930: 580–86.

Chen, Tina. "'Unraveling the Deeper Meaning': Exile and the Embodied Poetics of Displacement in Tim O'Brien's *The Things They Carried*." *Contemporary Literature* 39, no.1 (1998): 77–98.

Clare, Michael. *Beyond the "Vietnam Syndrome": U.S. Interventionism in the 1980s*. Washington, DC: The Institute for Policy Studies, 1981.

Clune, Michael. *American Literature and the Free Market 1945–2000*. New York: Cambridge University Press, 2010.

Cohen, Lizabeth. *A Consumer's Republic: The Politics of Mass Consumption in Postwar America*. New York: Knopf, 2003.

Cole, Andrew. "The Call of Things: A Critique of Object-Oriented Ontologies." *Minnesota Review* 80 (2013): 106–18.

Cole, Andrew. "Those Obscure Objects of Desire." *Artforum* (Summer 2015): 318–23.

Collins, Robert M. "David Potter's *People of Plenty* and the Recycling of Consensus History." *Reviews in American History* 16, no. 2 (1988): 321–35.

Collins, Robert M. *More: The Politics of Economic Growth in Postwar America*. Oxford: Oxford University Press, 2000.

Collins, Robert M. *Transforming America: Politics and Culture during the Reagan Years*. New York: Columbia University Press, 2007.

Christopher, Columbus. "Letter to Luis de Santangel Regarding the First Voyage." In *The Norton Anthology of American Literature Vol A*, edited by Nina Baym, 32. New York: Norton, 2007.

Cooke, Alistair. "America's Polluted Waters." *Letter from America* (BBC Radio), July 29, 1988. http://www.bbc.co.uk/programmes/articles/t08HyN6h55P3zTQ3Fw-cpfQ/ americas-polluted-waters-29-july-1988

Coplans, John. "Pop Art, USA." In *Pop Art: A Critical History*, edited by Stephen Henry Madoff, 97–102. Berkeley, Los Angeles, and London: University of California Press, 1997.

Corn, Wanda. M. *The Great American Thing: Modern Art and National Identity 1915–1935*. Berkeley and London: University of California Press, 1999.

Cowart, David. *Don DeLillo: The Physics of Language*. Athens: The University of Georgia Press, 2002.

Cowie, Jefferson. *Capital Moves: RCA's 70-Year Quest for Cheap Labor*. Ithaca: Cornell University Press, 1999.

Cowie, Jefferson. *Stayin' Alive: The 1970s and the Last Days of the Working Class*. London and New York: The New Press, 2010.

Cox, Matthew. "Pentagon Tells Congress to Stop Buying Equipment it Doesn't Need." *Military.com*, January 28, 2015. http://www.military.com/daily-news/2015/01/28/pentagon-tells-congress-to-stop-buying-equipment-it-doesnt-need.html.

Crowdus, Gary and Dan Georgakas, "Blue Collar: An Interview with Paul Schrader." *Cineaste* 8 (Winter 1977–78): 34–59.

Crowley, David and Jane Pavitt. *Cold War Modern: Design 1945–1970*. London: V&A Publishing, 2008.

Csikszentmihalyi, Mihayli and Eugene Rochberg-Halton. *The Meaning of Things: Domestic Symbols and the Self*. Cambridge and New York: Cambridge University Press, 1981.

Cusset, François. *French Theory: How Foucault, Derrida, Deleuze, & Co. Transformed the Intellectual Life of the United States*. Translated by Jeff Fort. Minneapolis and London: Minnesota University Press, 2008.

Danner, Mark. *The Massacre at El Mozote: A Parable of the Cold War*. New York: Vintage, 1994.

Danto, Arthur C. *Andy Warhol*. New Haven: Yale University Press, 2009.

Danto, Arthur C. *The Transfiguration of the Commonplace.* Cambridge, MA: Harvard University Press, 1981.

Dario, Rubén. "To Roosevelt." In *Keen's Latin American Civilization: History and Society, 1492 to the Present,* edited by Benjamin Keen, Robert Buffington, and Lila Caimari, 503–505.

Davies, William. "Reasons for Corbyn." *London Review of Books* 39, no. 14 (July 13, 2017), https://www.lrb.co.uk/v39/n14/william-davies/reasons-for-corbyn

Day, Robert H., David G. Shaw, and Steve E. Ignell. "The Quantitative Distribution and Characteristics of Neuston Plastic in the North Pacific Ocean, 1985–1988." In *Proceedings of the Second International Conference on Marine Debris,* edited by Richard S. Shomura and Mary Lynne Godfrey, 247–66. Honolulu: Conference Proceedings, 1990.

Dean, Jodi. *Democracy and other Neoliberal Fantasies.* Durham, NC and London: Duke University Press, 2009.

Debord, Guy. *The Society of the Spectacle.* Translated by David Nicholson-Smith. New York: Zone Books, 1994.

Deetz, James. *In Small Things Forgotten: The Archaeology of Early American Life.* Garden City, NY: Anchor, 1977.

DeLillo, Don. *Americana.* London: Penguin, 1990.

DeLillo, Don. "In the Ruins of the Future: Reflections on Terror and Loss in the Shadow of September." *Harper's* December 2001, 33–40.

DeLillo, Don. *The Names.* London: Picador, 1999.

DeLillo, Don. *Players.* London: Vintage, 1991.

DeLillo, Don. *Ratner's Star.* New York: Alfred A. Knopf, 1976.

DeLillo, Don. *Underworld.* London: Picador, 1999.

DeLillo, Don. *White Noise.* London: Picador, 1999.

Dewey, Joseph. *Beyond Grief and Nothing: A Reading of Don DeLillo.* Columbia, SC.: University of South Carolina, 2006.

Dewey, Joseph. *In a Dark Time: The Apocalyptic Temper in the American Novel of the Nuclear Age.* West Lafayette: Purdue University Press, 1990.

Didion, Joan. "Salvador." In *We Tell Ourselves Stories In Order To Live: Collected Non-Fiction,* 343–410. New York: Everyman's Library, 2006.

Diggins, John Patrick. *Ronald Reagan: Fate, Freedom, and the Making of History.* New York and London: Norton, 2007.

Dimock, Wai-Chee. *Through Other Continents: American Literature Across Deep Time.* Princeton: Princeton University Press, 2006.

DiPietro, Thomas, ed. *Conversations with Don DeLillo.* Jackson: University Press of Mississippi, 2005.

Doris, Sara. *Pop Art and the Contest over American Culture*. New York: Cambridge University Press, 2007.

Doss, Erika. "War, Memory, and the Public Mediation of Affect: The National World War II Memorial and American Imperialism." *Memory Studies* 1 no. 2 (2008): 227–50.

Douglas, Mary. *Purity and Danger: An Analysis of Concepts of Pollution and Taboo*. London and Henley: Routledge and Kegan Paul, 1966.

Douglas, Mary and Baron Isherwood. *The World of Goods: Towards an Anthropology of Consumption*. London and New York: Routledge, 1996.

Dower, John. *Embracing Defeat: Japan in the Wake of World War II*. New York: Norton/The New Press, 1999.

Durose, Lisa. "Marilynne Robinson: A Bibliography." *ANQ: A Quarterly Journal of Short Articles, Notes and Reviews* 10, no. 1 (1997): 31–46.

Duvall, John, ed. *The Cambridge Companion to Don DeLillo*. Cambridge: Cambridge University Press, 2008.

Eagleton, Terry. *After Theory*. New York: Basic Books, 2003.

Eggleston, William. *The Democratic Forest*. Göttingen: Steidl, 2015.

Ehrman, John. *The Eighties: America in the Age of Reagan*. New Haven: Yale University Press, 2005.

Eichman, Erich. "Will Raymond Carver Please be Quiet, Please?" *The New Criterion*, November 1983. http://www.newcriterion.com/articles.cfm/ Will-Raymond-Carver-please-be-quiet--please--6329

Ellis, Bret Easton. *American Psycho*. London: Picador, 2006.

Ellis, Bret Easton. *Less Than Zero*. London: Picador, 1986.

Emerson, Ralph Waldo. *The Portable Emerson*. London: Penguin, 1981.

Evans, David. "Taking Out the Trash: Don DeLillo's Underworld, Liquid Modernity, and the End of Garbage." *Cambridge Quarterly* 35, no. 2 (2006): 103–32.

Fardon, Richard. "Citations out of Place, or Lord Palmerston Goes Viral in the Nineteenth Century but Gets Lost in the Twentieth." *Anthropology Today* 29, no. 1 (2013): 25–27.

Fender, Stephen. *The American Poem: An Annotated Selection*. London: Edward Arnold, 1977.

Fender, Stephen. *Sea Changes: British Emigration and American Literature*. Cambridge: Cambridge University Press, 1992.

Firstman, Richard C. et al., *Rush to Burn: Solving America's Garbage Crisis?* Washington, DC and Covelo: Island Press, 1989.

Fisher, Mark. *Capitalist Realism: Is There No Alternative?* Winchester, UK and Washington, DC: Zero Books, 2009.

Fleeson, Lucinda. "Report from Sheffield, ALA.—From Success Story to Casualty." *Philadelphia Inquirer,* February 28, 1982, A02.

Foley, Michael Stewart. *Front Porch Politics: The Forgotten Heyday of American Activism in the 1970s and 1980s.* New York: Hill and Wang, 2013.

Fordham, Benjamin O. "Paying for Global Power: Assessing the Costs and Benefits of Postwar U.S. Military Spending." In *The Long War: A New History of U.S. National Security Policy Since World War II,* edited by Andrew Bacevich, 371–404. New York: Columbia University Press, 2007.

Foster, Hal. "The Future of an Illusion, or The Contemporary Artist as Cargo Cultist." In *Endgame: Reference and Simulation in Recent Painting and Sculpture,* edited by David Joselit and Elisabeth Sussman, 91–105. Cambridge, MA. And London: The MIT Press, 1986.

Foucault, Michel. *The Birth of Biopolitics: Lectures at the Collège de France, 1978–79.* Translated by Graham Burchell. Basingstoke and New York: Palgrave Macmillan, 2008.

Frank, Barney. *Frank: A Life in Politics from the Great Society to Same-Sex Marriage.* New York: Farrar, Straus and Giroux, 2015.

Frankenberry, Dennis., dir. *Harbor.* The Living Room Candidate: Presidential Campaign Commercials 1952–2008, Museum of the Moving Image. www.livingroomcandidate.org/commercials/1988/harbor.

Frost, Randy O. *Stuff: Compulsive Hoarding and the Meaning of Things.* Boston: Houghton Mifflin, 2010.

Frow, John. "A Pebble, A Camera, A Man." In *Things,* edited by Bill Brown, 246–361. Chicago and London: University of Chicago Press, 2004.

Fukuyama, Francis. "The End of History?" *National Interest* (Summer 1989): 3–18.

Galehouse, Maggie. "Their Own Private Idaho: Transience in Marilynne Robinson's *Housekeeping.*" *Contemporary Literature* 41, no. 1 (2000): 117–37.

Gallagher, Ann. *Still Life.* London: British Council, 2002.

Gallagher, Tess. "Carver Country." In *Carver Country: The World of Raymond Carver,* edited by Bob Adelman and Tess Gallagher, 8–19. London: Pan Books, 1991.

Gallup. "What is Your Religious Preference? [1948–2105]." http://www.gallup.com/poll/1690/religion.aspx

Gardner, Thomas. *A Door Ajar: Contemporary Writers and Emily Dickinson.* Oxford and New York: Oxford University Press, 2006.

Gentry, Marshall Bruce and William L. Stull, eds. *Conversations with Raymond Carver.* Jackson and London: University Press of Mississippi, 1990.

Gessen, Keith. *All the Sad Young Literary Men.* New York: Penguin, 2009.

Gibson, James William. *The Perfect War: Technowar in Vietnam.* Boston and New York: Atlantic Monthly Press, 1986.

Gibson, William. *Neuromancer.* London: Voyager, 1995.

Gideon, Sigfried. *Mechanization Takes Command: A Contribution to Anonymous History.* New York: Oxford University Press, 1948.

Gilman, Nils. "The Twin Insurgency." *The American Interest* 9, no. 6 (June 15, 2014). http://www.the-american-interest.com/2014/06/15/the-twin-insurgency/

Glickman, Leo, ed. *Consumer Society and American History: A Reader.* Ithaca: Cornell University Press, 1999.

Goff, Liz. "The Old Disaster: Queens' Garbage Standoff," *Queens Tribune* February 8, 2001.

Gornick, Vivian. *The Men in My Life.* Cambridge, MA. and London: MIT Press, 2008.

Gould, Richard A. and Michael B. Schiffer, eds. *Modern Material Culture: The Archaeology of Us.* New York and London: Academic Press, 1981.

Gramsci, Antonio. *Selections from the Prison Notebooks.* London: Electric Book Company, 2001.

Griswold, Charles. "The Vietnam Veterans Memorial and the Washington Mall: Philosophical Thoughts on Political Iconography." *Critical Inquiry* 12, no. 4 (1986): 688–719.

Grunenburg, Christoph and Max Hollein. *Shopping: A Century of Art and Consumer Culture.* Ostfildern-Ruit: Hatje Canze, 2002.

Hacker, Jacob. and Paul Pierson. *Winner-Take-All-Politics: How Washington Made the Rich Richer—And Turned Its Back on the Middle Class.* New York: Simon and Schuster, 2010.

Haddow, Robert. *Pavilions of Plenty: Exhibiting American Culture Abroad in the 1950s.* Washington and London: Smithsonian Institution Press, 1997.

Hallett, Cynthia. *Minimalism and the Short Story: Raymond Carver, Amy Hempel, and Mary Robison.* Lewiston, Queenston and Lampeter: Edwin Mellen Press, 1999.

Halpern, Martin. "Arkansas and the Defeat of Labor Law Reform in 1978 and 1994." *Arkansas Historical Quarterly* 57, no. 2 (Summer 1998): 99–133.

Hanley, Robert. "Many Beaches in Jersey Reopen; Source of Medical Waste is Sought," *New York Times,* August 16, 1987. http://www.nytimes.com/1987/08/16/nyregion/many-beaches-in-jersey-reopen-source-of-medical-waste-is-sought.html.

Hardt, Michael and Antonio Negri. *Empire.* Cambridge, MA.: Harvard University Press, 2000.

Harrison, Sylvia. *Pop Art and the Origins of Postmodernism*. Cambridge: Cambridge University Press, 2001.

Harvey, David. *A Brief History of Neoliberalism*. Oxford: Oxford University Press, 2005.

Harvey, David. *The Condition of Postmodernity: An Enquiry into the Origins of Social Change*. Cambridge, MA. and Oxford: Blackwell, 1990.

Harvey, David. *The Enigma of Capital and the Crises of Capitalism*. London: Profile, 2010.

Harvey, David. *The Limits of Capital*. London: Verso, 2006.

Harvey, David. *Rebel Cities: From the Right to the City to the Urban Revolution*. New York: Verso, 2012.

Heale, Michael. "Anatomy of a Scare: Yellow Peril Politics in America, 1980–1993." *Journal of American Studies* 43, no. 1 (2009): 19–47.

Hedrick, Tace. "On Influence and Appropriation." *The Iowa Review* 22, no.1 (1992): 1–7.

Heidegger, Martin. *What Is A Thing?* Translated by W.B. Barton and Vera Deutsch. Chicago: Henry Reguery, 1967.

Hendin, Jospehine. "Fictions of Acquisition." In *Culture in an Age of Money*, edited by Nicolaus Mills, 216–33. Chicago: Ivan R. Dee, 1990.

Henry, O. *Cabbages and Kings*. New York: McClure, Phillips, 1904.

Herr, Michael. *Dispatches*. London: Picador, 1979.

Hertzberg, Hendrick. "The Short Happy Life of the American Yuppie." In *Culture in an Age of Money*, edited by Nicolaus Mills, 66–82. Chicago: Ivan R. Dee, 1990.

Herzog, Tobey C. "Tim O'Brien's 'True Lies' (?)" *Modern Fiction Studies* 46, no. 4 (2000): 893–916.

Hillkirk, John. "Book Tries to Make 'Made in USA' Stick." *USA Today*, June 12, 1989, 2b.

Hirschman, Albert O. *The Passions and the Interests: Political Arguments for Capitalism before its Triumph*. Princeton and Oxford, Princeton University Press: 2013.

Hoberek, Andrew. "Foreign Objects, or, DeLillo Minimalist." *Studies in American Fiction* 37, no. 1 (2010): 101–25.

Hobson, J. A. *Imperialism: A Study*. Edinburgh: Ballantyne, Hanson & Co., 1902.

Hofstadter, Richard. *Anti-Intellectualism in American Life*. New York: Vintage, 1964.

Hooke, Robert. *Extracts from Hooke's Micrographia*. Oxford: Old Ashmolean Reprints, 1926.

Horkheimer, Max and Theodor Adorno. *Dialectic of Enlightenment*. Translated by John Cumming. London: Allen Lane, 1973.

Hornby, Nick. *Contemporary American Fiction*. London: Vision Press, 1992.

Inglehart, Ronald. *Culture Shift in Advanced Industrial Society*. Princeton: Princeton University Press, 1990.

Inter-Agency Group (Space). "Report on Orbital Debris for National Security Council," Washington DC, February 1989. https://web.archive.org/web/20170309004938/https://ntrs.nasa.gov/archive/nasa/casi.ntrs.nasa.gov/19900003319.pdf

Iyotake, Tatanka. "Behold, My Friends, the Spring is Come." In *Great Speeches by Native Americans*, edited by Bob Baisdell, 166. Mineola: Dover Publications, 2000.

Jacobs, Meg. *Panic at the Pump: The Energy Crisis and the Transformation of American Politics in the 1970s*. New York: Hill and Wang, 2016. Kindle edition.

James, William. *The Principles of Psychology, Vol. 1*. New York: Cosimo, 2007.

James, William. *Writings, 1878–1899*. New York: Library of America, 1992.

Jameson, Frederic. *Postmodernism, or, The Cultural Logic of Late Capitalism*. London and New York: Verso, 1991.

Jarraway, David R. "'Excremental Assault' in Tim O'Brien: Trauma and Recovery in Vietnam War Literature." *Modern Fiction Studies* 44, no.3 (1998): 695–711.

Jeffords, Susan. *The Remasculinization of America: Gender and the Vietnam War*. Bloomington and Indianapolis: Indiana University Press, 1989.

Jefferson, Thomas. *The Selected Writings of Thomas Jefferson*, edited by Wayne Franklin. New York: Norton, 2010.

Jelfs, Tim. "Marilynne Robinson's Turn to the 'Real World, That Is Really Dying': Reading the Nineteenth Century, National Difference, and the Health Hazards of Nuclear Waste in *Mother Country*." In *Environmental Crisis and Human Costs*, edited by Ufuk Özdağ and François Gavillon, 133–48. Alcalá: Biblioteca Benjamin Franklin, 2015.

Jelfs, Tim. "Matter Unmoored: Trash, Archaeological Consciousness and American Culture and Fiction in the 1980s." *Journal of American Studies* 51, no. 2 (2017): 553–71.

Jelfs, Tim. "'Something Deeper than Things': Some Artistic Influences on the Writing of Objects in the Fiction of Don DeLillo." *Comparative American Studies* 9, no. 2 (2011): 144–58.

Johnson, Chalmers. *Blowback: The Costs and Consequences of American Empire*. London: Time Warner, 2013.

Johnson, Chalmers. *MITI and the Japanese Miracle: The Growth of Industrial Policy, 1925–1975*. Stanford: Stanford University Press, 1982.

Johnson, Chalmers. *The Sorrows of Empire: Militarism, Secrecy and the End of the Republic.* London: Verso, 2006.

Jordan, Chris. "Midway: Message from the Gyre," *Chris Jordan: Photographic Arts.* http://www.chrisjordan.com/gallery/midway/#CF000313%2018x24.

Judge, Mike. dir. *Idiocracy.* Twentieth Century Fox/Ternion Pictures, 2006.

Kaivola, Karen. "The Pleasures and Perils of Merging: Female Subjectivity in Marilynne Robinson's *Housekeeping.*" *Contemporary Literature* 34, no. 4 (1993): 670–90.

Katz, Richard. *Japan: The System That Soured: The Rise and Fall of the Japanese Economic Miracle.* Armonk, NY and London: M.E. Sharpe, 1998.

Kaufmann, David. "Yuppie Postmodernism." *Arizona Quarterly* 47, no. 2 (1991): 93–116.

Keats, John. *Selected Poems.* London: Faber, 2000.

Keesey, Douglas. *Don DeLillo.* New York: Twayne, 1993.

Kellner, Douglas. "From Vietnam to the Gulf: Postmodern Wars?" In *The Vietnam War and Postmodernity,* edited by Michael Bibby, 199–236. Amherst: University of Massachusetts Press, 1999.

Kepel, Gilles and Jean-Pierre Milelli. *Al-Qaeda in Its Own Words.* Translated by Pascale Ghazaleh. Cambridge and London: Belknap Press, 2008.

Kiernan, V. G. *America: The New Imperialism: From White Settlement to World Hegemony.* London: Zed Press, 1978.

King, Jr., Martin Luther. "Beyond Vietnam: A Time to Break the Silence." In *Landmark Speeches on the Vietnam War,* edited by Gregory Allen Olson, 93–113. College Station: Texas A&M University Press, 2010.

Kirkby, Joan. "Is There Life After Art? The Metaphysics of Marilynne Robinson's *Housekeeping.*" *Tulsa Studies in Women's Literature* 5, no. 1 (1986): 91–109.

Klein, Naomi. *The Shock Doctrine: The Rise of Disaster Capitalism.* New York: Metropolitan Books/Henry Holt, 2007.

Knight, Peter. "DeLillo, Postmodernism, Postmodernity." In *The Cambridge Companion to Don DeLillo,* edited by John Duvall, 27–39. Cambridge: Cambridge University Press, 2008.

Kopytoff, Igor. "The Cultural Biography of Things: Commoditization as Process." In *The Social Life of Things: Commodities in Cultural Perspective,* edited by Arjun Appadurai, 69–91. Cambridge: Cambridge University Press.

Kouwenhoven, John. *Made in America: The Arts in Modern Civilization.* New York: Octagon, 1948.

Kouwenhoven, John. *Half a Truth is Better Than None.* Chicago: University of Chicago Press, 1982.

Kramer, Larry. *The Normal Heart*. London: Nick Hern Books, 1993.

Krugman, Paul. "Making Things in America," *New York Times*, May 19, 2011. http://www.nytimes.com/2011/05/20/opinion/20krugman.html.

Kushner, Tony. *Angels in America: A Gay Fantasia on National Themes*, First Combined Paperback Ed. New York: Theatre Communications Group, 2003.

Kurth, James. "Variations on the American Way of War." In *The Long War: A New History of U.S. National Security Policy Since World War II*, edited by Andrew Bacevich, 53–98. New York: Columbia University Press, 2007.

La Berge, Leigh Claire. *Scandals and Abstractions: Financial Fiction of the Long 1980s*. Oxford and New York: Oxford University Press, 2015.

Lainsbury, G. P. *The Carver Chronotope: Inside the Life-World of Raymond Carver's Fiction*. New York and London: Routledge, 2004.

Lasch, Christopher. *The Culture of Narcissism: American Life in An Age of Diminishing Expectations*. New York: Norton, 1991.

Laswell, Harold. *Who Gets What, When, How*. New York: Whittlesey House, 1936.

Latour, Bruno. "News from the Trenches of the Science Wars." In *Philosophy of Technology-The Technological Condition: An Anthology*, edited by Robert C. Scharff and Val Dusek, 126–37. Malden, MA and Oxford: Blackwell, 2003.

Latour, Bruno. *Reassembling the Social: An Introduction to Actor-Network Theory*. Oxford: Oxford University Press, 2005.

Latour, Bruno. *We Have Never Been Modern*. Translated from French by C. Porter. Cambridge, MA: Harvard University Press, 1993.

Laurence, Alexander and David Strauss. "An Interview with Nicholson Baker." *The Write Stuff*, 1994. http://www.altx.com/interviews/nicholson.baker.html.

Law, John and John Hassard. *Actor-Network Theory and After*. Oxford: Blackwell, 1999.

LeClair, Thomas. "Fiction Chronicle: January to June." *Contemporary Literature* 23, no. 1 (1981): 83–91.

LeClair, Thomas. *In the Loop: Don DeLillo and the Systems Novel*. Urbana: University of Illinois Press, 1987.

Lee, Spike, dir. *Do The Right Thing*. 40 Acres and a Mule, 1989.

Lehman, Daniel W. "Symbolic Significance in the Stories of Raymond Carver." *Journal of the Short Story in English*, 46 (2006): 75–88.

Lenin, V. I. "Imperialism: The Highest Stage of Capitalism." In *Selected Works, Vol.1*, 667–766. Moscow: Progress Publishers, 19163. *Marxists Internet Archive*, https://www.marxists.org/archive/lenin/works/1916/imp-hsc/

Lentricchia, Frank. "Tales of the Electronic Tribe." In *New Essays on White Noise*, edited by Frank Lentricchia, 87–113. Cambridge: Cambridge University Press, 1991.

Lethem, Jonathan. *Fear of Music*. London: Bloomsbury, 2012.

Levin, Carl and Sen. John McCain, "Offshore Profit Shifting and the U.S. Tax Code—Part 2 (Apple Inc.): Memorandum to Members of the U.S. Senate's Permanent Subcommittee on Investigations," *Permanent Subcommittee on Investigations*, https://www.hsgac.senate.gov/subcommittees/investigations/hearings/offshore-profit-shifting-and-the-us-tax-code_-part-2

Lewis, Michael. "The End: How Wall Street Did Itself In," *Portfolio*, November 11, 2008. http://upstart.bizjournals.com/news-markets/national-news/portfolio/2008/11/11/the-end-of-wall-streets-boom.html?page=all

Lewis, Michael. "Greed Never Left: Michael Douglas on Wall Street, in Lower Manhattan," *Vanity Fair*, April 2010. http://www.vanityfair.com/hollywood/2010/04/wall-street-201004

Lewis, Michael. *Liar's Poker*. London: Hodder and Stoughton, 2006.

Life. "Sixty Pictures that Changed Us Forever," October 1996. http://www.maryellenmark.com/text/magazines/life/905W-000-057.html

Lippard, Lucy. *Pop Art*. London: Thames and Hudson, 1966.

Lloyd, Rosemary. *Shimmering in a Transformed Light: Writing the Still Life*. Ithaca: Cornell University Press, 2005.

Lomperis, Timothy. *"Reading the Wind": The Literature of The Vietnam War— An Interpretative Critique*. Durham, NC: Duke University Press, 1987.

Lukács, Georg. *Studies in European Realism*. Translated by Edith Bone. London: Merlin Press, 1972.

Lyotard, Jean-François. *The Postmodern Condition*. Translated by Geoff Bennington and Brian Massumi. Manchester: Manchester University Press, 1999.

Macaulay, David. *Motel of the Mysteries*. London: Hutchinson, 1979.

Macaulay, David. *The Way Things Work*. Boston: Houghton Mifflin, 1988.

Madoff, Steven Henry. *Pop Art: A Critical History*. Berkeley, Los Angeles, and London: University of California Press, 1997.

Madsen, Michael, dir. *Into Eternity*. Magic Hours Films, 2010.

Maguire, James H. *Reading Marilynne Robinson's Housekeeping*. Boise: Boise State University Western Writers Series, 2003.

Mallon, Anne-Marie. "Sojourning Women: Homelessness and Transcendence in Housekeeping." *Critique* 30, no. 2 (1989): 95–105.

Maltby, Paul. "The Romantic Metaphysics of Don DeLillo." *Contemporary Literature* 37, no. 2 (1996): 258–77.

Manchester, Elizabeth, "Three Ball Total Equilibrium Tank (Two Dr J Silver Series, Spalding NBA Tip-Off)," *Tate.org*. http://www.tate.org.uk/art/artworks/

koons-three-ball-total-equilibrium-tank-two-dr-j-silver-series-spalding-nba-tip-off-t06991/text-summary.

Mao, Douglas. *Solid Objects: Modernism and the Test of Production*. Princeton: Princeton University Press, 1998.

Marcuse, Herbert. *One-Dimensional Man*. Boston: Beacon Press, 1991.

Marling, Karal Ann and Robert Silberman. "The Statue near the Wall: The Vietnam Veterans Memorial and the Art of Remembering." *Smithsonian Studies in American Art* 1, no. 1 (1987): 5–29.

Martin, Bradford D. *The Other Eighties: A Secret History of America in the Age of Reagan*. New York: Hill and Wang, 2011.

Martucci, Elise. *The Environmental Unconscious in the Fiction of Don DeLillo*. London: Routledge, 2007.

Masters, J. J. "Race and the Infernal City in Tom Wolfe's *Bonfire of the Vanities*." *Journal of Narrative Theory* 29, no. 2 (1999): 208–27.

Marx, Karl. *Capital Vol. I*. Translated by Ben Fowkes. London: Penguin, 1990.

Marx, Karl and Friedrich Engels. *The Communist Manifesto*. Translated by Samuel Moore. London: Penguin, 1985.

Mason, Bobbie Ann. *In Country*. New York: Perennial, 1993.

Mayer, Thomas. *Monetary Policy and the Great Inflation in the United States*. Cheltenham: Edward Elgar, 1998.

Mazzucato, Mariana. *The Entrepreneurial State: Debunking Public vs Private Sector Myths*. London: Anthem Press, 2013.

McCarthy, Tom. "Book of a Lifetime," *Independent*, July 30, 2010. http://www.independent.co.uk/arts-entertainment/books/reviews/book-of-a-lifetime-le-parti-pris-des-choses-by-francis-ponge-2038686.html

McCaffery, Larry. *After Yesterday's Crash: The Avant-Pop Anthology*. New York: Penguin, 1995.

McCaffery, Larry and Sinda Gregory. *Alive and Writing: Interviews with American Authors of the 1980s*. Urbana and Chicago: University of Illinois Press, 1987.

McClay, Wilfred M., "Where Have We Come Since the 1950s?" In *Rethinking Materialism: Perspectives on the Spiritual Dimensions of Economic Behavior*, edited by Robert Wuthnow, 25–71. Grand Rapids: William B. Eerdmans, 1995.

McCracken, Grant. *Culture and Consumption: New Approaches to the Symbolic Character of Consumer Goods and Activities*. Bloomington: Indiana University Press, 1988.

McFadden, Robert D. "Garbage Barge Returns in Search of a Dump," *New York Times*, May 18, 1987. http://www.nytimes.com/1987/05/18/nyregion/garbage-barge-returns-in-search-of-a-dump.html

McHale, Brian. *Postmodernist Fiction*. London and New York: Routledge, 1993.

McInerney, Jay. *Bright Lights, Big City*. London: Flamingo, 1986.

McInerney, Jay. *Brightness Falls*. London: Bloomsbury, 1992.

McInerney, Jay. "Raymond Carver: A Still, Small Voice," *New York Times*, August 6, 1989. http://www.nytimes.com/books/98/09/27/specials/mcinerney-carver.html.

McKibben, Bill. *The End of Nature: Humanity, Climate Change and the Natural World*. London: Bloomsbury, 2003.

Macpherson, C. B. *The Political Theory of Possessive Individualism: Hobbes to Locke*. Oxford: Oxford University Press, 1962.

Mark, Mary Ellen. "Streets of the Lost: Runaway Kids Eke Out a Mean Life in Seattle," *Life*, July 1983: 36–42.

Mattson, Kevin. *What the Heck Are You Up To, Mr. President? Jimmy Carter, America's "Malaise," and the Speech that Should Have Changed the Country*. New York: Bloomsbury, 2009.

Mecoy, Don. "Equipment Damaged At Hitachi Plant Site," *The Oklahoman*, May 28, 1986. http://infoweb.newsbank.com/resources/doc/nb/news/0EB42270DBE7B748?p=AWNB.

Meikle, Jeffrey L. *American Plastic: A Cultural History*. New Brunswick: Rutgers University Press, 1995.

Meikle, Jeffrey L. "Ghosts in the Machine: Why It's Hard to Write about Design." *Technology and Culture* 46, no. 2 (2005): 385–92.

Meikle, Jeffrey L. "Material Virtues: On the Ideal and the Real in Design History." *Journal of Design History* 11, no. 3 (1998): 191–99.

Michaels, Walter Benn. "The Beauty of a Social Problem," *The Brooklyn Rail*, October 3, 2011. http://www.brooklynrail.org/2011/10/art/the-beauty-of-a-social-problem.

Michaels, Walter Benn. "Going Boom," *Bookforum* February–March 2001. http://www.bookforum.com/inprint/015_05/3274.

Michaels, Walter Benn. "Meaning and Affect: Phil Chang's *Cache Active*," *nonsite.org*, March 13, 2012. http://nonsite.org/feature/meaning-and-affect-phil-changs-cache-active.

Michaels, Walter Benn. *The Trouble With Diversity*. New York: Metropolitan Books, 2006.

Mile, Sian. "Femme Foetal: The Construction/Destruction of Female Subjectivity in *Housekeeping*, or NOTHING GAINED." *Genders* 8 (1990): 129–36.

Miller, Daniel. *Material Culture and Mass Consumption*. Oxford: Blackwell, 1987.

Miller, Laura. 1996. "Lifting Up The Madonna." *Salon* 23 March, 1996. http://www.salon.com/1996/03/23/baker/.

Mills, Nicolaus, ed. *Culture in an Age of Money: The Legacy of the 1980s in America.* Chicago: Ivan R. Dee, 1990.

Mirowski, Philip. *Never Let A Serious Crisis Go To Waste: How Neoliberalism Survived the Financial Meltdown.* London and New York: Verso, 2013.

Mirowski, Philip and Dieter Plehwe, eds. *The Road From Mont Pèlerin: The Making of the Neoliberal Thought Collective.* Cambridge and London: Harvard University Press, 2009.

Mitchell, Timothy. *Carbon Democracy: Political Power in the Age of Oil.* Rev. ed. London and New York: Verso, 2013.

Moffitt, Kimberly R. and Duncan A. Campbell, eds. *The 1980s: A Critical and Transitional Decade.* Lanham: Lexington, 2011.

Moore, Charles. "Trashed: Across the Pacific Ocean, Plastics, Plastics Everywhere." *Natural History* 112, no. 9 (November 2003): 1–11.

Morris, Narelle. *Japan-Bashing: Anti-Japanism since the 1980s.* Abingdon and New York: Routledge, 2011.

Morrison, Toni. *Song of Solomon.* London: Triad Panther, 1980.

Mosler, Warren. "Now Versus the 1970s." *The Center of the Universe*, February 21, 2008. http://moslereconomics.com/2008/02/21/now-versus-the-1970s/

Mosler, Warren. *Seven Deadly Innocent Frauds of Economic Policy.* St. Croix, VI: Valance, 2010.

Munby, Johnathan. *Under A Bad Sign: Criminal Self-Representation in African-American Culture.* Chicago and London: Chicago University Press, 2011.

Mumford, Lewis. *Technics and Civilization.* New York: Harcourt, Brace, 1940.

New, David S. *Christian Fundamentalism in America: A Cultural History.* Jefferson, NC: McFarland, 2012.

Newman, Charles. *The Post-Modern Aura.* Evanston: Northwestern University Press, 1985.

New York Times. "Noted With Pleasure." December 4, 1988. http://www.nytimes.com/1988/12/04/books/noted-with-pleasure.html.

New York Times. "Suffolk Votes A Bill to Ban Plastic Bags." March 30, 1988. http://www.nytimes.com/1988/03/30/nyregion/suffolk-votes-a-bill-to-ban-plastic-bags.html.

Nichols. John and Robert McChesney. *Dollarocracy: How the Money and Media Election Complex is Destroying America.* New York: Nation Books, 2013.

Norman, Donald A. *The Psychology of Everyday Things.* London: MIT, 1988.

O'Brien, Tim. *Going After Cacciato.* New York: Broadway Books, 1978.

O'Brien, Tim. *If I Die in a Combat Zone, Box Me Up and Ship Me Home.* London: Granada, 1980.

O'Brien, Tim. "The Magic Show." In *Writers on Writing*, edited by Robert Pack and Jay Parini, 175–83. Hanover and London: Middlebury College Press/University Press of New England, 1991.

O'Brien, Tim. *The Things They Carried*. London: Flamingo, 1991.

Office of Management and Budget. *Historical Tables: Budget of the U.S. Government* (FY 2016). https://www.whitehouse.gov/sites/default/files/omb/budget/fy2016/assets/hist.pdf

O'Hara, Frank. *Selected Poems*. London: Penguin, 1994.

Oldenburg, Claes and Emmett Williams. *Store Days: Documents from The Store, 1961, and Ray Gun Theater, 1962*. New York: Something Else Press., 1967.

Olson, Charles. *Call Me Ishmael*. New York: Reynal and Hitchcock, 1947.

Oppen, George. *Collected Poems*. New York: New Directions, 1975.

Osteen, Mark. *American Magic and Dread: Don DeLillo's Dialogue with Culture*. Philadelphia: University of Pennsylvania Press, 2000.

Overton, Bridget. "Too Much Misogyny For Comfort," *Los Angeles Times*, October 29, 1988: 5-12. http://infoweb.newsbank.com/resources/doc/nb/news/0EB42A5166926450?p=AWNB

Owen, Diane S. "Deregulation in the Trucking Industry." *Federal Trade Commission Economic Issues Paper* (May 1988). https://www.ftc.gov/policy/reports/policy-reports/economics-research/issue-papers.

Packard, Vance. *The Waste Makers*. Harmondsworth: Penguin, 1963.

Packer, Matthew J. "At the Dead Center of Things in DeLillo's *White Noise*: Mimesis, Violence, and Religious Awe." *Modern Fiction Studies* 51, no. 3 (Fall 2005): 648–66.

Polanyi, Karl. *The Great Transformation: The Political and Economic Origins of Our Time*. Boston: Beacon Press, 2001.

Panitch, Leo and Sam Gindin. *The Making of Global Capitalism: The Political Economy of American Empire*. London and New York: Verso, 2012.

PBS Newshour. "Greenspan Admits 'Flaw' to Congress, Predicts More Economic Problems," October 23 2008. http://www.pbs.org/newshour/bb/business-july-dec08-crisishearing_10-23/.

Pearlman, Alison. *Unpackaging Art of the 1980s*. Chicago and London: University of Chicago Press, 2003.

Pelecanos, George. "Bad Dreams," *The Wire*, season 2, episode 11, directed by Ernest Dickerson, aired August 17, 2003 (Burbank, CA: Warner Home Video, 2008), DVD.

Perl, Jed. "The Cult of Koons." *New York Review of Books* LXI, no. 14 (September 25–October 8, 2014): 14–18.

Petroski, Henry. *Small Things Considered: Why There Is No Perfect Design.* New York: Alfred A. Knopf, 2003

Petroski, Henry. *The Pencil: A History of Design and Circumstance.* New York: Alfred A. Knopf, 1989.

Phillips, Jayne Anne. "Crowding Out Death," *New York Times,* January 13, 1985. http://www.nytimes.com/books/97/03/16/lifetimes/del-r-white-noise.html.

Phillips, Jayne Anne. *Machine Dreams.* London: Faber, 1993.

Plato. *The Republic.* Translated by Benjamin Jowett. Chichester: Capstone Classics, 2012.

Piketty, Thomas. *Capital in the Twenty-First Century.* Translated by Arthur Goldhammer. Cambridge and London: Belknap Press, 2014.

Piketty, Thomas and Emmanuel Saez. "The Evolution of Top Incomes: A Historical and International Perspective." *American Economic Review* 96, no. 2 (Apr–May 2005), 200–205.

Plunket, Robert. "Howie and the Human Mind," *New York Times,* February 5, 1989. http://www.nytimes.com/books/01/04/15/specials/baker-mezzanine.html.

Ponce de Leon, Charles. "The New Historiography of the 1980s." *Reviews in American History* 36 (2008): 303–14.

Poore, Patricia. "America's 'Garbage Crisis': A Toxic Myth," *Harper's,* March 1994: 24–28.

Potter, David. *People of Plenty: Economic Abundance and the American Character.* Chicago: University of Chicago Press, 1954.

Powers, Richard. *Gain.* London: Vintage, 2001.

Price, Joanna. *Understanding Bobbie Ann Mason.* Columbia, SC: University of South Carolina Press, 2000.

Rathje, William L. and Cullen Murphy. *Rubbish! The Archaeology of Garbage.* Tucson: University of Arizona Press, 2001.

Rathje, William L. 1996. "The Garbage Project & 'The Archaeology of Us.' Symmetrical Archaeology." In *Yearbook of Science and the Future 1997,* edited by Charles Ciegelski, 158–77. New York: Encyclopaedia Britannica, 1996.

Ravits, Martha. "Extending the American Range: Marilynne Robinson's *Housekeeping.*" *American Literature* 61, no. 4 (1989): 644–66.

Reagan, Ronald. "Address Accepting the Presidential Nomination at the Republican National Convention in Detroit," July 17, 1980. *The American Presidency Project.* http://www.presidency.ucsb.edu/ws/?pid=25970.

Reagan, Ronald. "Remarks and a Question-and-Answer Session With the Students and Faculty at Moscow State University," May 31, 1988. *The American Presidency Project.* http://www.presidency.ucsb.edu/ws/?pid=35897.

Reagan, Ronald. "Remarks at Dedication Ceremonies for the Vietnam Veterans Memorial Statue," November 11, 1984. *The American Presidency Project*. http://www.presidency.ucsb.edu/ws/?pid=39414.

Rebein, Robert. *Hicks, Tribes and Dirty Realists: American Fiction after Postmodernism*. Lexington: University Press of Kentucky, 2001.

Reed Jr., Adolph. "*Django Unchained*, or, *The Help*: How 'Cultural Politics' Is Worse Than No Politics at All, and Why," *Nonsite.org* 9, February 25, 2013. http://nonsite.org/feature/django-unchained-or-the-help-how-cultural-politics-is-worse-than-no-politics-at-all-and-why.

Reeves, Hope. "The Way We Live Now: 2-12-01: Map; A Trail of Refuse," *New York Times*, February 12, 2001. http://www.nytimes.com/2001/02/18/magazine/the-way-we-live-now-2-18-01-map-a-trail-of-refuse.html

Reynolds, Simon. *Pop Culture's Addiction to Its Own Past*. London: Faber, 2011.

Riesman, David. *Abundance for What? and Other Essays*. London: Chatto and Windus, 1964.

Rilke, Rainier Maria. *The Best of Rilke*. Translated by Walter Arndt. Hanover and London: University Press of New England, 1989.

Robinson, Marilynne. *The Death of Adam: Essays on Modern Thought*. New York: Picador, 2005.

Robinson, Marilynne. *Housekeeping*. London: Faber, 1981.

Robinson, Marilynne. "Language is Smarter than We Are," *New York Times*, January 11, 1987. http://www.nytimes.com/1987/01/11/books/about-books-language-is-smarter-than-we-are.html.

Robinson, Marilynne. "Marriage and Other Astonishing Bonds," *New York Times*, May 15, 1988. http://www.nytimes.com/1988/05/15/books/marriage-and-other-astonishing-bonds.html.

Robinson, Marilynne. *Mother Country*. London: Faber, 1989.

Rodgers, Daniel T. *Age of Fracture*. Cambridge, MA and London: Belknap Press, 2011.

Rogin, Michael. "'Make My Day!': Spectacle as Amnesia in Imperial Politics." In *Cultures of United States Imperialism*, edited by Amy Kaplan and Donald E. Pease, 499–534. Durham, NC: Duke University Press, 1990.

Roosevelt, Theodore. "Citizenship in a Republic," April 23, 1910. *Almanac of Theodore Roosevelt*. http://www.theodore-roosevelt.com/images/research/speeches/maninthearena.pdf.

Runyon, Randolph. *Reading Raymond Carver*. Syracuse: Syracuse University Press, 1992.

Ryan, Barbara T. "Decentered Authority in Bobbie Ann Mason's *In Country*." *Critique* 31, no. 3 (1990): 199–212.

Saltzman, Arthur. "To See a World in a Grain of Sand: Expanding Literary Minimalism," *Contemporary Literature* 31, no. 4 (1990): 423–33

Saltzman, Arthur. *Understanding Nicholson Baker*. Columbia, SC: University of South Carolina Press, 1999.

Saltzman, Arthur. *Understanding Raymond Carver*. Columbia, SC: University of South Carolina Press, 1988.

Sargent, Daniel J. *A Superpower Transformed: The Remaking of American Foreign Relations in the 1970s*. Oxford and New York: Oxford University Press, 2015.

Schapp, Alain. *The Discovery of the Past*. Translated by Ian Kinnes and Gillian Varndell. London: British Museum Press, 1996.

Schaub, Thomas. "An Interview with Marilynne Robinson." *Contemporary Literature* 35, no. 2 (1994): 231–51.

Schifferes, Steve. "Toyota, an All American Car Company?" *BBC News*, January 12, 2007. http://news.bbc.co.uk/1/hi/business/6247479.stm.

Schlereth, Thomas J. *Material Culture Studies in America*. Nashville: The American Association for State and Local History, 1982.

Schnabel, Julian. *Paintings 1975–1986*. London: Whitechapel, 1986.

Schor, Naomi. *Reading in Detail: Aesthetics and the Feminine*. New York and London: Methuen, 1987.

Schulman, Bruce. *The Seventies: The Great Shift in American Culture, Society and Politics*. New York: Free Press, 2001.

Schulman, Bruce. "Slouching Towards the Supply Side: Jimmy Carter and the New American Political Economy." In *The Carter: Policy Choices in the New Deal Era*, edited by Gary M. Fink and Hugh David Graham, 51–71. Lawrence: University of Kansas Press, 1998.

Schumpeter, Joseph. *Social Classes/Imperialism*. New York: Meridian, 1958..

Schuster, Marc. *Don DeLillo, Jean Baudrillard, and the Consumer Conundrum*. Youngstown, NY: Cambria Press, 2008.

Schwenger, Peter. *The Tears of Things: Melancholy and Physical Objects*. Minneapolis and London: University of Minnesota Press, 2006.

Selz, Peter, 1997. "The Flaccid Art." In *Pop Art: A Critical History*, edited by Stephen Henry Madoff, 85–87. Berkeley, Los Angeles and London: University of California Press, 1997.

Sewall, Gilbert, ed. *The Eighties: A Reader*. Reading, MA: Perseus, 1997.

Shapiro, Walter. "What's Wrong: Hypocrisy, Betrayal and Greed Unsettle the Nation's Soul." *Time,* May 25 1987. http://www.time.com/time/magazine/article/0,9171,964432-1,00.html.

Shi, David. *The Simple Life: Plain Living and High Thinking in American Culture.* New York and Oxford: Oxford University Press, 1985.

Shonkwiler, Alison and Leigh Claire La Berge, eds. *Reading Capitalist Realism.* Iowa City: University of Iowa Press, 2014.

Silbergleid, Robin. "Making Things Present: Tim O'Brien's Autobiographical Metafiction." *Contemporary Literature* 50, no. 1 (2009): 129–55.

Simmons, Phillip E. *Deep Surfaces: Mass Culture and History in Contemporary American Fiction.* Athens: University of Georgia Press, 1997.

Simmons, Phillip E. "Toward the Postmodern Historical Imagination: Mass Culture in Walker Percy's *The Moviegoer* and Nicholson Baker's *The Mezzanine.*" *Contemporary Literature* 33, no. 4 (1992): 601–24.

Solomon, Alan. "The New Art." In *Pop Art: A Critical History,* edited by Stephen Henry Madoff, 90–96. Berkeley, Los Angeles and London: University of California Press, 1997.

Sorrentino, Gilbert. "Kitsch Into 'Art': The New Realism." In *Pop Art: A Critical History,* edited by Stephen Henry Madoff, 47–56. Berkeley, Los Angeles and London: University of California Press, 1997.

Springsteen, Bruce. *Born in the USA.* Columbia Records, 1984.

Stallybrass, Peter. "Marx's Coat." In *Border Fetishisms: Material Objects in Unstable Spaces,* edited by Patricia Spyer, 183–207. New York and London: Routledge, 1995.

Stockholm International Peace Research Institute. "SIPRI Arms Industry Database 2002–2014." https://www.sipri.org/databases/armsindustry.

Stanton, Andrew. dir. *Wall-E.* Pixar Animation Studios/Walt Disney Pictures, 2008.

Stegner, Wallace. *Discovery! The Search for Arabian Oil!* Vista, CA: Selwa Press, 2007.

Stein, Judith. *Running Steel: Race, Economic Policy, and the Decline of Liberalism.* Chapel Hill and London: University of North Carolina Press, 1998.

Steinbeck, John. *Steinbeck: A Life in Letters.* Edited by Elaine A. Steinbeck and Robert Wallsten. New York: Viking Press, 1975.

Steinberg, Bruce. "The Mass Market Is Splitting Apart." In *The Eighties: A Reader,* edited by Gilbert Sewall, 121–28. Reading, MA: Perseus, 1997.

Stewart, James. *Den of Thieves.* New York and London: Simon and Schuster, 1991.

Strait, Guy. "What Is A Hippie?" In *"Takin' it to the Streets": A Sixties Reader*, edited by Alexander Bloom and Wini Breines, 310–12. New York and Oxford: Oxford University Press, 1995.

Strasser, Susan. *Waste and Want: A Social History of Trash*. New York: Metropolitan Books, 1999.

Sturken, Marita. "The Wall, the Screen, and the Image: The Vietnam Veterans Memorial." *Representations* 35 (1991): 118–42.

Summers, Larry. "Let Them Eat Toxics: Leaked Memo." *Harper's*, May 1992: 26–27.

Suplee, Curt. "Sayonara, Apple Pie. Auf Wiedersehen, Detroit: We're on the Guilt-Edged Road to Deficit City." *Washington Post*, August 4, 1982: B1.

Swenson, Gene. "What is Pop Art? Part I." In *Pop Art: A Critical History*, edited by Stephen Henry Madoff, 103–11. Berkeley, Los Angeles and London: University of California Press, 1997.

Talking Heads. *Talking Heads: 77*. Sire, 1977.

Talking Heads. *More Songs About Buildings and Food*. Sire, 1978.

Talking Heads. *Fear of Music*. Sire, 1979.

Talking Heads. *Remain in Light*. Sire, 1980.

Talking Heads. *Naked*. EMI, 1988.

Thompson, Graham. *American Culture in the 1980s*. Edinburgh: Edinburgh University Press, 2007.

Thompson, Graham. *Male Sexuality under Surveillance: The Office in American Literature*. Iowa City: University of Iowa Press, 2003.

Thompson, Helen. *Oil and the Western Economic Crisis*. E-book. Palgrave Macmillan, 2017.

Thompson, Michael. *Rubbish Theory: The Creation and Destruction of Value*. Oxford: Oxford University Press, 1979.

Thoreau, Henry David. *I to Myself: An Annotated Selection from the Journal of Henry D. Thoreau*. New Haven and London: Yale University Press, 2007.

Tocqueville, Alexis de. *Democracy in America and Two Essays on America*. London: Penguin Classics, 2003.

Tomkins, Calvin. "The Art World: The Antic Muse." *The New Yorker*, August 17, 1981: 80–83.

Troy, Gil. *Morning in America: How Ronald Reagan Invented the 1980s*. Princeton, NJ: Princeton University Press, 2005.

Trump, Donald. "Transcript: Donald Trump Speaks at Victory Rally." *NPR.org*, November 9, 2016. http://www.npr.org/2016/11/09/500715254/transcript-donald-trump-speaks-at-victory-rally

Turner, Frederick Jackson. *The Frontier in American History*. New York: Dover, 1996.

Twain, Mark. *Following the Equator and Anti-Imperialist Essays.* New York and London: Oxford University Press, 1996.

Updike, John. *Rabbit at Rest.* London: Penguin Classics, 2006

Updike, John. *Rabbit is Rich.* London: Penguin Classics, 2006.

United States Census Bureau, Economic Indicator Division. "U.S. Trade in Goods and Services 1960–2015." https://www.census.gov/foreign-trade/statistics/historical/gands.pdf.

Untitled Editorial. *Cape Cod Times,* n.d. https://web.archive.org/web/20131006034125/http://jconoverjr.com/html/the_garbage_barge.html

Veblen, Thorstein. *The Theory of the Leisure Class.* London & Unwin, 1970.

Verley, Claudine. "'Errand,' or Raymond Carver's Realism in a Champagne Cork." *Journal of the Short Story in English* 46 (2006): 147–63.

Vernon, Alex. *Soldiers Once and Still: Ernest Hemingway, James Salter, and Tim O'Brien.* Iowa City: University of Iowa Press, 2004.

Vidal, Gore. "American Plastic." *New York Review of Books,* July 15, 1976. http://www.nybooks.com/articles/1976/07/15/american-plastic-the-matter-of-fiction/

Vogel, Ezra. *Japan as Number One: Lessons for America.* Cambridge, MA and London: Harvard University Press, 1979.

Wagner, Kathryn D. "Medical Wastes and the Beach Washups of 1988: Issues and Impacts." Second International Conference on Marine Debris. April 2–7, 1989, Honolulu, Hawaii. http://swfsc.noaa.gov/publications/TM/SWFSC/NOAA-TM-NMFS-SWFSC-154_P811.PDF

Walters, Ian. "Vietnam Zippos." *The Journal of Material Culture* 2, no. 1 (1997): 61–75.

Weisman, Alan. *The World Without Us.* London: Virgin, 2007.

White, Leslie. "The Function of Popular Culture in Bobbie Ann Mason's *Shiloh and Other Stories* and *In Country.*" *The Southern Quarterly* 26, no. 4 (1988): 69–79.

Whiting, Cécile. *Pop Art, Gender, and Consumer Culture.* Cambridge: Cambridge University Press, 1997.

World Bank. "GDP Growth (Annual %): United States 1981–1990." http://data.worldbank.org/indicator/NY.GDP.MKTP.KD.ZG?end=1990&locations=US&start=1981&view=chart.

Whoriskey, Peter. "Bright Idea of Tire Reef Now Simply a Blight." *Washington Post,* October 2, 2006. http://www.washingtonpost.com/wp-dyn/content/article/2006/10/01/AR2006100101090_pf.html

Wigglesworth, Michael. "God's Controversy with New England." In *The Puritans in America: A Narrative Anthology,* edited by Alan Heimart and Andrew

Delbanco, 229–36. Cambridge, MA and London: Harvard University Press, 1985.

Wilcox, Leonard. "Baudrillard, DeLillo's *White Noise*, and the End of Heroic Narrative." *Contemporary Literature* 32, no. 3 (1991): 346–65.

Wilde, Alan. *Middle Grounds: Studies in Contemporary American Fiction.* Philadelphia: University of Pennsylvania Press, 1987.

Wilentz, Sean. *The Age of Reagan: A History, 1974–2008.* New York: Harper Collins. 2008.

Wilson, Woodrow. "Address to the Salesmanship Congress, Detroit, Michigan," July 10, 1916. http://www.presidency.ucsb.edu/ws/?pid=117701

Winner, Langdon. "Do Artefacts Have Politics?" *Daedalus* 109 (1980): 121–36.

Witko, Christopher. "How Wall Street Became a Big Chunk of the U.S. Economy— And When The Democrats Signed on." *Washington Post,* March 29, 2016. https://www.washingtonpost.com/news/monkey-cage/wp/2016/03/29/how-wall-street-became-a-big-chunk-of-the-u-s-economy-and-when-the-democrats-signed-on

Wolfe, Tom. *The Bonfire of the Vanities.* London: Picador, 1990.

Wolfe, Tom. "The 'Me' Decade and the Third Great Awakening." *New York,* August 23, 1976. http://nymag.com/news/features/45938/

Wolfe, Tom. "Stalking the Billion-Footed Beast: A Literary Manifesto for the New Social Novel." *Harper's,* November 1989.

Zalasiewicz, Jan et al. "The Geological Cycle of Plastics and Their Sse as a Stratigraphic Indicator of the Anthropocene." *Anthropocene* 13 (March 2016): 4–17.

Zaretsky, Natasha. *No Direction Home: The American Family and the Fear of National Decline, 1968–1980.* Chapel Hill: University of North Carolina Press, 2007.

Index

Abbey, Edward, 97
Abstract Expressionism, 56, 64
ACT UP, 5
aestheticism of objects, 16
Afghanistan, 142
Agent Orange, 75
AIDS (acquired immune deficiency
    syndrome), 5, 79, 164n11
airplanes, 58, 102, 109, 117, 121, 138
alcoholism, 69
alienation, 58, 113
All American Men of War (comic book
    series), 118
Allende, Salvador, 6
All in The Family (TV show), 46
All The Sad Young Literary Men (Gessen),
    99
Althusser, Louis, 7
America (Baudrillard), 14–15
Americana (DeLillo), 87
American Civil War, 3
American culture: capitalist realism, 50;
    engagement with material things, 1,
    10–12, 16, 19–21, 143, 148;
    materialism, 145; neoliberalism, 7,
    16, 143; peace with things, 22, 99,
    101; rhopography and realism, 53,
    54, 59, 61; structural
    transformations, 37. See also culture
American dream, 47
American expansionism, 3, 4, 29
American imperialism: ideal and material,
    10; militarism, 121, 122, 130;
    neoliberalism and oil, 24–26, 29–31;
    weight on nation, 116
American Psycho (Ellis), 47, 163n70
American Studies, 1, 13

Ammons, A. R., 95
Anderson, Perry, 10
Andersonville Diary, 126
Angels in America (Kushner), 79
Anglo-Persian Oil Company (now BP), 29
Annesely, James, 64, 163n70
anti-materialism, 42, 76, 101, 108, 145,
    149
Apocalypse Now (film), 124
Apollo 13 (space mission), 119
Apple, 120
Applefield, David, 69
Arabian Peninsula, 23, 24, 28, 141
Arab-Israeli conflict, 33
Aramco (American Arabian Oil
    Company), 23, 25–29, 42, 141
archaeological consciousness, 22, 78,
    84–90, 95, 96, 100
"Archaic Torso of Apollo" (Rilke), 72
Arendt, Hannah, 25, 81–82, 83, 156n19
"Are These Actual Miles?" (Carver), 67, 68
argument about things: after the great
    transformation, 38–51; American
    culture and material things, 142–47;
    American history, 1–5; complexity
    of, 1; definition, 2; mass culture,
    43–46, 49; matter unmoored, 77–97;
    militarism and materialism,
    117–140; in 1980s, 5–6, 9, 13, 20–22;
    neoliberalism, 22, 35, 37, 142, 143,
    146, 147; at peace with things,
    98–116; reanimation of argument,
    38, 39, 41, 43; rhopography and
    realism, 52–76; technological
    progress, 168n48; triumph of
    neoliberalism, 23–37
arms industry, 31, 117, 118, 120, 121

ARPANET, 120
art: archaeological consciousness, 78,
    85–86; criticism, 11, 12, 65; history,
    56; Koons, Jeff, 11, 21, 54–56, 57, 58,
    60, 75; neoliberal era, 20; painting,
    56, 61, 85–86; photography, 52–53,
    62–63, 149; Pop Art, 56–57, 59–60,
    62, 64–65, 75, 118, 144; rhopography
    and realism, 21, 52–53, 54–57, 59,
    61–62, 65, 76
Atlantic, The, 105
Augustine, St., 2
Aurelius, Marcus, 107, 114, 115
Auster, Paul, 88, 89
authenticity, 126
avant-garde culture, 39, 53, 57, 58

Bacevich, Andrew, 142
Bahrain, 26, 142
Baker, Nicholson: "Changes of Mind," 105,
    106, 111; *Checkpoint*, 117–18;
    Fermata, The, 112, 168n37; *Human
    Smoke*, 118; *Mezzanine, The*, 100,
    101–5, 106–8, 109–12, 114–16,
    167n11, 168n37, 168n46; peace with
    things, 22, 100–109, 110–16; and
    Petroski, 167n11; "Rarity," 112;
    Room Temperature, 100, 102–7,
    109–13, 115–17; "Size of Thoughts,
    The," 105, 106; *U and I*, 104, 107,
    114; *Vox*, 112
ballpoint pens, 112–13
banking sector, 43
Barr, Roseanne, 46
Barth, John, 63, 64–65, 161n40
Barthelme, Frederick, 66, 161n40
Barthes, Roland, 67, 82, 88
Basel Convention on the Control of
    Transboundary Movements of
    Hazardous Waste and their Disposal,
    80
basketballs, 11, 54, 55, 56, 129
Baudrillard, Jean, 14–15, 82, 154n71,
    154n73, 155n74
Bawer, Bruce, 12
Beattie, Ann, 12, 64, 161n40
Bechtel, 24, 26

Beddoes, Thomas Lovell, 97
Beginners (Carver), 162n61
Bell, Martin, 46
Bellamy, Ralph, 49, 118
Benedict, Ruth, 4
Benjamin, Walter, 86, 107
Bennett, Jane, 16
Bercovitch, Sacvan, 2, 40, 159n8
Bic pens, 112–13
"Big Country, The" (Talking Heads song),
    58, 136
"Big Yellow Taxi" (Mitchell song), 59
Bilton, Alan, 16
Binschtok, Viktoria, 52–53, 61
biodegradation, 81, 83
Birth of Biopolitics, The (Foucault), 17
Blank Fictions (Annesley), 163n70
Bloom, Allan, 113
blowback, 30, 40
Blue Collar (film), 44–46, 48, 50, 51
Blyth, Mark, 9, 33, 159n13
bodies, 5, 132, 133, 137, 138
Boeing, 117
Boesky, Ivan, 36, 43, 47, 98, 158n58, 164n3
Boland Amendment, 121
Bonfire of the Vanities, The (Wolfe), 48, 49
"Born in the USA" (Springsteen song),
    170n33
Born on the Fourth of July (Kovic), 124
Boston harbor, 79
BP, 29
brand names, 65–66, 73–76, 102, 143, 144,
    163n70
"bratpack" fiction, 12, 22, 64, 122
Bretton Woods system, 29, 30, 31
Bright Lights, Big City (McInerney), 71–73
Brightness Falls (McInerney), 92, 96
Brown, Bill, 13, 15, 16, 147
Brown, Wendy, 34
Bumpers, Dale, 42
burial, 139, 140
Burke, Kenneth, 52
Bush, George H. W., 20, 36, 39, 79, 98,
    101, 138–141
Bush, George W., 118
Byrne, David, 35, 58–59, 60, 62, 75

Cabbages and Kings (Henry), 25, 129–130
California Arabian Standard Oil Company
  (now Chevron), 23
cameras, 146, 147
capital, 14, 16, 30, 32, 34, 142, 147
Capital (Marx), 154n71
capitalism: archaeological consciousness,
  95–96; Baker novels, 22, 101, 115,
  117; Carter "malaise" speech, 40;
  commodity fetishism, 15;
  communicative capitalism, 115;
  cultural debate, 11, 12, 37, 38;
  inequality, 61, 62, 149; mainstream
  culture, 21, 44, 50; materialism, 13,
  149; militarism, 129, 130, 136;
  neoliberalism, 8–10, 19–20, 25, 30,
  35, 37, 147; post-Cold War 1990s,
  141, 147; reconfiguration of, 9–10,
  20, 61, 101, 115, 117, 141;
  rhopography and realism, 53, 55, 57,
  60–62, 73; Schumpeter defense of,
  156n19
capitalist realism, 18, 50
carbon emissions, 77, 96
Carlin, George, 11, 90
Carter, Howard, 85
Carter, Jimmy: anti-materialism, 50, 76,
  109, 142, 143, 145, 149; Carter
  Doctrine, 26; deregulation, 42;
  garbage panics, 85; "malaise" speech,
  20, 35, 37–39, 40–42, 158n5;
  militarism, 121, 139; neoliberalism,
  6, 20, 35–37
Carver, Raymond: "Are These Actual
  Miles?," 67, 68; Barth on
  minimalism, 161–62n40; *Beginners*,
  162n61; *Cathedral*, 70; and DeLillo,
  90; "Fat," 72; fictions of acquisition,
  12; rhopography and realism, 22, 64,
  65–71, 72–74, 76; "Serious Talk, A,"
  70; "Small Good Thing, A," 72; "Tell
  the Women We're Going," 70;
  "Vitamins," 70–71; *What We Talk
  About When We Talk About Love*, 67,
  68; "Why Don't You Dance?," 69;
  Will You Please Be Quiet, Please? 67
Castle (Macaulay), 84

Cathedral (Carver), 70
Cathedral (Macaulay), 84
Cather, Willa, 126
Cato Institute, 35
Central America, 25, 124
Challenger disaster, 92
Chambers, Ross, 104, 107
"Changes of Mind" (Baker), 105, 106, 111
Chapman, Tracy, 46
Chase, Stuart, 81
Checker cab plant, 44, 51
Checkpoint (Baker), 117–18
Chekhov, Anton, 66
Chen, Tina, 129, 132
Chen, Vincent, 51
Chevron, 23
"Chicago Boys," 6, 32
Chicago School, 17
Chile, 6, 32
China, 95
Christianity, 2
Chrysanthemum and the Sword, The
  (Benedict), 4
CIA (Central Intelligence Agency), 6, 26,
  27, 32
Cimino, Michael, 124
Cineaste (magazine), 44
cinema, 11, 43–50, 79, 122–24
Civil War, 3
Clare, Michael T., 121
class divisions: art, 55, 59; Baker novels,
  111, 116; *Blue Collar* film, 44–46;
  Carver stories, 65, 67–69, 71; *Do The
  Right Thing* film, 48; garbage panics,
  95, 96; inequality, 41, 49, 116, 149;
  neoliberalism, 35; solidarity, 44, 45;
  underclass, 50; Wolfe, 49; working
  class, 46, 50
classical liberalism, 17
Closing of the American Mind, The
  (Bloom), 113
Clune, Michael, 12
coal power, 27, 42
Coca-Cola (Coke), 56, 61, 65, 73, 75
cocaine, 122
cognition, 105, 106
Cohen, Lizabeth, 62

Cold War: Baker novels, 101; global capitalism, 30, 35; militarism, 117–121, 124, 130; neoliberalism, 10, 32; oil and imperialism, 30, 31, 32; peace with things, 22, 98, 101; Soviet Union, 31
Cole, Andrew, 14, 99, 106, 148
Collins, Robert M., 9
colonialism, 2, 27
Columbus, Christopher, 2
comic strips, 57
commercialism, 73
commodification, 11, 16
commodities, 14, 16, 20, 60, 109
commodity fetishism, 15, 49, 55, 99, 108, 154n71
common objects, 56, 66, 70, 71, 104
communicative capitalism, 115
communism, 129
complexity of thought, 105
conatus, 16
conceptual art, 55
Connally, John, 51
connections, 113, 114–15
consumer capitalism, 60, 73, 78
consumer culture, 5, 11, 55, 57, 96
consumer goods: Baker novels, 100, 103; cultural representation, 11, 12; DeLillo, 60; Koons, 11, 54; Mason, 74; militarism and materialism, 120; peace with things, 99, 100, 103; Pop Art, 56; rhopography and realism, 21, 54, 56, 60, 62, 74
consumerism: Baker, 100; and consumption, 13, 62; cultural criticism, 11; DeLillo, 90; inequality and poverty, 62, 63; literary culture, 143; and materialism, 8; rhopography and realism, 62, 63, 73; trash, 77, 90
consumption: age of things, 3; Baker novels, 100, 103, 107; capitalism, 15; Carter "malaise" speech, 40; and consumerism, 13; cultural criticism, 149; inequality and poverty, 62; militarism, 129; rhopography and

realism, 54, 62, 63, 73; trash, 78, 81, 83, 85, 90, 96
Cooke, Alistair, 79, 80
Coover, Robert, 63
Coppola, Francis Ford, 124
corporate tax revenues, 169n6
Costello, Elvis, 118
cost-push inflation, 33
counter-culture, 123
Cowie, Jefferson, 31–32
credit, 40, 45
Crichton, Michael, 160n32
crime, 48, 49
criticism, cultural, 11, 12, 65, 67, 148, 149
crude oil, 24, 33. *See also* oil
Csikszentmihalyi, Mihalyi, 107, 145
Cubism, 56
cultural criticism, 11, 12, 65, 67, 148, 149
cultural history, 99, 104
culture: capitalist realism, 50; engagement with material things, 1, 10–13, 15–16, 19–21, 143, 145, 148–49; mainstream culture, 21, 43, 46, 48–50; militarism, 22, 122, 123–24; and neoliberalism, 7, 16, 20–21, 143; neo-Realism, 74–76; peace with things, 22, 99, 101; and politics, 38; rhopography and realism, 53, 54, 59–61, 74–76; structural transformations, 37; and trash, 78, 84, 93, 97
Cusset, François, 154n73

Damms family, 46
Danner, Mark, 121
Danto, Arthur C., 11, 55, 61
Dario, Rubén, 3
DARPA, 120
Davenport, James, 2, 4, 48
D.C. Comics, 118
Dean, Jodi, 115
death, 20, 88, 132–37
Debord, Guy, 154n71
debt, 43, 50, 62
deep time, 19
Deer Hunter, The (film), 124

Defense Advanced Procurements Agency (DARPA), 120
defense spending, 121
deindustrialization, 6, 43, 66, 118, 130–31
DeLillo, Don: *Americana*, 87; American culture and material things, 11, 143, 145–46, 147, 148; archaeological consciousness, 86–87, 92, 95, 96; *Names, The*, 87–88; *Players*, 14, 16; *Ratner's Star*, 87; rhopography and realism, 21, 59–60, 75; *Underworld*, 95, 145–46, 147; *White Noise*, 11, 14, 59–60, 87–90, 92, 96, 129, 148
dematerialization, 14, 15, 77
demilitarization, 117
democracy, 27
Democratic Forest, The (Eggleston), 62
Democratic Party, 42, 50
deregulation, 6, 34, 41, 42, 43
Descartes, René, 107
Desert Solitaire (Abbey), 97
designer goods, 71–72, 73, 103, 143
Design History Society, 168n46
design of things, 110, 115, 116, 168n46
Dewey, Joseph, 85
Dharhan, 28
diapers, 81, 82
Didion, Joan, 121
"Diet-Pepsi minimalism," 162n40
digitization, 114, 147
Dimock, Wai-Chi, 19
dirty realism, 77
discourse, 39
Discovery! The Search for Arabian Oil (Stegner), 23
Dispatches (Herr), 124, 135
disposable cameras, 147, 148
disposable diapers, 81, 82
dispossession: mass culture, 46; neoliberalism, 20, 21; rhopography and realism, 61, 63, 67, 70, 75; riots, 49
documentary truth, 126
domestic waste, 81, 90, 96
Donahue, Phil, 79
Do The Right Thing (Lee), 48, 49

double movement, 33
Douglas, Mary, 45, 145, 164n7
Douglas, Michael, 47
"dreck," 20
drift, 158n51
drinking straws, 100, 102, 109, 110
drugs trade, 122
Duchamp, Marcel, 12, 54
duct tape, 119
Dukakis, Michael, 79
durability of things, 81–84, 86, 91–93, 95, 96
Dutch artists, 59

Eagleton, Terry, 12
East India Company, 25
Ecclesiastes, 146
Eckhart, Meister, 148
economic nationalism, 32, 50, 55, 115, 117, 150
economics, 17, 34
economy: capitalism, 8; deindustrialization, 6, 43, 66, 118, 130–31; deregulation, 6, 41; militarism, 118, 119, 120, 130–31; neoliberalism, 14, 31, 33, 35, 119; "new economy," 114, 115; post-war economic expansion, 4; Wall Street crash, 92; waste economy, 82
Eggleston, William, 62–63, 67, 73, 149
Eisenhower, Dwight D., 118
Eliot, T. S., 38
Elkin, Stanley, 71
Ellis, Bret Easton: American culture and material things, 12, 143, 163n70; *American Psycho*, 47, 163n70; *Less Than Zero*, 71; materialism, 47; narco-culture, 122; rhopography and realism, 71, 73
El Salvador, 121
embedded liberalism, 33
embodiment, 5
Emerson, Ralph Waldo, 3
empire, 29–30
End of Nature, The (McKibben), 165n30
environment, 23, 83, 91, 98

ephemerality of things, 86, 92, 93, 96, 147
eroticism of objects, 16, 104
European imperialism, 130
Evans, David, 89
everyday objects, 11, 16, 22, 54, 100, 103, 106, 144
Evolution of Useful Things, The (Petroski), 167n11
existential self, 38
expansionism, 3, 4, 29
experimental culture, 53
ExxonMobil, 23, 150
Exxon Valdez oil spill, 77

"F-111" (Rosenquist artwork), 118–19
Fadiman, Anne, 46
Falklands War, 118
falling objects, 133, 135, 137, 138
fascism, 33
"Fast Car" (Chapman song), 46
"Fat" (Carver), 72
Fear of Music (Talking Heads album), 58
Federal Reserve, 34, 41
Federal Trade Commission, 42
feminism, 9
Fermata, The (Baker), 112, 168n37
fetishism, 12, 13–14, 15, 16, 89. *See also* commodity fetishism
fiction: archaeological consciousness, 86–87; "bratpack" fiction, 12, 22, 64, 122; "hick chic," 64, 74, 162n40; literary fiction, 12, 16, 91, 99, 102; mass culture, 12; new realism, 64–67, 74, 149; rhopography and realism, 63–67, 76
fictional truth, 126
"fictions of acquisition," 12
Field, Sally, 44
Fields of Fire (Webb), 124
film, 11, 43–50, 79, 122–24
financial crisis (2008), 7, 43, 150
financial fiction, 64
financialization, 118, 131
Finch, Peter, 51
Fisher, Mark, 18
Fitzgerald, F. Scott, 5

flight metaphor, 135–36, 137, 138, 171n66
Ford, Richard, 64
foreign direct investment, 51
fossil fuels, 34, 82
Foster, Hal, 11, 12
Foucault, Michel, 17
found objects, 54
Frank, Barney, 149, 150
Frankfurt School, 12, 168n46
Frantz, Chris, 58
Franzen, Jonathan, 52
freedom, 18, 138, 149
free markets, 6, 17, 34
Friedman, Milton, 8
Fukuyama, Francis, 7

Gaddis, William, 63
Gain (Powers), 146, 147, 148
Gallagher, Tess, 68
gangsta rap, 47
garbage: archaeological consciousness, 22, 84, 85, 89, 91; capitalist system, 1, 20; cultural critique, 148, 149; DeLillo, 89, 90, 96, 129; durability of, 81–84, 86, 91–93, 95, 96; "garbage discourse," 91, 96, 98; garbage glut, 80, 83; Great Pacific Garbage Patch, 77, 83, 96; *Khian Sea* garbage barge, 78–80, 95; *Mobro 4000* garbage barge, 77–81, 83, 91–92, 95–96; O'Brien, 129; panics, 81, 90, 95, 98; Updike, 91
"Garbage" (Ammons poem), 95
Garbage Project, 81
gas markets, 41
Gas Policy Act, 159n11
gay subcultures, 5
gender roles, 49, 57
Gentlemen Prefer Blondes (film), 47
gentrification, 49
geopolitical power, 10, 28
Gere, Richard, 49, 118
Gessen, Keith, 99
Gibson, James William, 129
Gibson, William, 122
Gideon, Siegfried, 13

Gilbert, James, 151n4
Gilded Age, 71, 96
Gilman, Nils, 48
Gindin, Sam, 29
Glaucon, 3
global capitalism: Baker novels, 22, 101, 115, 117; cultural debate, 37, 38; inequality, 62; mainstream culture, 21; militarism, 130; neoliberalism, 10, 19, 37, 147; post-Cold War 1990s, 141, 147; reconfiguration of, 9–10, 20, 61, 101, 115, 117, 141; victims of, 61. *See also* capitalism
globalization, 34, 55, 142
Going After Cacciato (O'Brien), 124, 129, 133, 171n66, 171n71
gold standard, 29
Goldwater, Barry, 19
Gorbachev, Mikhail, 120
Gornick, Vivian, 70, 71
Gramsci, Antonio, 143
Grandmaster Flash, 122
grand narratives, 18, 127
gravity metaphor, 131, 132, 133, 134, 138
Great Depression, 7, 9, 46, 63
Great Gatsby, The (Fitzgerald), 5
Great Pacific Garbage Patch, 77, 83, 96
Great Recession, 7, 46
Great Transformation, The (Polanyi), 33
greed, 36, 47
Green Berets, The (film), 123
Greenpeace, 81
Greenspan, Alan, 7, 19
Grenada, 122
grief, 94
Griswold, Charles L., 122, 123, 125
Gulf War, 5, 120, 138, 141

habitus, 62
Haiti, 80
Hardt, Michael, 29
Harrington, Michael, 61
Harrison, Jerry, 58
Hart, Frederick, 123
Harvey, David, 14
Hayek, Friedrich, 17

heaviness, 131, 133, 134, 135, 136
Heidegger, Martin, 10, 11
helicopters, 121, 135, 137, 138
Helprin, Mark, 65
Hemingway, Ernest, 65, 66, 162n40
Henry, O., 25, 26, 129–130
Heritage Foundation, 35
Herr, Michael, 124, 135, 138
Heston, Charlton, 87
"hick chic," 64, 74, 162n40
Higginson, John, 2
hippies, 4
history of objects, 104
Hitachi, 51
Hitler, Adolf, 88
Hoarders (TV show), 14
Hoberek, Mark, 65
Hobson, J. A., 25, 156n19
Hollywood, 11, 49, 139
homelessness, 63, 124
home loans, 45
Hoover brand, 55
Hope, Bob, 56
Hornby, Nick, 74
hospital waste, 79
Housekeeping (Robinson), 93–94, 95
housing, 61, 149
human agency, 138
Human Condition, The (Arendt), 81–82
humanities, material turn in, 13–16, 19, 99, 100
Human Smoke (Baker), 118
hydrocarbons, 141

Iacocca, Lee, 36
Ibn Saud, 28
idealism, 2, 7
ideas, 9, 10
identity, 37, 40, 128
ideology, 7, 9
Idiocracy (film), 85
If I Die in a Combat Zone, Box Me Up and Ship Me Home (O'Brien), 124, 133
immateriality, 15, 16
immaterial labor, 114
immortality, 82

imperialism: American, 10, 24–26, 29–31,
116, 121–22, 130; and capitalism, 20;
European, 130; materialism, 3, 10;
militarism, 22, 116, 119–122,
129–130; neoliberalism, 6, 10, 21, 35,
142; neoliberalism and oil, 24–26,
27, 29–31; nineteenth century,
156n19; weight on nation, 22, 116
In Country (Mason), 73–75, 88–89, 124,
163n80
Indiana, Robert, 56
individualism, 3, 8, 18
industrial design, 115, 116, 144
industrialization, 3, 44
industrial landscape, 130
Industrial Revolution, 8
industrial waste, 80
inequality: Baker novels, 116; Carver
stories, 68; cultural criticism, 149;
and debt, 43; drift, 158n51;
mainstream culture, 46, 49, 50;
marginalization, 5; neoliberalism, 6,
62, 116; nostalgic materialism, 49;
poverty, 62; rhopography and
realism, 62, 68; trash, 80, 96
inflation, 24, 33–35, 37, 39, 40–42, 45, 50
information technology, 114–15, 147
Inglehart, Ronald, 9
insider trading, 98
interest rates, 34, 41
Internet, 120
intimacy, 112
Invention of Solitude, The (Auster), 88
investment banks, 31, 43, 47, 92
iPads, 120
Iran, 26, 28, 31, 33, 35, 40, 98, 121
Iran-Contra affair, 98, 121
Iraq, 84, 142
Isherwood, Baron, 45, 145
Islamism, 142

Jacobs, Meg, 157n33
James, William, 107, 108, 109, 110
Jameson, Fredric, 15, 119
Japan, 4, 31, 91, 116, 160n32
Japan as Number One (Vogel), 160n32

Japan: The System That Soured (Katz),
160n32
Jarvis, Howard, 19
Jefferson, Thomas, 3, 99, 151n15
Jeffords, Susan, 122, 124
jeremiads, 40, 85, 159n8
"John Button Birthday" (O'Hara), 148
Johnson, Chalmers, 30, 31, 160n32
Jordan, Chris, 96
Judge, Mike, 85
junk, 77, 83, 85, 129
junk bonds, 77
junk food, 77, 91

Katz, Richard, 160n32
Kaufmann, David, 69, 72
Keats, John, 89, 148
Keitel, Harvey, 44
Kennedy, Ted, 138
Khian Sea garbage barge, 78–80, 95
Kiernan, G. K., 29, 42
Kilhefner, Don, 5
King, Jr., Martin Luther, 4, 49, 152n23
Kipling, Rudyard, 24
Kissinger, Henry, 30
"K-Mart realism," 64, 162n40
knowledge, 148
knowledge economy, 114
Koch, Charles, 35
Koch, David, 35
Koons, Jeff, 11, 21, 54–56, 57, 58, 60, 75
Korean steel, 31
Korean War, 117, 119, 120
Kotto, Yaphet, 44
Kouwenhoven, John, 13
Kovic, Ron, 124
Kramer, Hilton, 65
Kramer, Larry, 5, 164n11
Krugman, Paul, 1
Kushner, Tony, 79
Kuwait, 141

labels, 73, 103
La Berge, Leigh Claire, 7, 64
labor, 27–28, 31, 33, 40, 42–43, 50, 53, 62
Lainsbury, G. P., 69
landfill sites, 81, 82, 83, 89

Lange, Dorothea, 46
language, 64, 70, 100, 147
Larsa, 84
Lasch, Christopher, 8, 11, 38, 39, 109
Laswell, Harold, 9
late capitalism, 19
Latin America, 3, 31, 122
Latour, Bruno, 13
Lear, Norman, 46
Lebenswelt (life-world), 11, 62
LeClair, Thomas, 67
Lee, Spike, 48, 49
Lenin, Vladimir, 25, 156n19
Lentricchia, Frank, 89, 148
Less Than Zero (Ellis), 71
Lethem, Johnathan, 58
"Letter from America" (radio show), 79
Lewis, Michael, 7, 36, 47
LGTBQ rights, 5, 9
Liar's Poker (Lewis), 7, 36, 47
liberalism, 17, 33, 61
Libya, 142
Lichtenstein, Roy, 60, 65, 118
"Life During Wartime" (Talking Heads song), 58
life-world, 11, 62
Lin, Maya, 75, 120, 122, 123, 125
Lish, Gordon, 69, 70
literary criticism, 65, 67
literary culture, 10, 25, 63, 64, 66, 100, 120, 136
literary fiction, 12, 16, 91, 99, 102
literary postmodernism, 63, 64
literary realism, 22, 65, 67, 149
"Little Boxes" (Reynolds song), 149
loans, 45
Lockheed Martin, 117
Lomperis, Timothy, 124
"long 1980s": capitalism reconfiguration, 21; mainstream culture, 21, 39, 41, 46, 48, 50; materialism, 85, 143; narrative culture, 113, 116; neoliberalism, 7, 34, 36, 37; origin of term, 7; rhopography and realism, 53, 54, 56, 58, 60–63, 65, 66, 70, 76; simulacra, 15; trash, 77, 78, 85, 96

Love Canal scandal, 80
Lukács, Georg, 16, 113–14, 115
luxury, 3

Macaulay, David, 84
Machine Dreams (Phillips), 136–37
Machine in the Garden, The (Leo Marx), 168n48
Macpherson, C.B., 2
Made in America (Kouwenhoven), 13
Madonna (singer), 36, 46, 47, 49
mainstream culture, 21, 46, 53
"malaise" speech (Carter), 20, 35, 37–39, 40–42, 158n5
manifest destiny, 3
manufacturing, 1, 3, 30, 43, 115, 118, 130, 144
Marcuse, Herbert, 101, 107, 108, 109
marine environments, 98
Mark, Mary Ellen, 46, 149
markets, 8, 18, 33
Marling, Karal Ann, 125, 126
Marshall Plan, 24, 30
Marx, Karl, 14, 15, 60, 154n71
Marx, Leo, 168n48
Marxism, 12, 20, 108
masculinity, 70, 71, 122, 124
Mason, Bobbie Ann: archaeological consciousness, 88–89; Barth on minimalism, 162n40; *In Country*, 73–75, 88–89, 163n80; rhopography and realism, 22, 73–75; *Shiloh and Other Stories*, 163n80
mass consumption, 54, 78, 85, 90, 149
mass culture, 46, 49, 57, 74
mass market, 43
Masters, J. J., 49
material culture, 13, 59, 86, 97, 100
"Material Girl" (Madonna song), 36, 46–47, 49
materialism: American culture and material things, 10, 141, 143, 145, 148, 149; archaeological consciousness, 78, 85, 97; Baker novels, 22, 101, 107, 116; dematerialization, 14, 15, 77; and idealism, 2; mainstream culture, 39,

materialism (*continued*)
  50; material turn in humanities,
    13–16, 19, 99, 100; militarism, 120,
    143; neoliberalism, 7–10, 18–20, 36,
    37, 143; "1980s materialism," 8, 10,
    19, 97; peace with things, 22, 98, 99,
    101, 107, 116; rhopography and
    realism, 63, 73, 76
materiality of the body, 132
materiality of things, 14–16, 19, 90
material self, 110
material things: American cultural
    engagement, 1, 3, 10–16, 19–21, 143,
    145, 148–49; Baker novels, 100, 101,
    104–6, 108, 109; Bush speech, 36;
    Carter "malaise" speech, 40–41;
    dematerialization, 14, 15; materiality,
    14–16, 19, 90; militarism and
    materialism, 125, 126, 127;
    neoliberalism, 19, 20; peace with
    things, 98, 100, 101, 104–6, 108, 109;
    rhopography and realism, 70, 76
material turn in humanities, 13–16, 19, 99,
    100
Matrix, The (film), 154n73
matter, 9, 10, 16, 83, 89
Mazzucato, Mariana, 119
McCarthy, Tom, 15
McEvilley, Thomas, 86
McInerney, Jay: archaeological
    consciousness, 92, 96; *Bright Lights,
    Big City*, 71–73; *Brightness Falls*, 92,
    96; literary fiction, 12, 143; narco-
    culture, 122; rhopography and
    realism, 22, 66–67, 71–73
McKibben, Bill, 77, 83, 165n30
meaning of things, 74, 87, 90, 145, 148
Mechanization Takes Command (Gideon),
    13
"Me" decade, 8
media, 12, 15, 44, 55, 118
medical waste, 77, 78, 79
Meditations (Aurelius), 107, 114
Meikle, Jeffrey L., 82, 167n11, 168n46
Melville, Herman, 93
memories, 126, 140

mergers, 43
metaphor, 144
methane gas, 78
methodological fetishism, 13
Mexico, 3
Mezzanine, The (Baker), 100, 101–5,
    106–8, 109–12, 114–16, 167n11,
    168n37, 168n46
Michaels, Walter Benn, 15, 18, 52–53, 60,
    61
microhistory of objects, 104
Middle East, 23, 26–32, 35, 42, 142
Middle East Export Press, 23
Midway atoll, 96
militarism, 118, 120, 121, 130, 139,
    152n23
militarization, 119, 131
military aid, 122
military expenditure, 43, 119, 130, 142
military imperialism, 31, 116
military-industrial complex, 118
military-industrialization, 120, 130
military intervention, 26, 121, 141–42
military Keynesianism, 117, 118
military objects, 129, 130
military power, 4, 27, 28, 117, 119, 130
military production, 118, 130, 144
military spending, 43, 119, 130, 142
Milken, Michael, 43, 48, 77, 164n3
Miller, Daniel, 12
mind, 106, 107, 108, 109
mindless materialism, 116
"Mine All Mine Decade," 8
minimalism, 64–66, 71, 74, 77, 102,
    161n40
Mirowski, Philip, 17
Mitchell, Joni, 59
Mitchell, Timothy, 27, 28, 30, 31
MITI and the Japanese Miracle (Johnson),
    160n32
Mobil, 23
Mobro 4000 garbage barge, 77–81, 83,
    91–92, 95–96
Moby-Dick (Melville), 93
modernism, 63
modernity, 15

Mondale, Walter, 51
monetarism, 41, 157n44
money, 4, 14, 34, 36
Monroe, Marilyn, 47
Mont Pèlerin Society, 6, 17
More Music About Buildings and Food
(Talking Heads album), 58
Morrison, Toni, 52, 136, 137
"mortality" of things, 90, 91
Mosler, Warren, 33, 159n11
Mossadegh, Mohammad, 26
Motel of the Mysteries (Macaulay), 84–85
Mother Country (Robinson), 93, 94–95
Motor Carrier Act (1980), 41
"Mountains O' Things" (Chapman song),
46
movies, 11, 43–50, 79, 122–24
MTV, 46
"Mud in Mudanza, The" (Schnabel
painting), 86
Mumford, Lewis, 100
Murphy, Cullen, 83
music, 43, 46, 47, 58, 149, 159n27
muteness, 148
"My Hometown" (Springsteen song),
170n33
mysticism, 99, 148

Naked (Talking Heads album), 59
Names, The (DeLillo), 87–88
"narco-culture," 122
narrative culture, 11, 20, 100
NASA, 83, 119
nation, 38
national culture, 60–61
national identity, 37, 115
nationalism, 32
nationalization, 28
National Mall, 75, 122
Natural Gas Policy Act (1978), 41
Negri, Antonio, 29
neoclassical economics, 17
neoliberalism: American culture and
material things, 16, 19, 21, 142–44,
147, 148; definitions, 5–6, 16–17;
mainstream culture, 39, 41, 50;

militarism, 117, 119, 128, 130; oil
and geopolitics, 24, 32, 33, 37; peace
with things, 113, 114, 115;
rhopography and realism, 52, 53,
60, 62, 68, 75; rise of, 5–7, 9–10, 12,
14, 16–22; trash, 77, 80; triumph of,
10, 19, 21, 23–37
"Neoliberal Thought Collective," 17
neo-Platonism, 76
neo-Realism, 64, 65, 71, 163n70
Network (film), 51
networks, 115
New, David S., 2
New, The (Koons art series), 54
New Criterion, The (journal), 65
New Deal, 33, 42, 62
"new economy," 114, 115
New England, 2, 6
new Gilded Age, 77, 96
New Jersey, 77, 79, 80
New Left, 4, 39
new realism, 64, 65, 66, 74, 149
Newsweek, 73, 80, 83
New World, 1, 2
New York, 48, 80, 81
New York Times, 89
Nicaragua, 124
9/11 attacks, 119, 142
"1980s materialism," 8, 10, 19, 97
Nixon, Richard, 29, 40
Nixon shock, 29, 32, 51, 157n32
Noriega, Manuel, 122
Normal Heart, The (Kramer), 5, 164n11
Norman, Donald, 103
Norma Rae (film), 44
nostalgic materialism, 49, 50, 51, 116, 117
"Nothing But Flowers" (Talking Heads
song), 59
nuclear industry, 42–43, 85, 94, 95

Oakes, Urian, 1
Objectivist poets, 38, 39
object-oriented ontologies, 99, 101, 106,
114
objects: aestheticism of, 16; American
culture and material things, 143,

objects (*continued*)
145; archaeological consciousness, 87, 88, 90; common objects, 66, 70, 71, 104; eroticism of, 16, 104; everyday objects, 11, 16, 22, 54, 100, 103, 106, 144; falling objects, 133, 135, 137, 138; found objects, 54; history of, 104; materiality of, 14–16, 19, 90; militarism, 126, 127, 130, 131, 132, 140; peace with things, 98–99, 100, 102, 104; rhopography and realism, 55, 70, 71; and self, 38. *See also* things

O'Brien, Tim: *Going After Cacciato*, 124, 129, 133, 171n66, 171n71; *If I Die in a Combat Zone, Box Me Up and Ship Me Home*, 124, 133; *Things They Carried, The*, 120–21, 124–130, 131–36, 137–140, 141, 171n71

ocean dumping, 79, 80

"Ode on a Grecian Urn" (Keats), 89, 148

"Of Being Numerous" (Oppen), 38

O'Hara, Frank, 148

oil: and Carter, 40, 42; history in Middle East, 6; ideological politics, 142; Jacobs on, 157n33; plastics, 82; shocks, 28–29, 32, 33, 35, 40, 150, 157n32; spills, 77; Stegner on, 23–28, 30, 32, 34, 35, 141; triumph of neoliberalism, 21, 23–30, 32, 33, 35

OK Harris Gallery, 85

Olson, Charles, 80

"Once in A Lifetime" (Talking Heads song), 58

ontbijtjes (still lifes of the table), 59

OPEC (Organization of the Petroleum Exporting Countries), 29

Operation Desert Storm, 141

Oppen, George, 38, 39

organized labor, 27, 42, 50

Other America, The (Harrington), 61

painting, 56, 61, 85–86

Panama, 122

Panic at the Pump (Jacobs), 157n33

Panitch, Leo, 29

PATCO union (Professional Air Traffic Controllers Organization), 43

peace with things, 22, 98–116

Pearlman, Alison, 11, 12, 55, 56

Pencil, The (Petroski), 98–99, 100, 104, 105

Perfect War, The (Gibson), 129

Persian Gulf, 26, 42, 121

Persian Gulf War, 5, 120, 138, 141

Petroski, Henry, 98–99, 100, 103, 104, 105, 119, 167n11

Philadelphia Inquirer, The, 51

Phillips, Jayne Anne, 136–37, 138

photography, 46, 52–53, 62–63, 149

Pikkety, Thomas, 157n47

Pixar, 85

Planet of the Apes (film), 87

plantations, 25, 26, 51

plastic bags, 81, 82, 95

plastics, 81–85, 88, 95–96, 113, 148, 165n30

plate paintings, 86

Plato, 2, 3

Players (DeLillo), 14, 16

Plehwe, Dieter, 17

poetry, 38, 39

Polanyi, Karl, 33, 34

political discourse, 20, 21, 41, 79, 98

political economy, 7, 16, 17, 18, 31, 53

political power, 10, 27, 28

politics, 9, 38, 53, 149

pollution, 77, 91, 95, 98, 147

Ponce de Leon, Charles, 9

Poore, Patricia, 80

Pop Art, 56–57, 59–60, 62, 64–65, 74–75, 118, 144

popular music, 11, 43, 46

postmaterialism, 9, 18

postmodernism, 15, 18, 19, 63, 119, 127, 154n67, 155n74

postmodernity, 14, 15, 19

postpostmodernism, 19

post-structuralism, 17

poverty, 5, 46, 55, 61–63, 69, 74, 76

Powell, Lewis, 34

Powers, Richard, 146, 147, 148

Pretty Woman (film), 49–50, 118

Price, Joanna, 163n80
principle of limitation, 17
Principles of Psychology, The (James), 107, 108
privatization, 41
progress, 168n48
pronkstilleven (Dutch still lifes), 59
"Prop 13" campaign, 19
property crime, 48, 49
property rights, 2, 17, 18, 34
Pryor, Richard, 44, 79
Psychology of Everyday Things, The (Norman), 103
public health, 79–80
Puritanism, 2, 6, 159n8
Pygmalion myth, 49
Pynchon, Thomas, 63–64

Quayle, Dan, 79

Rabbit at Rest (Updike), 91, 92
racial tensions, 9, 48, 51
Radical Faeries, 5
"Radio, Radio" (Costello song), 118
radioactive waste, 95
Rambo movies, 124
Rand, Ayn, 19
Ransom, John, 126
rap music, 149, 159n27
"Rarity" (Baker), 112
Rathje, William, 81, 82, 83, 89, 96
Ratner's Star (DeLillo), 87
RCA, 32
Reagan, Ronald: and Bush, 36, 98; and Carter, 35, 36, 41, 42; Carver writings, 66, 68; and Gorbachev, 120; housing policy, 61; inflation, 45; legacy of, 8; militarism, 120, 121, 123, 130, 131; neoliberalism, 6, 19, 41; "new economy" and digitization, 114, 115, 147; Reaganism/ Reaganomics, 41, 76; reelection, 71, 92; speechmaking, 42–43; Strategic Defense Initiative, 120, 131, 170n35; tax policy, 61; Vietnam Veterans' Memorial, 123

realism, 18, 22, 48, 63–67, 74–75, 126
reality effects, 67, 126
Rebein, Robert, 63, 64, 68
recession, 7, 37, 40, 43, 46, 61, 150
recycling, 83, 95
Reed, Adolph, Jr., 18
refuse. *See* garbage; trash
Reich, Robert, 43
religion, 2, 8
remasculinization, 122, 124
remembrance, 125, 126, 139
Republic, The (Plato), 3
Republican National Convention, 98
resource imperialism, 29
retromania, 46
Revenue Act (1978), 41
revolution of things, 25
Reynolds, Malvina, 149
Reynolds, Simon, 46
Rhode Island School of Design, 58
rhopography (aesthetic rendering of small and trivial things), 54, 56, 58, 59, 61, 65, 76
rhopos, 57, 59, 61, 62, 67
Rilke, Rainer Maria, 72
riots, 48, 49
rising bodies, 137, 138
Rising Sun (Crichton), 160n32
Roberts, Julia, 49
Robinson, Marilynne: *Housekeeping*, 93–94, 95; *Mother Country*, 93, 94–95
Robison, James, 162n40
Robison, Mary, 162n40
Rochberg-Halton, Eugene, 107, 145
Rogin, Michael, 118
role of things, 12, 21
Rolling Stone magazine, 48
Roman Empire, 2
Room Temperature (Baker), 100, 102–7, 109–13, 115–17
Roosevelt, Theodore, 3–4
Roseanne (TV show), 46
Rosenquist, James, 118
Roth, Philip, 52
rubbish. *See* garbage; trash

Rubbish Theory (Thompson), 83
Russell, Bertrand, 19

Saez, Emmanuel, 157n47
Saltzman, Arthur M., 67, 104, 110, 167n11
sanitary landfill sites, 82, 83, 89
Sargent, Daniel J., 30, 31
Saturday Night Live (TV show), 118
Saudi Arabia, 21, 23–25, 26–29, 31, 42, 141
Savonarolo, Girolamo, 2, 48
Scaife, Richard Mellon, 35
Scarface (film), 122
Schapp, Alain, 84
Schnabel, Julian, 11, 85–86, 92
Schrader, Paul, 44, 48, 50
Schulman, Bruce, 58
Schumpeter, Joseph, 25, 156n19
Scorsese, Martin, 44
Scruggs, Jan, 123
SDI. *See* Strategic Defense Initiative
"Sea, The" (Schnabel painting), 86
Second World War, 4, 116, 118
See No Evil, Hear No Evil (film), 79
self, 21, 38, 101, 107–10
Seltzer, Mark, 62
semiotics, 15, 62
"Serious Talk, A" (Carver), 70
settlers, 1, 2
sex, lies and videotape (film), 79
sexual politics, 49
Shah of Iran, 40
Shapiro, Walter, 98
Sheen, Martin, 47
Shiloh and Other Stories (Mason), 163n80
"Shipbuilding" (song), 118
shoelaces, 101, 109, 111, 112, 113
shopping malls, 9, 59, 62, 103
short story form, 72
"Significance of the Frontier in American History, The" (Turner), 3
sign-values, 15
Silbergleid, Robin, 126, 131
Silberman, Robert, 125, 126
silicon chip, 114, 115
simulacra, 15

Sitting Bull (Tatanka Iyotake), 3
"Size of Thoughts, The" (Baker), 105, 106
slavery, 3, 5, 136
"Small Good Thing, A" (Carver), 72
Small Things Considered (Petroski), 167n11
Snyders, Frans, 59
social being, 113, 114, 115
social engineering, 24
social mobility, 55
social networks, 21, 115
social realism, 46, 63, 68, 69
society, 33, 34
Society of the Spectacle (Debord), 154n71
Socrates, 3
Soderbergh, Steven, 79
Solomon, Alan R., 57
"Song of Myself" (Whitman), 38
Song of Solomon (Morrison), 136, 137
Sorrentino, Gilbert, 56
sovereign debt, 31, 43
Soviet Union, 31, 85, 118, 130
space, lack of, 80–81
space debris, 77, 83
space missions, 119
Spalding basketball brand, 54, 55
speech, 148
Speer, Albert, 88, 90
Splendors of the Sohites (Weiner installation), 85
Springsteen, Bruce, 46, 130, 170n33
stagflation, 34, 40, 50, 130
Stallone, Sylvester, 124
Stallybrass, Peter, 15, 154n71
state role: Carter deregulation, 41; militarism, 119–120, 128; neoliberalism, 17, 27, 30, 34, 115
status symbols, 72, 103
steel industry, 31, 32
Stegner, Wallace, 23–28, 30, 32, 34, 35, 141
Stein, Judith, 31
Steinbeck, John, 4
Steinberg, Bruce, 43
Stevenson, Adlai, 4
still life art, 56, 59, 62, 87, 146, 147
Stone, Oliver, 36, 47, 122, 154n73, 164n3

Strait, Guy, 4
Strategic Defense Initiative (SDI), 120, 131, 170n35
straws, drinking, 100, 102, 109, 110
Streetwise (documentary), 46
strikes, 28
structural poverty, 62
"stuff," 11, 14, 90
Sturken, Marita, 169n17
subject–object relations, 15, 38, 100–101, 103
Summers, Larry, 80–81
supermarkets, 56, 59, 60, 62
superpowers, 119
supply-side economics, 34
Swenson, Gene, 56
Syria, 26, 142
System of Objects, The (Baudrillard), 82

Taft Hartley Act (1947), 42
Talking Heads (band), 21, 35, 58–59, 136
Tapline (Trans-Arabian Pipeline), 24, 26
Tatanka Iyotake (Sitting Bull), 3
taxation, 6, 41, 61, 169n6
Taxi Driver (film), 44
Taylor, Frederick Winslow, 44
Technics and Civilization (Mumford), 100
technology, 14, 100, 108, 111
Tehran agreement, 28, 31
television, 11, 43, 46, 61
"Tell the Women We're Going" (Carver), 70
Texaco, 23
texts, 114, 125
Thatcherism, 41
Thiebaud, Wayne, 59
"thingness of things," 16
things: American cultural engagement, 1–5, 10–16, 19–21, 143–46, 148–49; archaeological consciousness, 87, 90, 93, 94; Baker novels, 100–102, 105–9, 113, 114; Carver stories, 70; DeLillo novels, 60, 87, 90; design of, 110, 115, 116, 168n46; durability of, 81–84, 86, 91–93, 95, 96; ephemerality of, 86, 92, 93, 96, 147; love of, 2, 3;

mainstream culture, 38, 39, 40, 45, 46, 49; materiality of, 14–16, 19, 90; meaning of, 74, 87, 90, 145, 148; militarism and materialism, 22, 125, 131–36; neoliberalism, 19, 20–21, 25–26, 35–37; peace with, 22, 98–116; rhopography and realism, 56, 58, 60, 65, 70, 76; role of, 12, 21; thingness of, 16; thing theory, 13, 147; transience of, 144–47; weight of, 131–36, 137, 138; worth of, 145. *See also* argument about things; material things
Things They Carried, The (O'Brien), 120–21, 124–130, 131–36, 137–140, 141, 171n71
thing theory, 13, 147
"Thing Theory" (Brown), 147
thinking, 20, 100–101, 104–9, 114–15, 144
think tanks, 17, 35
Thompson, Graham, 168n37
Thompson, Helen, 142, 150
Thompson, Michael, 83
Thoreau, Henry, 99, 100
thought, 20, 100–101, 104–9, 114–15, 144
"Three Fightingmen" (Hart statuary), 123
Three Mile Island, 43
Time magazine, 8
time–space compression, 14
"time's shipwreck," 84, 86, 94
Tocqueville, Alexis de, 1
"To Roosevelt" (Dario), 3
toxic waste, 79, 80, 81, 95
Toyota, 51, 70, 91, 115
trade, 21, 27, 31
Trans-Arabian Pipeline, 24, 26
transience of things, 144–47
trash: archaeological consciousness, 22; DeLillo, 89, 90, 92, 96, 148; durability of, 81–84, 86, 91–93, 95, 96; in films, 85; Great Pacific Garbage Patch, 77, 83, 96; Jordan images, 96; *Mobro 4000* garbage barge, 77–81, 83, 91–92, 95–96; Robinson, 93, 95; Updike, 91. *See also* garbage
Treasures of Tutankhamun exhibition, 85

Tripoli agreement, 28
Troy, Gil, 8, 9
truckers, 41, 42
True Stories (Talking Heads album/book/film), 58, 62
Trump, Donald, 36, 150
truth, and authenticity, 126
Turkle, Sherry, 115
Turner, Frederick Jackson, 3
Tutankhamun, 85
Twain, Mark, 24

U and I (Baker), 104, 107, 114
underclass, 50
Underworld (DeLillo), 95, 145–46, 147
unemployment, 40
unions, 44, 45, 50
United Fruit Company, 25
United States, historical overview, 1–5. *See also* American culture; American imperialism
United States Navy, 26, 124, 142
"Unpacking My Library" (Benjamin), 107
Updike, John, 61, 91, 92, 102, 104, 114, 115
urbanization, 3
urban space, 49
"utopian" Marxism, 12
Utrecht, Adriaen van, 59

vacuum cleaners, 11, 54, 56
value, 145
values, 8, 98, 103
vanitas symbols, 146
vanity of all things, 146
Veterans' Memorial. *See* Vietnam Veterans' Memorial
Vidal, Gore, 20
"Vietnam Experience in American Literature" conference, 124
"Vietnam syndrome," 121
Vietnam Veterans' Memorial, 75, 89, 120, 122–23, 125, 126, 169n17
Vietnam War: Mason, 73–75; militarism and materialism, 22, 120–22, 123–130, 131–36, 137–140, 141; neoliberalism, 30, 33; O'Brien,
120–21, 124–130, 131–36, 137–140, 141; rhopography and realism, 73–75
"Vietnam Zippos" (Walters), 170n28
virtual realities, 147
visual culture, 10, 11, 20
"Vitamins" (Carver), 70–71
Vogel, Ezra, 160n32
Volcker, Paul, 41, 159n11
Vox (Baker), 112
vulture capitalism, 57

Wachowskis, 154n73
wages, 9, 33
Wall-E (film), 85
Wall Street, 77, 92
Wall Street (film), 36, 47, 57, 164n3
Walters, Ian, 135, 170n28
Walton, Sam, 36
"Wand 1" (Binschtok photograph), 52, 53
war: Civil War, 3; Japan, 4, 116; Mexico, 3; militarism, 22, 117–123, 131–38, 140; neoliberalism, 20, 30, 33; Persian Gulf War, 5, 120, 138, 141; post-war economic expansion, 4; Second World War, 4, 116, 118; simulacra, 15. *See also* Vietnam War
Warhol, Andy, 56, 57, 58, 59, 60, 61
Washington consensus, 31
Washington Monument, 123
Washington Post, 43
waste: archaeological consciousness, 85, 95; durability of, 81–84, 86, 91–93, 95, 96; mass consumption, 11; militarism and materialism, 128–29, 133, 134; *Mobro 4000* garbage barge, 77–81, 83, 91–92, 95–96. *See also* garbage; trash
"Waste Land, The" (Eliot), 38
Wayne, John, 123
WD-40, 119
wealth, 9, 34, 37, 41, 49, 80, 96, 98, 150
weaponry, 117, 119
Webb, Jim, 124
weight of things, 131–36, 137, 138
Weiner, Sam, 85, 93
welfare state, 33

Welty, Eudora, 62–63
Western imperialism, 26
Weymouth, Tina, 58
"Whaam!" (Lichtenstein artwork), 118
"What Is A Hippie?" (Strait), 4
What We Talk About When We Talk About Love (Carver), 67, 68
White, Leslie, 163n80
"White Lines (Don't Do It)" (Grandmaster Flash song), 122
White Noise (DeLillo), 11, 14, 59–60, 87–90, 92, 96, 129, 148
Whitman, Walt, 38
"Why Don't You Dance?" (Carver), 69
Wilder, Gene, 79
Wild Palms (TV series), 154n73
Williams, William Carlos, 39
Will You Please Be Quiet, Please? (Carver), 67

Wilson, Woodrow, 26
Wilson basketball brand, 54, 55
Wire, The (TV series), 1
Wojnarowicz, David, 5
Wolfe, Tom, 8, 48, 49, 64
Wolff, Tobias, 162n40
working class, 46, 50
Works Progress Administration, 62
worth of things, 145
Wyatt, Robert, 118

xenophobia, 51, 150

Yardley, Jonathan, 74
Yemen, 142
"yuppie" culture, 71, 72

Zarestsky, Natasha, 39
Zippo lighters, 126, 170n28

CPSIA information can be obtained
at www.ICGtesting.com
Printed in the USA
FSHW04n0001300318
46064FS